TRADE FACILITATION

A Handbook for Trade Negotiators

Prepared by **Vinod Rege,**
Former Director (WTO) and Multilateral Trade Adviser
financed by the Commonwealth Secretariat to the
Geneva Group of Commonwealth Developing Countries

in cooperation with **Isabella Kataric**
Consultant, Commonwealth Secretariat-International
Trade Centre (ITC) Joint Project

Commonwealth Secretariat
Marlborough House
Pall Mall
London SW1Y 5HX
United Kingdom

Published by the Commonwealth Secretariat
Designed by kc gan designs
Printed by Hobbs the Printers, Totton, Hampshire, UK

Views and opinions expressed in this publication are the
responsibility of the authors and should in no way be attributed
to the institutions to which they are affiliated.

Wherever possible, the Commonwealth Secretariat uses paper
sourced from sustainable forests or from sources that minimise
a destructive impact on the environment.

Copies of this publication may be obtained from

The Publications Section
Commonwealth Secretariat
Marlborough House
Pall Mall
London SW1Y 5HX
United Kingdom
Tel: +44 (0)20 7747 6342
Fax: +44 (0)20 7839 9081
E-mail: publications@commonwealth.int
Web: www.thecommonwealth.org/publications

ISBN: 978-0-85092-855-6

FOREWORD

Trade Facilitation has formed a part of the WTO work programme since 1996, when the Singapore Ministerial Conference instructed the WTO Goods Council to initiate its analysis and examination of four subjects: Trade Facilitation, Trade and Investment, Trade and Competition Policy, and Transparency in Government Procurement. These so-called 'Singapore Issues' were included in the Doha Development Agenda in 2001. However, no significant progress was made in launching negotiations on these issues, mainly due to the opposition of a number of developing countries.

Following the failure of the Cancun Ministerial Conference in 2003, a General Council Decision was taken on 1 August 2004 providing a new mandate for the negotiations – the 'July Package.' After this, WTO members formally agreed to commence negotiations on Trade Facilitation. It was also agreed that negotiations on the three remaining Singapore Issues would not take place during the Doha Round.

The main aim of the negotiations on Trade Facilitation is to clarify and improve the provisions of three GATT 1994 Articles – Article V (Freedom of Transit); Article VIII (Fees and Formalities connected with Importation and Exportation); and Article X (the Publication and Administration of Trade Regulations) – with a view to expediting the movement, release and clearance of goods through customs. The negotiations also aim at providing technical assistance to developing and least developed countries with a view to strengthening their technical capacities for the application of innovative techniques and methods in the clearance of goods, and for the gradual acceptance of the obligations and new rules that may be adopted in the Doha Round.

This Handbook on Trade Facilitation was written by Mr Vinod Rege (Geneva-based Multilateral Trade Adviser financed by the Commonwealth Secretariat) in cooperation with Ms Isabella Kataric (Consultant, joint ITC-Commonwealth project). Its aim is to provide background information and to identify the points that may need further examination by the negotiating parties in order to adopt a suitable negotiating approach on the issues raised in the proposals that have been tabled in the Negotiating Group on Trade Facilitation. The Handbook also contains suggestions on how the negotiating approaches adopted under other WTO Agreements (such as the Agreement on Customs Valuation, Rules of Origin, Technical Barriers to Trade and Sanitary and Phytosanitary Measures), could be taken into account while developing new rules in this area.

The Handbook takes into account the comments and views expressed at meetings of the Geneva Group of Commonwealth Developing Countries.[1] In addition to being attended by the delegations of Commonwealth Developing Countries, these meetings also had delegates from a number of other developing countries.

In addition, a one-day meeting, 'Briefing Session on Trade Facilitation', was organised to brief the delegations on the issues analysed and discussed in the Handbook. The meeting was arranged jointly by the Commonwealth Secretariat, the Geneva ACP Office and the Agency for International Trade Information and Cooperation (AITIC) and was held on 21 July 2006. It was attended by representatives of developing country members of the three agencies, as well as by representatives of the donor countries and of intergovernmental and non-governmental organisations.

---

1   All Commonwealth developing countries that have established Permanent Missions in Geneva are Members of the Group. At present, the following 25 countries are its Members: Bangladesh, Barbados, Belize, Botswana, Brunei Darussalam, Cameroon, Ghana, India, Jamaica, Kenya, Lesotho, Malaysia, Mauritius, Mozambique, Namibia, Nigeria, Pakistan, Singapore, Sri Lanka, South Africa, Swaziland, Tanzania, Trinidad and Tobago, Uganda and Zambia.

There appeared to be general consensus among the participants in the meeting that the approach suggested in the Handbook provides a good basis for further examination and discussions, *inter alia*, on the following issues:

- The modalities that could be adopted in future negotiations on rule making;
- The techniques that could be utilised to ensure that the timing and extent of commitments are related to the implementation capacity of each developing country;
- The operationalisation of commitments assumed by developed countries in the course of the negotiations to provide technical assistance and, subsequently, for the application of the rules of the Agreement; and for the implementation of commitments which developing and least developed countries may have assumed.
- The adoption of special procedures for the settlement of disputes.

The participants were also of the view that the Handbook's analysis of the issues raised in the tabled proposals for clarification of the existing GATT rules would require careful examination at the national level, in order to decide upon the approach that could be adopted in the negotiations. The Report on the discussions was presented to the Negotiating Group in Trade Facilitation by the Chairman of the Geneva Group of Commonwealth Developing Countries.

In conclusion, we would like to emphasise that the analysis in the Handbook is only intended to provide a basis for further examination and discussion, and does not reflect the official position of any of the delegations that participated in the discussions on the drafts of the Handbook, or the views of the Commonwealth Secretariat.

It is our hope and expectation that further in-depth discussions on the points raised in the Handbook would greatly contribute towards a more informed and effective dialogue and participation in Trade Facilitation negotiations by all countries, especially by the developing and least developed countries. Moreover, even though the Handbook is primarily intended as a source of reference for trade negotiators at the WTO and senior officials in country capitals, we hope that it would also be of interest to the business community and the public in general by increasing the understanding of issues arising in the area of trade facilitation.

Charles T. Ntwaagae
Ambassador, Permanent Representative of the Republic of Botswana and Former Chairman of the Group of Commonwealth Developing Countries in Geneva

George Saibel
Director, Special Advisory Services Division, Commonwealth Secretariat, London

Gomi T. Senadhira
Ambassador, Permanent Representative of Sri Lanka to the WTO and Present Chairman of the Geneva Group of Commonwealth Developing Countries

ACKNOWLEDGEMENTS

This Handbook has benefited from comments by the Ambassadors to the WTO and other Trade Representatives of the Group of Commonwealth Developing Countries in Geneva, Switzerland.

Special thanks to

Mr George Saibel, Director of the Special Advisory Services Division (SASD), Commonwealth Secretariat; and

Mr Nikhil Treebhoohun, Adviser and Head, Trade Section;

Ms Angela Strachan, Adviser, Trade;

Mr Elvis Gannon, Programme Co-ordinator and Head of Programme Support Team; and

Mrs Manel Herath, Programme Assistant (SASD).

Mr Kunio Mikuriya, Deputy Secretary General of the World Customs Organization (WCO);

Mr Tadatsugu Matsudaira, Senior Officer, WCO;

H.E. Amb. Marwa Kisiri, Head of the Geneva ACP Office;

Ms Esperanza Duran, Executive Director of the Agency for International Trade Information and Cooperation (AITIC);

Mr Sergio Delgado, Senior Trade Affairs Adviser, AITIC;

Mr Siva Palayathan, Minister Counsellor, Deputy Representative of the African Union in Geneva;

Mr Nigel Balchin, Vice President, Société Générale de Surveillance SA (SGS);

Mr Alexandre Schaffner, Delegate, International Federation of Inspection Agencies (IFIA);

Mr L. Alan Winters, Director, Development Research Group, World Bank;

Mr Gerard McLinden, Senior Trade Facilitation Specialist, International Trade Department, World Bank;

Mr John S. Wilson, Lead Economist, Development Research Group, World Bank;

Mr Rajesh Aggarwal, Senior Adviser, International Trading System, International Trade Centre (ITC); and

Dr Preeti Singh, who edited the Handbook.

CONTENTS

Abbreviations Used

ACP	African, Caribbean and Pacific Group of States
APEC	Asia-Pacific Economic Cooperation
CAC	Codex Alimentarius Commission
CTF	Committee on Trade Facilitation
DSU	Dispute Settlement Understanding
DTIS	Diagnostic Trade Integration Studies
ECOWAS	Economic Community of West African States
EC	European Communities
EDI	Electronic Data Interchange
EU	European Union
GATT	General Agreement on Tariffs and Trade
HSCC	Harmonized System of Customs Classification
ICAO	International Civil Aviation Organization
IDA	International Development Assistance
IEC	International Electrotechnical Commission
IFIA	International Federation of Inspection Agencies
IMF	International Monetary Fund
IMO	International Maritime Organisation
ISO	International Organization for Standardization
ITU	International Telecommunication Union
LDCs	Least Developed Countries
NGOs	Non-governmental organisations
OECD	Organisation for Economic Cooperation and Development
PSI	Preshipment Inspection
SADC	Southern African Development Community
S & D Treatment	Special and Differential Treatment
SNEP	Single National Enquiry Point
SPS Agreement	Agreement on Sanitary and Phytosanitary Measures
TBT Agreement	Agreement on Technical Barriers to Trade
TPRB	Trade Policy Review Body
TPRM	Trade Policy Review Mechanism
UNCTAD	United Nations Conference on Trade and Development
UN/CEFACT	United Nations Centre for Trade Facilitation and Electronic Business
UNECE	United Nations Economic Commission for Europe
UNDP	United Nations Development Programme
WCO	World Customs Organization
WTO	World Trade Organization

OVERVIEW

The Issues Discussed in
Trade Facilitation — a Handbook
for Trade Negotiators

1. General

This overview aims at providing a comprehensive picture of the issues discussed in the Handbook. It will be particularly useful to readers, at the management level, who are interested in knowing the issues needing further examination while deciding the negotiating approach to be adopted in the WTO negotiations regarding the proposals on the clarification and improvement of GATT Articles V, VIII and X.

The overview is divided into two sections.

Section I contains a summary of Chapters 1-7 in the Handbook. It provides background information on the inclusion of the subject of trade facilitation in the negotiating agenda; describes the modalities that could be adopted for further negotiations, and also contains a brief description of the work of organisations other than WTO that are actively working in this area.

Section II (Annex) contains a summary of the Chapters 8-16 analysing the proposals that have been tabled for the clarification of the above mentioned GATT provisions. The analysis in this section is presented in the form of tables, displaying the proposals alongside the issues that need further examination at the national level.

SECTION I: BACKGROUND INFORMATION AND THE MODALITIES FOR THE NEGOTIATIONS

2. Background information

Chapter 1 provides the historical background of the inclusion of the subject of trade facilitation in the WTO work programme for study and analysis, and examines the reasons for the initial reluctance of developing countries to include it in the Doha Development Agenda. The chapter explains how the frank and open discussions that have occurred since the adoption of the Agenda have eliminated some previous misgivings. It goes on to describe the provisions that were included in Annex D of the 2004 General Council Decision – known as the 'July Package' – to meet the main concerns of developing countries, and to ensure that these countries are provided technical assistance to build capacity for the application of any new WTO rules that may be adopted. It also states that the extent and timing of the obligations they are required to accept under such rules are related to their implementation capacities.

Since the work of other international organisations in this area has a bearing on the work proposed to be undertaken for the development of new trade facilitation rules at the WTO, **Chapter 2** provides an overview of the work done, *inter alia*, by the World Customs Organization (WCO), the UN Economic Commission for Europe (UNECE), United Nations Centre for Trade Facilitation and Electronic Business UN/CEFACT, the United Nations Conference on Trade and Development (UNCTAD), and other organisations.

3. Adoption of modalities for the negotiations

Chapter 3 describes the possible legal forms that could be used for the codification of the results of the negotiations. It suggests that after taking into account the number of new rules that may be adopted and that technical assistance for capacity building is effectively provided to those countries that need it, the form of the 'multilateral agreement' may be selected.

The chapter also explains how, in the trade negotiations, it is accepted practice to adopt 'modalities' after the issues on which substantive negotiations are to take place have been identified by the concerned Negotiating Group in the initial phase of the negotiations. Such modalities are adopted both in areas where the aim of the negotiations is the liberalisation of the trade itself, as well as in areas where new rules are to be adopted.

In the area of trade facilitation, the identification stage was reached with the adoption of the Hong Kong Ministerial Declaration in December 2005. Annex E on trade facilitation lists the measures on which new rules may be adopted for the clarification and improvement of the provisions of GATT Articles V, VIII and X. After taking into account the aims and objectives of the negotiations, it may be necessary to adopt modalities in the following four areas:

- Modalities for negotiations on rule making;
- Modalities to ensure that countries are not required to accept obligations that do not correspond to their implementation capacities;
- Modalities for negotiations on the provision of technical assistance and capacity building; and
- Modalities for negotiations on the settlement of differences/disputes through conciliation (not through the WTO dispute settlement procedures).

3.1   Modalities for negotiations on rule making

Chapter 4 explains that, for the purpose of agreeing on the modalities for the negotiations on the development of rules, it may be desirable to divide the measures listed in Annex E of the Hong Kong Declaration into the following categories:

- **Category 1**: Measures that primarily raise trade policy issues (e.g. the application of the non-discrimination principle, or the level of fees and charges for services provided by customs) and the establishment of appeals procedures.
- **Category 2**: Measures relating to the techniques and modalities which customs should apply in the day-to-day administration of the customs procedures (e.g. the application of risk assessment systems, the designation of authorised importers, and the use of post-clearance auditing).

The negotiations on the measures falling into **Category 1**, which mainly raise trade policy issues, should take place entirely in the WTO Negotiating Group. However, trade policy is not the main feature of the measures falling under **Category 2**. For most of such measures, the WCO, UNECE, UN/CEFACT and other international organisations have developed international standards or recommendations in cooperation with customs experts. Thus, it would be desirable if the modalities provide a mandate for the Negotiating Group to examine the possibility of linking the WTO rules to these international standards for maximizing synergy while avoiding the duplication of efforts between the organisations.

This would be consistent with the approach adopted under the Agreements on Technical Barriers to Trade (TBT) and Sanitary and Phytosanitary Measures (SPS). These two Agreements impose an obligation on WTO Members to apply the standards developed by international standardisation bodies.

The obligations under these Agreements to use international standards are open-ended and apply to all adopted standards – current and future.

The operational experience of these two Agreements shows that such open-ended obligations pose practical implementation problems. Thus, the proposed Agreement on Trade Facilitation could limit the obligation to a number of selected standards that apply to the measures falling in **Category 2**.

The modalities should also provide the criteria for the selection of international organisations and standards that should be brought under the scope of the proposed agreement. Negotiations for the identification of such standards should take place in 'special sessions' organised by the Negotiating Group, and be dedicated to the examination of a selected standard or standards. Sufficient advance notice of such meetings should be given to ensure attendance by customs experts from as many developing and least developed countries as possible.

The main advantages in requiring countries to apply standards that have been developed by the WCO and other international organisations are the following:

- The standards adopted by these organisations are not as prescriptive as the WTO rules;
- The standards adopted by these bodies are complemented by implementation guidelines;
- The formulation of such standards requires the active participation of the representatives of the trading and business community. The WCO and other organisations permit open and active participation by all interested stakeholders in the work on the formulation of customs related standards. In contrast, under the WTO rules, participation is confined only to government representatives; and
- Experience has shown that standards have to be under continuous review, especially in the light of technological developments that have occurred since their adoption.

However, there could be a few cases in which – after being examined in the special sessions of the Negotiating Group – it is found that the standards adopted by WCO or other international organisations need reviewing. Such a review may be found necessary, *inter alia*:

- When the discussions in the Negotiating Group find that the standard has failed to take into account certain aspects, or
- Because a majority of developing countries have not been able to participate in the technical level discussions in the relevant organisation regarding the formulation of the standard.

It is expected that such cases are likely to be few since these standards have been adopted by the WCO and in the UNECE after discussions and negotiations lasting many years, and in which customs experts from many countries participated. In these (few) cases, the modalities for the negotiations should provide for the standards/recommendations being referred back to the organisation that had adopted them for review at the technical level. This review should take into account the proposals tabled in the Negotiating Group and the views expressed in the discussions. In remitting the standard for review, the WTO shall indicate the period within which the results of the negotiations at the technical level should be communicated to the Negotiating Group.

4. Modalities for the operationalisation of the provision of technical assistance (TA) and capacity building (CB)

Chapter 4 states that one of the important features of the mandate for negotiations is that developed countries have undertaken to provide technical assistance to developing and least developed countries to build up their capacities, e.g. for participation in the negotiations. They have also agreed – after the negotiations are completed – to provide these countries with assistance which is precise, effective, and operational, and reflects their needs and priorities regarding the successful implementation of the results of the negotiations and of the commitments that may be assumed by them. The mandate also recognises that the implementation of certain commitments may require assistance for infrastructural development.

4.1 Assistance for participation in the negotiations

Assistance for improving the participation of developing countries in the WTO negotiations on trade facilitation is currently being provided by the WTO Secretariat itself; by multilateral organisations dealing with trade issues, such as UNCTAD, ITC, OECD and the Commonwealth Secretariat; and by international financial institutions such as the World Bank and the IMF in the form of specialised workshops or seminars on trade facilitation.

As suggested earlier, these measures could be complemented by meeting the travel costs and the subsistence allowance of national negotiators with special expertise in customs affairs, who attend:

- Special sessions arranged at the WTO for the identification of standards adopted by other organisations to which the provisions of the WTO Agreement should apply; and
- Meetings at WCO for technical review of the standards referred to it by the WTO Negotiating Group.

4.2 Assistance for the reform and modernisation of customs procedures

In considering the modalities to be adopted to provide assistance after the negotiations are completed, it may be desirable to bear in mind that, over the last two decades, a considerable amount of technical assistance for the reform and modernisation of customs clearance procedures has been (and is being) provided by international financial institutions such as the World Bank and IMF, international organisations such as the WTO, WCO, UNCTAD, UNECE and other organisations, such as the Commonwealth Secretariat, as well as by donor countries on a bilateral basis.

In adopting a new institutional framework at the WTO for providing additional programmes for assistance in accordance with the mandate for negotiations, the past experience of providing assistance must be taken into account. In particular, it is necessary to ensure that:

- There is a greater degree of transparency in the assistance provided by different agencies, and greater coordination in granting it.
- The programmes are need-based and driven by the countries receiving the assistance, and not by international organisations or donors, as seems to be the case at present.
- Experts or consulting firms selected for providing assistance are able to relate their expertise and experience to the environment in which customs officials in the receiving countries work and to the trading realities in these countries, and not merely suggest the adoption of procedures with which they may be familiar.

4.2.1 Differing views

Today, widely differing views are being expressed in academic circles, by international financial institutions, international trade organisations, donor countries as well as developing countries regarding how the greatly expanded aid for trade could be provided effectively, and how while providing the above, predictability, country ownership, and coherence can be ensured. One view is that the existing mechanism should continue, particularly the Integrated Framework (IF), by establishing 'character funds' under a separate window for providing assistance in such areas as the 'erosion of preferential margins' and 'trade facilitation,' as well as broadening the span of countries to include others besides least developed countries to which assistance could be given under its present mandate.

The proposals for the establishment of 'dedicated funds' under the umbrella of the Integrated Framework do not find favour with the staff of the World Bank and the IMF, as well as by the Development Committees of both institutions. Donor countries have also indicated that they are not in favour of establishing such funds. The main reasons for their reluctance are the following.

- They consider the establishment of such funds as unnecessarily bureaucratizing the process of granting aid, and
- The establishment of such funds may require them to change the existing systems for the provision of assistance. As noted above, both international financial institutions and donor countries are already providing significant amounts of assistance in the area of trade facilitation. They would prefer to continue with their own existing procedures and priorities even after the proposed Agreement is adopted.

These objections would also apply if such a fund were to be established as a separate window, or a pillar of the Integrated Framework, or even as a standalone fund.

From the point of view of developing countries as a group, the Integrated Framework poses more serious limitations. The assistance under the programme is directed entirely to the least developed countries. Staff of the World Bank and IMF have suggested that country eligibility could be extended to cover other relatively less developed countries that are eligible for international development assistance (IDA) at concessional interest rates. The adoption of the IDA-only criteria could increase the number of developing countries that would be eligible for assistance. However, this would still exclude a large number of developing countries and transitional economies.

4.2.2 A separate Fund

Any discussions or negotiations regarding the institutional framework which should be adopted for the provision of technical assistance in the area of trade facilitation will have to take into account the views described above.

However, there does appear to be a strong case for the establishment of a separate dedicated Fund or Facility for the provision of assistance in the area of trade facilitation for the following reasons:

- Developing countries have agreed to accept new and additional disciplines in this area only if the assistance required by them to build technical capacities for the application of the rules, and for the implementation of the commitments which they may assume, is made available to them, and
- Developed countries have already given commitments to provide assistance for the above purposes, including that needed for related infrastructural development.

The establishment of a separate Fund would help greatly in ensuring that both the developed and developing countries fulfil their commitments.

In fact, these considerations appear to have influenced the Group of African, Caribbean and Pacific (ACP) countries to propose the establishment of a special Trade Facilitation Assistance and Capacity Building Fund to the Negotiating Group on Trade Facilitation. The proposal envisages that the required resources should be contributed by 'bilateral and multilateral donors,' and should be managed by an inter-agency coordinating body consisting of 'international, regional and sub-regional organisations such as (but not limited to) UNCTAD, UNECE, WTO, WCO, and the World Bank.'

If such a Fund is established, its initial size would have to be negotiated taking into account the rough assessment of needs that are being made by the World Bank, the WCO, and other organisations.

Moreover, because developed countries and international financial institutions are likely to insist on continuing with their existing procedures and practices for providing assistance in the area of trade facilitation, the procedures should provide that, while pledging resources, they should clearly indicate which ones are being allocated:

- For providing assistance on a bilateral basis, and
- As contributions to the Fund.

The procedures should also provide for at least [X] % (to be negotiated) of the resources to be disbursed through the Fund. This requirement is considered necessary for two reasons.

- For political and other reasons, donor countries often focus their aid to particular countries as, for instance, those with whom they have close historical ties. This often results in other countries being given low priority as far as the provision of aid is concerned, and

- Countries with which aid giving countries do not have friendly political relations are often excluded by law from the list of countries to which aid can be given. If aid giving countries were required to contribute some proportion of their resources to the Fund, an equitable disbursement of aid could be facilitated.

The resources from the Fund shall be available to provide assistance for:

- Diagnostic studies on the identification of needs, and for the preparation of project documents, and

- The implementation of projects aimed at building technical capacities, *inter alia*, for

  - The application of the rules of the GATT Articles V, VIII and X, and the new rules which may be adopted under the proposed Agreement on Trade Facilitation, and
  - The implementation of the commitments that may be assumed by countries during the course of the negotiations for the adoption of the Agreement.

Of relevance here is that the mandate recognises that the negotiations could lead to certain commitments whose implementation would require support for infrastructural development. Developed countries have undertaken to provide such assistance, but have also stated that their undertaking is not open ended.

It should also be clearly recognised that the assistance provided from the Fund for infrastructural development would have to be limited to that which is directly needed for the application of the rules of the Agreement and the implementation of the commitments. In most cases, such assistance would focus on the introduction and adoption by customs of information technology, of new and innovative methods such as the application of risk management techniques in the physical checking of imported goods, and in the scrutiny of documents.

Trade facilitation is often understood in a broad sense to include the development of infrastructure at ports and airports, the development of warehousing facilities and, in the case of countries where roads for internal traffic are not developed, the construction of such roads, particularly in transit countries. However, any assistance needed for such purposes would have to continue to be provided, as is currently the case, by the World Bank and/or bilateral donors, or from the Global Trade Facility that may be established under the Aid for Trade Programme, and not from the Fund that is proposed to be established.

4.2.3   The establishment of a Mentoring and Twinning arrangement under the umbrella of the Fund

Moreover, to ensure transparency in the assistance provided and to allow a greater degree of choice in deciding upon which agencies or countries would be most suited to providing such assistance, it may be necessary to establish a complementary mechanism – under the umbrella of the Fund – that would facilitate the exchange of information between the country in need of assistance and the country or agency which has the necessary technical competence to provide such assistance. Such partnerships could take the form of a Mentoring and Twinning arrangement.

The meaning of the term 'mentor' is 'experienced and trusted adviser.' 'Twinning' is a process by which 'similar bodies or agencies' are brought together. Thus, a 'Mentoring and Twinning arrangement' applies to an agreement under which a country with the technical capacity to provide assistance in a particular field agrees to do so to countries in need of it.

Under such arrangements, the international organisation establishing the arrangement plays the role of the coordinator or catalyst: it brings together countries that can act as 'mentors' providing the advice and 'twins' them with the countries needing the assistance. The actual areas of assistance, and the terms and conditions, are left to be negotiated on a bilateral or a plurilateral basis, between the interested mentor country and the country or countries wishing to obtain the assistance. The main advantages of such arrangements include:

- Countries will have the opportunity to select the mentor country they consider best equipped to provide them with the type of assistance they need;
- Countries may have the opportunity to seek assistance from other developing countries if they consider that the assistance provided is likely to be more responsive to their needs, taking into account such factors as similarities in their trading environments; and
- Since the assistance would be obtained through bilateral agreements, it is possible that mentoring and twinning countries will develop a relationship for mutual cooperation on a long term and continuing basis, e.g. help solve any problems arising in the period following the completion of the assistance project.

The Forum, jointly organised by the Development Committee of the OECD and the UNDP in February 2005, has also recommended that one of the ways for the international community to utilise the expertise available in developing countries for providing assistance to other developing countries is to enter into 'trilateral development cooperation arrangements.' In these arrangements, an international financial institution, organisation, or bilateral donor agency, agrees to provide the required financial assistance to a developing country (or to a consultancy firm from such a country) with the technical capacity to provide assistance to another developing country.

5. Modalities for the extension of special and differential (S&D) treatment to developing countries to ensure that countries are not required to accept obligations that do not correspond to their implementation capacities

5.1   Present techniques for providing S&D treatment

The issues relating to the extension of special and differential treatment to developing countries to ensure that they are not required to accept obligations for which they do not have technical capacities are discussed in Chapter 5. When a new Agreement is adopted in trade negotiations, it is accepted practice under the WTO system to provide one/two years for its implementation at the national level. This period is intended to give time to countries to adopt national legislations for the implementation of the new rules, establish institutional arrangements, and arrange for the training of officials.

Most WTO Agreements also provide special and differential treatment to developing countries by providing longer transitional periods to prepare themselves for the acceptance of the obligations. In some cases, least developed countries are provided longer periods than those normally provided to developing countries. Some Agreements also provide longer periods for the application of rules in certain specified areas as compared to the time provided for the general application of rules.

In the past, developing countries were not under any obligation to apply the rules during the validity of the transitional period. The obligation to apply them arose only on the termination of this period. Because of this, many developing countries postponed taking action at the national level for the adoption of the required legislation, or for the training of officials, until almost the end of the transitional period. This resulted in countries accepting obligations without building up institutional and technical capacities for the application of the rules. In some cases, this also resulted in requests for the extension of the transitional period.

5.2   The new mandate

Past experience with the application of the 'transitional period technique' for the extension of S&D treatment has resulted in other provisions being incorporated in the mandate for negotiations in the area of trade facilitation. These include:

- S&D treatment should extend beyond the granting of a transitional period;

- Developing and least developed countries should be provided technical assistance to help them prepare for the application of the rules of the proposed Agreement, and for the implementation of any commitments they may assume during the negotiations;

- The extent and timing of developing and least developed countries entering into commitments should be related to their implementation capacities; and

- Least developed countries should only be required to undertake those commitments consistent with their individual development, their financial and trade needs, and their administrative or institutional capacities.

5.3 Complementing the transitional period technique with the GATS scheduling technique

These specific provisions suggest that, in addition to one standard transitional period, techniques that take into account the technical capacities of individual developing countries (to implement the rules) would have to be adopted while extending S&D treatment to them. It may be possible to achieve these aims by combining the transitional period technique with the scheduling technique used for recording the commitment assumed under the General Agreement on Trade in Services (GATS). The main advantage of using this technique is that it would enable developing countries to decide on the level and nature of the obligation they would like to undertake on a rule-by-rule basis.

The use of the scheduling technique in undertaking obligations should be available only to developing countries. Developed countries are expected to accept the obligations which the Agreement imposes on a binding basis from the day it becomes operational. Those developing countries which feel they can accept, on a binding basis, all of the obligations which the Agreement imposes from the time it becomes effective, may decide on not taking advantage of the scheduling technique.

All developing countries, except those which accept the Agreement on a fully binding basis, will have a separate schedule. The schedule of each country will be divided into two parts. **Part I** will list all those rules which do not present serious problems of acceptance by developing and least developed countries. Rules raising trade policy issues, and which have been classified under Category I mentioned above, will be listed in this part. Most of these rules aim at adding more specificity and precision to the obligations which the GATT Articles V, VIII and X impose. Since all countries are currently bound by the basic obligations which these articles impose, they are expected to accept the additional new obligations imposed by the new rules adopted at the conclusion of the Round within the one/two years provided for their acceptance at the national level.

However, some countries – especially least developed countries – may require time to prepare themselves for the acceptance of the obligations imposed by a few of the rules falling in the Part I category. A transitional period of five/seven years, beginning from the date of the adoption of the Agreement, should be available to these countries.

Part II of the schedule will list all the rules adopted regarding the techniques and modalities which have been classified under Category II above, and which the custom administrations would be required to follow in the clearance of goods. Currently, there are no WTO rules regarding most of these techniques and modalities. The international norms or standards which do exist have been developed by international organisations such as the WCO and UNECE. Only a few developing countries are applying them on a *de jure* basis. The technical capacities currently available for the application of these standards and norms in these developing countries vary. The capacity of countries to effectively apply any new rules that may be adopted in the course of the present ongoing negotiations will also depend on how widespread the use of information technology is in its business community. Thus, many countries may need assistance for the development of IT infrastructure.

For the measures listed in Part II of the schedule, a longer maximum transitional period of 15 years for the acceptance of obligations on a binding basis by all countries, may have to be provided.

For the rules listed in Part I and II of the schedule, it shall be left to developing countries to choose the level of obligation they wish to assume during the specified transition periods. These countries would also have to lay down conditions to ensure that they are not required to accept obligations for which they do not have the technical capacity to implement. The choice which developing and least developed countries could exercise in accepting obligations on a rule by rule basis would, *inter alia*, include the following:

- Undertake no obligation to apply the rule;
- Undertake to apply the rule after a specific number of years;
- Make the application of the rule conditional on the provision of technical assistance and indicate the type and nature of assistance required; and
- Commit to apply the rule on a binding basis.

The final decision regarding which rules should be included in Part I (needing a shorter transitional period for compliance) and which in Part II (needing a longer transitional period for compliance) would have to be decided through negotiations which take into account the criteria used in classifying the rules into the two categories mentioned above, as well as such factors as:

- The degree of difficulty that may be faced by developing countries in accepting the rule, and
- The resources and capacity required for implementation.[2]

An example of such a schedule is provided in **Annex II** to **Chapter 5.**

All schedules would be based on the self-assessment made by each concerned country regarding the nature and type of obligation it is prepared to assume, and of its technical assistance needs. Countries would be required to submit these schedules to the WTO within the one/two years provided between the date of the adoption of the Agreement and the date of its becoming operational. This would ensure that negotiations on securing technical assistance from international agencies or donor countries are completed, and most of the assistance needed is made available to the country concerned before the Agreement becomes operational.

The WTO secretariat would be expected to prepare a consolidated document listing all schedules and to publish it in the concerned country's website on the WTO Internet portal.

The commitments assumed in the schedule shall be subject to periodic reviews – once in two years – in the Committee on Trade Facilitation. The purpose of such reviews will be to assess the effectiveness of the technical assistance provided under the Agreement in facilitating the implementation of its rules, especially the application of new methods for the clearance of goods through customs. Such reviews will also help in finding out whether it is possible for countries which have not undertaken fully binding commitments, to improve the level of commitments they have assumed under their schedules.

---

2   See also the proposal by the Republic of China, India, Pakistan and Sri Lanka for a further description of the criteria mentioned above (TN/TF/W/82).

5.4 Comparison of the proposals with those tabled by other delegations

Among the proposals tabled on S&D treatment, perhaps the two most comprehensive are the proposals tabled by the Core Group of Developing Countries on Trade Facilitation (CGDCTF),[3] and by a group consisting of developed and developing countries.[4]

There are some important differences between the two proposals, both in substance and nuance. The proposal by the Core Group envisages that for developing, least developed and low income countries in transition, special and differential treatment would be provided on the basis of the nature of the obligations. These would be divided into two categories.

- Category 1 would include those obligations which developing, least developed, and low income countries in transition would have to implement from the date the Agreement enters into force. The first of such obligations would be agreed upon in the negotiations. However, it may be possible for these countries to avail of a transitional period to prepare themselves for the implementation of such obligations. Such a transitional period would have to be determined in the negotiations, and would not exceed [X] years.

- Category 2 would include all the obligations not included in Category 1. It is quite possible that in respect of some of the obligations in this category, developing, least developed and low income countries in transition may require technical assistance for capacity building. Countries needing such assistance would be expected to prepare capacity building plans, and to notify them to the WTO Secretariat before the Agreement enters into force. The transitional period required for the acquisition of implementation capacity should be specified in these plans. Thus, the transitional periods so required could vary from country to country.

At the end of the implementation period, each country would be expected to assess whether the assistance provided has resulted in the acquisition of the required capacity. If the capacity building plans provide for their involvement, both the donor country and the implementing agency should be associated in making such an assessment. When such an assessment is able to conclude that the country receiving the assistance has acquired the necessary capacity, it shall notify the WTO Committee on Trade Facilitation. After such notification, the country would be under obligation to apply the measure or rule.

It is envisaged that, in practice, there would only be a few cases in which the assistance receiving country – after assessment and evaluation – comes to the conclusion that 'capacity has yet to be entirely acquired.' In such cases, the assistance receiving country and the donor country should bring the matter to the notice of the Trade Facilitation Technical Assistance and Capacity Building Support Unit (TFTACBSU). After reviewing the matter, the Unit could make appropriate recommendations.

The proposals further envisage that for some of the obligations falling under category 2, the Agreement may not impose a binding requirement to apply the rules. It may only require countries to make their best endeavours to implement them (taking into account their individual capacity) as soon as possible after the Agreement enters into force.

---

3   TN/TF/W/142, submitted by Bangladesh, Botswana, Cuba, Egypt, India, Indonesia, Jamaica, Kenya, Malaysia, Mauritius, Namibia, Nepal, Nigeria, Philippines, Rwanda, Tanzania, Trinidad & Tobago, Uganda, Venezuela, Zambia, and Zimbabwe.

4   TN/TF/W/137, submitted by Armenia, Canada, Chile, China, Dominican Republic, Ecuador, the European Communities, Georgia, Guatemala, Honduras, Japan, Kyrgyz Republic, Mexico, Moldova, Nicaragua, Pakistan, Paraguay, Peru, Sri Lanka, Switzerland, and Uruguay.

5.5 The advantage of the scheduling technique over the technique suggested in the tabled proposals

Even though there are a number of common elements in the two proposals tabled by the delegations (described above) and the approach suggested in the Handbook, there are some important differences. For instance, the scheduling technique would provide a structured framework to a developing or least developed country to decide, on a rule-by-rule basis, for the level of obligation it wishes to undertake during the course of the transitional period, after taking into account its technical capacity for implementation. The experience gained during the application of the relevant rules would also make for a learning process and, thus, assist countries in improving the nature and the level of obligations being gradually undertaken by them, the ultimate goal being their accepting fully all binding obligations by the end of the transitional period of 15 years.

These two proposals are also based on the assumption that the verification exercise – undertaken on a bilateral (or trilateral) basis when the project is about to be completed – will, in most cases, result in an agreement that the capacity to accept a binding commitment to apply the relevant rules has been developed.

However, past experience has shown that even when reform programmes are adopted after a careful identification of the needs of a country, they have often failed to achieve the desired results, or have met with only partial success. This is so because of a number of extraneous factors.

These considerations have made World Bank economists like Michael Finger and John S. Wilson – with much experience in the administration and disbursement of aid for development – to point out that in practice it is often difficult to separate the benefits achieved in the area of trade facilitation from the improvements in the domestic business environment and the progress made in the development of infrastructure of the aid receiving country. This makes it necessary to exercise extreme caution in making direct links between the receipt of assistance for capacity building on the one hand, and the acceptance of a binding obligation to implement them on the other.

5.6 Some tentative ideas on the multilateral mechanism that could be adopted for review and evaluation

The above factors suggest that it would be necessary to leave the aid receiving country to itself assess whether or not the necessary capacity has been developed and whether it is ready to accept obligations to apply the relevant rules on a binding basis. Consultations arranged on a multilateral basis should examine those cases in which the aid receiving country considers that the assistance provided has not resulted in the full development of the required capacity for implementation.

Also, any multilateral mechanism that may be established in the WTO for the review and evaluation of how far the aid provided is contributing towards building implementation capacities would have to draw a balance between the WTO approach of imposing binding obligations, and the difficulties of applying such an approach in areas where the capacity to implement rules and commitments is dependent on many development related extraneous factors. It may be possible to draw such a balance by ensuring that the same principles as are applied to reviews undertaken, on a country-by-country basis, by the WTO's Trade Policy Review Mechanism (TPRM) of developments in trade policy are also applied to reviews undertaken in the area of trade facilitation. These reviews are carried out against the background of the 'wider economic and developmental needs, policies and objectives of the Member concerned' as well as the external environment it faces. [5]

6. Modalities for the adoption of rules on the settlement of disputes

The chapter on Dispute Settlement (Chapter 6) states how a number of developing countries appear to consider that the WTO provisions regarding the settlement of disputes should not be applicable for at least the first 10-15 years. The main reason for this reluctance is that the primary objective of the Agreement is to gradually prepare least developed countries as well as other countries at a middle or lower stage of development to accept the obligations of the Agreement by providing them the technical assistance needed to build up their implementation capacities. Thus, it would be undesirable and inappropriate to apply the WTO dispute settlement procedures during the transitional period provided for accepting the Agreement on a fully binding basis.

A tentative suggestion is that the solution may lie in the adoption of a 'two-track' approach under the proposed Agreement for the settlement of any differences and disputes arising in the transitional period.

The Committee on Trade Facilitation which would be established under the Agreement would be responsible for the consideration of any complaints regarding the non-compliance of its provisions.

- If requested by the complaining country, the Committee shall authorise it to invoke the WTO dispute settlement procedures if, after a preliminary examination of the complaint, the Committee has reasons to believe that:
  - In the case of a complaint against a developed country, it is in breach of the obligations under the Agreements and/or under GATT Articles V, VIII and X; and
  - In the case of a complaint against a developing country, it is in breach of the obligations which it has accepted under the Agreement on a binding basis and/or of the obligations under GATT Article V and VIII and X.

- In all other cases, the Committee shall aim at settling disputes through conciliation.

- Where the Committee finds that the failure to comply with the rules of the Agreement or to abide by the commitments is due to the lack of technical competence on the part of the 'defendant' (the party against which the complaint is made), it shall examine the case and make appropriate recommendations for the provision of technical assistance.

It should be emphasised that the main purpose of the procedures suggested above is to avoid dispute settlement procedures being applied to developing countries which do not have the technical capacity to implement the rules. Developed countries also recognise that it would be futile to insist on the application of the WTO dispute settlement system to complaints brought against such countries.

However, the procedures would permit the WTO's dispute settlement mechanism being invoked in cases of non-compliance of the provisions of the Agreement by a developed country, including in cases where it is alledged that it has failed to abide by the commitment it has assumed to provide technical assistance to developing countries for capacity building.

---

5   See the Agreement Establishing the WTO, Annex 3 A 'Objectives', para (ii) on the Trade Policy Review Mechanism.

7. Relevance of the Single Undertaking for the negotiations in the area of trade facilitation

Chapter 7 points out that, in establishing the modalities for negotiations in the above areas, it is important to remember that the negotiations relating to trade facilitation commenced only in the latter part of 2004, while the negotiations in other areas of the Doha Round (e.g. relating to trade in agricultural and non-agricultural products and in services) began in 2001. Because of this late start as well as the complexity of the issues that have to be addressed, it may be necessary to continue with the negotiations 'in certain clearly defined subject areas' after the Agreement on Trade Facilitation is adopted at the conclusion of the Round.

The Doha Ministerial Declaration stipulates that the 'conduct, conclusion and entry into force of the outcome of the negotiations shall be treated as parts of a single undertaking.'[6] Thus, this 'single undertaking' principle implies that the negotiations on the Agreement on Trade Facilitation would have to be completed at the same time as the negotiations on other subjects of the Doha Round. However, past experience of the application of this principle shows that in certain areas of the negotiations, the WTO members have agreed to continue the negotiations even after the closure of a Round. For instance, in the past (the Uruguay Round), it was agreed that the negotiations on certain 'unfinished business' in the General Agreement on Trade in Services (GATS) should continue after the Round, and be completed within specific periods.

In the area of trade facilitation, even though it may be possible to adopt an Agreement containing basic rules at the same time as the negotiations in other areas of the Round are concluded, it may become necessary to agree that negotiations on a limited number of specified areas of a highly technical nature (and for which participating countries consider more time is required for study and analysis) would be continued after the conclusion of the Round, for example for a period of two years. The practice described above was followed in the past in the application of the Single Undertaking concept and suggests that it may be possible to continue such negotiations by adopting a suitable Decision at the end of the Round.

A tentative structure of the Agreement that could be adopted if the negotiations are undertaken on the basis of the modalities described above is provided in the chapter.

---

6   See paragraph 47 of the Doha Ministerial Declaration, (WT/MIN(01)/DEC/1).

SECTION II: ANNEX

ANNEX

Analysis of the Proposals Tabled for the Clarification and Improvement of the Provisions of Articles V, VIII and X

This section summarises chapters 8-16 of the Handbook which provide an analysis of the proposals. The summaries are presented in the form of tables (see Annex below), displaying the proposals alongside the issues that need further examination. The proposals included in the tables are listed below.

I.   Proposals relating to measures primarily raising trade policy issues

A.   Publication obligations;

B.   The level of fees;

C.   The formalities and procedures applicable in the clearance of goods through customs;

D.   The establishment of a mechanism for the exchange of customs related information among WTO members; and

E.   Preshipment inspection.

II.   Proposals relating to techniques and modalities which customs could adopt to facilitate the release of goods

A.   Facilitating the release of goods through customs by adopting risk assessment and management techniques, and other new innovative methods, and

B.   Other measures to facilitate the imports and exports of goods.

III.   Transit trade and the special problems of landlocked countries

I. Proposals relating to measures primarily raising trade policy issues

A. *Publication obligations*

GATT Rules

Article X imposes an obligation to publish all laws, regulations, judicial decisions, administrative rulings of general application, and those pertaining to the classification or the valuation of products for customs purposes, to the rates of duties, to taxes and other charges, to requirements, restrictions and the prohibition of imports and exports etc. (Para 1).

It further requires the maintenance or adoption (as soon as possible) of judicial, arbitral and administrative tribunals or procedures for the purpose, inter alia, of the prompt review and correction of administrative actions relating to customs matters (Para 2).

Tabled proposals	Points for consideration
1. The scope and content of these obligations should be widened to cover information on, *inter alia*: ▓ The practices followed by customs in internal decision making; ▓ The substantive content of measures affecting foreign trade; ▓ Border related agency processes; and ▓ Administrative guidelines.	The present obligation is confined to the publication of laws, regulations, and judicial decisions. The widening of the obligation to cover 'information' about such matters as the internal decision making process, border related agency processes, and administrative guidelines would put a heavy administrative burden on customs. These proposals would have to be examined against the current trend of many governments confining themselves to publishing only basic rules and regulations, and leaving it to the Chambers of Commerce or Trade Associations to bring out manuals or guides which explain customs clearance procedures and documentary requirements in detail, and provide other relevant information. Thus, it may be desirable to consider that instead of imposing an obligation on governments to publish 'information' on the processes used while applying rules, the rules should call on the customs to encourage business associations in their countries to bring out guides or manuals about how customs operate. They could also be asked to provide the financial resources needed to cover the costs of such publications wherever necessary. This would be in keeping with the proposals made for public-private partnership in the formulation and application of rules, and in the dissemination of information about customs practices.
2. Customs administrations should publish their reform plans.	Improvement in the effectiveness and efficiency of the services provided by the government is a management function. The concerned government departments are expected to take measures for the modernisation and improvement of services they provide on a continuous basis. Thus, in actual practice, it may be difficult for the authorities to decide which of their programmes should be treated as 'reform programmes' about which information should be published for the knowledge of the general public as well as the governments of other countries. Any decision about whether the measures adopted for the improvement of services should be published – and if published, the amount of publicity to be extended – should be left to the country concerned. In some cases, customs administrations may be reluctant to publicise the reform measures being undertaken until they are fully implemented because of the uncertainty about the continued availability of financial resources.

3. Standard time for release of goods:

Members shall measure and publish their own average time for the release of goods in a consistent manner on a periodic basis, based on the WCO Time Release Study.

Members shall endeavour to continuously reduce such average release time.

In case of a significant delay in the release of goods, Members shall provide the traders who have made written requests with the reasons for the delay except when such notification would impede the pursuance of legitimate policy objectives.

The average time taken for the clearance of goods varies from country to country, depending on the prevalence of factors such as customs malpractices (e.g. the tendency on the part of importers to undervalue imported goods), and whether the imports are made in bulk by a few large firms or by numerous smaller companies. Differences in the composition of imports can also influence variations in clearance time. Countries in which a high proportion of imports require approvals before clearance from the Ministries of Industry or Health, the average time taken for the clearance of all imports may be longer than in countries where such imports constitute only a small proportion.

Experience has also shown that countries which have been able to reduce the time taken for the clearance and release of goods following the adoption of a reform programme have not been able to maintain the speed of clearance as a result of the inability of the government to provide the required financial resources after the termination of the assistance programme.

Thus, a number of countries seem to consider it premature to be required to publish the average time it takes to clear goods through customs and to also explain periodically the reasons for variations in the standard clearance period.

---

4. The obligation to publish should apply to publication on the Internet.

Internet publication is only one of the ways by which laws, rules and regulations could be published, and relevant information made available to the public. Currently, Internet publication would be suitable only for a few developing countries where the use of IT among traders and the business community is widely prevalent. In other countries, more traditional methods of publication may be necessary.

---

5. The rules should impose an obligation on countries to take into account the views and comments of the business sector, consumer associations, academics, professionals, and other stakeholders when formulating new rules or assessing them.

There is increasing recognition on the part of most governments (including those of developing countries) of the need to consult all interested stakeholders when formulating new laws and regulations, or when reviewing existing ones. However, as one of the proposals recognises, it would be necessary to leave it to the judgement of the concerned country about how such consultations should be arranged, and whether any views expressed by traders or other stakeholders should be accepted. Any requirement imposing an obligation on governments to justify why the views of their traders have not been accepted may put them in awkward and embarrassing situations, particularly in relation to laws and regulations dealing with customs matters. Many of these regulations are aimed at striking a balance between the control functions of the customs (that the revenues due are fully collected and that there is full compliance with customs rules) and the interests of the traders who would like to see such controls kept to the minimum in order to facilitate trade.

The right to comment should also be available to the governments of other countries.

The idea of giving the right to comment to the governments of other countries appears to have been borrowed from the Agreements on TBT and SPS. The agreements require countries to provide an opportunity to other countries to comment on the draft TBT regulations and SPS Measures in all cases where they are not based on international standards.

The country adopting new laws or regulations should be under obligation to provide an explanation to traders and other WTO members as to why their comments have not been taken into account.

Any examination of whether this concept should be applied while adopting rules relating to customs procedures will have to bear in mind that the basic condition applicable to the adoption of technical regulations and SPS measures – viz. that they should ordinarily be based on international standards – does not apply to customs related laws and regulations. These are adopted by governments after taking into account the views and needs of their customs authorities and, where considered desirable and appropriate, the views of the industry, trade associations, and other stakeholders. In other words, they are tailored to the trade situation prevailing in the country, and aim at striking a balance between the need for controls on import and export transactions, (given the prevalence of malpractices such as the undervaluation of goods, and other forms of customs related corruption) and the desire of the business community to keep such controls to the minimum in order to facilitate trade. Consequently, the approach adopted, and the detailed provisions included in the laws and regulations, vary greatly from country to country.

Thus, many countries are apprehensive about giving the right to other member countries to comment on their domestic laws and regulations. This could lead to unnecessary tensions, particularly if a country is put under obligation to give reasons for its non-acceptance of the comments of other governments while adopting the legislation or regulation. In the case of laws, such a requirement may be considered as unnecessary interference by a foreign government in the work of its national parliament.

---

6. All countries should establish enquiry points or a single national enquiry point (SNEP) which can supply information regarding documentation requirements, duties and other charges payable on imported and exported products etc. to interested traders and other stakeholders.

The subjects about which information may be requested by traders, and other members of the business community, are handled by different departments in the customs administration itself, and by national standards institutions, the Ministry of Health, and other departments which play a role in the clearance of goods. The effective working of the enquiry point, and its ability to provide the requested information promptly and efficiently, depends greatly on how far it receives cooperation from other departments and Ministries.

The TBT and SPS Agreements also impose an obligation on countries to establish enquiry points to provide information, *inter alia*, on all technical regulations and SPS measures. In some countries these enquiry points are playing a useful role; in others they are not able to provide useful services because of the inability of the government to provide the financial resources required for recurring expenditure on staff, computers, and other related facilities.

In discussions on this subject, some delegations have suggested that technical and financial assistance should be provided by donor agencies for the establishment of such enquiry points only if the country concerned is able to provide an undertaking that it will be able to meet the recurring expenditure after the termination of the technical assistance project. Further, the need for the establishment of such a point, and its location should be left to the judgement of the country concerned. It should also be recognised that the information provided by such an enquiry point does not have any legal consequences.

B.   *The level of fees*

GATT Rules

Arts. X and VII stipulate that countries should ensure that the fees and charges levied by them in connection with importation and exportation should be:

● *Limited to the approximate costs of services rendered, and*

● *Should not represent indirect protection to domestic products or taxation on imports or exports for fiscal purposes.*

Tabled proposals	Points for consideration
1. The rules relating to the level of fees should be clarified to ensure that the fees charged do not exceed the costs of services rendered.	In addition to customs duties, a number of developing countries currently levy fees and taxes, such as:

In addition to customs duties, a number of developing countries currently levy fees and taxes, such as:

▓ Customs surcharge;
▓ Tax on foreign exchange transactions procedures;
▓ Stamp tax;
▓ Import license fee;
▓ Consular invoice fee;
▓ Statistical tax;
▓ Tax on transport facilities;
▓ Taxes or charges on sensitive products;
▓ Surcharge for the development of port facilities and of housing for fishermen; and
▓ Fees charged to finance the activities of the Regional Trade Area Secretariats.

There are doubts about whether some of the fees and charges being levied meet the criteria in Article VIII.

The issue of limiting fees and charges to the approximate cost of the services rendered by customs was discussed and debated during the revision of the WCO Kyoto Convention. However, no standard could be agreed upon due to the divergence of views among countries on, *inter alia*, how the cost for determining the fees should be calculated.

A major constraint faced by many developing countries while adopting new and innovative methods in customs clearance – such as the application of risk management techniques, post- audit, and the recognition of authorised traders – is the lack of financial resources. In this context, the proposal made by one of the delegations suggesting that both the direct costs (for equipment, material, and utilities) and the indirect costs (recurring expenditure on the maintenance of equipment, rent for office premises, etc.) should be included in the calculation of costs, could provide a useful basis for further examination. It may also be necessary to consider whether the costs should include other elements, such as expenditure on the training and salaries of additional staff that may have to be employed as a result of the adoption of the reform programme. To ensure that the fees or charges calculated on such a basis do not impose a heavy additional burden on importers and exporters, the recovery of direct costs should be spread over a 'reasonable' period of time. However, the determination of how long this should be should be left to the country concerned.

The rules should also recognise that any fee aimed at recovering the direct costs of the reform programme as well as meeting the recurring expenditure on its implementation should not be considered as constituting the 'direct protection of the domestic industry' or as 'taxation of imports for fiscal purposes,' provided that:

- The fees levied do not exceed the actual expenditure incurred on meeting direct and recurring costs, and
- In the case of direct costs, the recovery of such costs is spread over a reasonable period of time.

2. The rules should impose an obligation on countries to notify fees to the WTO.	Whether the rules should impose an obligation on countries to notify fees to the WTO is a question that may need careful consideration. The main purpose of requiring notification is to ensure transparency. As countries start publishing information regarding customs laws and regulations on the Internet, interested traders and the governments of other countries will have easy access to such information. The imposition of an obligation to notify fees to the WTO could impose an unnecessary and avoidable additional administrative burden on the governments of member countries.

C.   *Appeals Procedures*

GATT Rules:
Para 3(b) of Article X requires countries to maintain judicial arbitral or administrative tribunals or procedures for the purpose, inter alia, of the prompt review and correction of administrative action relating to customs matters.

Tabled Proposals	Points for consideration
New rules should be adopted to provide: - The right of appeal; - Transparency; - Standard time for the resolution of minor appeals; and - The costs of minor appeals be kept to the minimum.	The need to adopt new rules in this area would have to be considered, taking into account that the provision of the rights of traders to appeal first to a higher authority within the customs administration or a tribunal and, if necessary, to a judicial body, already exist in GATT as well as in the Agreement on Customs Valuation. The Kyoto Convention also contains detailed provisions on all aspects of appeals procedures. The proposals requiring countries to fix a 'standard time for the resolution of minor appeals' and to ensure that the costs of appeal are kept low may, however, pose problems for many developing countries in which there are backlogs of undecided cases due to many reasons, including a shortage of staff. Likewise, the costs of appeal depend largely on the level of fees charged by lawyers specialising in the field of customs law. Thus, there are limits to government intervention in keeping the costs of appeal as low as possible. Another question relating to the above is how to identify 'a minor appeal.' According to some proposals, the obligation to fix a standard time is expected to apply only to this category of appeals. The proponents of the proposals have clarified that minor appeals may be defined as covering those cases involving low value consignments, imports by individuals, payment of duties of less than EUR 1000, and others raising minor legal issues.

D. *Formalities and procedures applicable in the clearance of goods through customs (Art VIII)*

GATT Rules
In addition to the rules relating to how the level of fees should be determined, Article VIII contains rules which call on countries to:

- *Minimise the incidence and complexity of import and export formalities;*

- *Simplify import and export documentation; and*

- *Review disciplines and formalities, if requested by another member country.*

Tabled Proposals	Points for consideration
1. A commitment to apply non-discriminatory treatment should be built into the design and application of import/export formalities.	The proposals recognise that customs authorities may often have to exercise rigorous controls in the examination of goods originating in certain countries. Such rigorous controls involving documentation scrutiny and physical checking are generally applied to imports from countries where past experience has shown that their exporters are routinely engaging in undervaluation or other customs frauds. Customs may decide to apply such controls on the basis of risk assessment criteria or, where it has not been possible for them to adopt such a technique, on the basis of the confidential information it has been able to collect. Thus, in actual practice, it would be difficult to apply the principle of non-discrimination to procedures followed by customs in the clearance of goods.

In this context it is relevant to note that para 3(a) of Article X imposes an obligation on countries to administer all their laws, regulations, and decisions relating to customs matters in a 'uniform, impartial and reasonable way.' The difficulties that customs would encounter in abiding by the non-discrimination principle in the clearance of goods appears to have made the drafters of these provisions to not include the application of the principle, and only state that such rules should be applied in an impartial and reasonable manner. |
| 2. Consular formalities should be abolished. | Consular formalities in which embassy officials in the exporting countries seek to verify whether the value displayed on the invoice reflects the correct value of the goods being exported have become outdated This is so because it is becoming increasingly possible for customs officials in importing countries to carry out such checks using the data available on prices charged in the past, and other price data.

Such formalities are also inconsistent with the rules of the Agreement on Customs Valuation which, *inter alia*, require that except in cases where there are doubts about the truth or accuracy of the value declared by the importer, customs shall use it as a basis for determining the customs duty payable by the importer. Moreover, as such duties are currently being charged only by a few countries, it may be possible to adopt a rule prohibiting their use. |

3. Members periodically review fees, charges, formalities, and other requirements at reasonable intervals.	Keeping the procedures adopted for the implementation of rules (and whether they apply in the area of customs or other areas) constantly under review is a management function and an important element in good governance. Thus, it should be left to each country to decide whether there is a need for review and if so, when it should be undertaken. International rules requiring countries to undertake reviews on a periodical basis could be counterproductive, and add unnecessary administrative burdens and costs. Thus, it would be desirable to consider carefully whether the existing rules requiring countries to undertake such reviews – if requested by another country which considers the procedures being applied in certain areas are causing barriers to its trade – should be broadened to impose an obligation for undertaking periodic reviews, even if such requests are not made.
4. Countries should minimise documentation requirements by using the UN Layout Key.	Taking into account the experience of the application of the UN Layout Key, the WCO has developed the Single Goods Declaration (SGD) in 1990. The form has also been adopted (with minor modifications) by the European Union to meet the requirements of the customs administrations of its member countries.
	The UN Layout Key has been adopted by some developing countries as the format to be used by importers. However, a number of other developing countries appear reluctant to adopt it. Past experience with the adoption of the UN Layout Key format by EU members and other countries has shown that it may have to be modified to suit the specific trading realities and conditions prevailing in the country choosing to use it. Thus, it may be necessary to examine – by sending a questionnaire to the countries which have not adopted the format so far– the practical difficulties that they feel they may encounter in using the format.
	In addition to the main declaration, a number of developing countries also require other supporting documents. While some of these may be redundant, in countries where undervaluation and customs fraud are widely prevalent, the customs authorities consider them essential for ascertaining the authenticity of the information provided in the importer's declaration.
5. The complexity of export and import formalities and documentation requirements should not be "more trade restrictive than necessary to fulfil the legitimate objectives."	Under WTO jurisprudence, the 'necessity test' refers to the criteria which countries are expected to apply in determining whether the measures used at the national level are not more trade restrictive than necessary to fulfil legitimate objectives.
	The TBT and SPS Agreements prescribe rules clarifying how the necessity test should be applied in adopting technical regulations and SPS measures. In particular, they state that the standards used in such regulations and measures must be based on 'scientific evidence.' The obligation to base standards on science is more explicit in the case of SPS measures than in the case of technical regulations. Because of this, in judging whether SPS measures are justified and 'necessary,' it is possible to make a relatively objective judgement since the physical and chemical sciences, with their more theoretical foundations and well defined methods for analysis provide more objective criteria while applying the necessity test than would be the case if they were not based on scientific analysis.
	In the case of trade facilitation, investigating authorities would not have such scientifically predictable and definitive criteria while applying the necessity

test. The customs determine the extent of control they wish to exercise over imports/exports through the scrutiny of documentation, physical checking, or on the basis of information derived from an importer's past records of compliance with customs rules. Even though such information may be collected by applying methods that are scientific, the final judgment on the nature, type, and extent of control involves a large degree of discretion. Also, as some of the information which customs rely upon may be of a confidential nature, they may not wish to disclose it to external investigating authorities. Thus, in practice, it would be difficult for an outside body to be objective when determining whether the procedures adopted for imports/exports are 'more trade restrictive than necessary.'

E. The Establishment of a mechanism for the exchange of customs related information among WTO members

Tabled Proposals	Points for consideration
1. It is proposed (by India and USA) that a multilateral mechanism should be established for the exchange of a "defined universe of trade transaction information". Such information could include "documentation" or "data elements" that relate to the movement of goods across the border (e.g. the name of the importing or exporting party, the origin of goods, the description of goods, their classification, their declared value, the shipment company etc).	The genesis of this proposal can be traced to the initiatives taken by the Group of 7 – the seven largest economically developed countries. A Group of customs experts established by them have developed customs data models 'to standardise and reduce the amount of data necessary to meet customs requirements.' The Model developed by the Group was transmitted to the WCO and its application by other countries and by other international trade and development organisations was encouraged. The main objective of the WCO Data Model is to standardise the information needed by customs, both for the clearance of goods and for the security of borders, by developing 'data sets' for cargo reports, for import and export data, and for aligning the standards adopted in electronic transmission systems. This enables traders to submit import/export declarations electronically. Also, the adoption of such techniques as 'single window' and 'authorised importers' facilitates the speedy clearance of goods. The ability of countries to participate in the system for the exchange of information based on the WCO Data Model will depend greatly on how far the use of information technology is developed and spread among the trading community. Thus, the participation in the system will have to remain optional for a number of countries that do not have information technology available to traders to submit the data required for the clearance of goods through customs, as its use has not yet penetrated the business community.
2. In addition to the establishment of the general mechanism for the exchange of data information described above, a separate proposal, tabled by India, envisages the supply of information by the exporting countries to importing countries in a "limited number of cases," where the investigating	This proposal is not new. A similar proposal, tabled by India at the Doha Ministerial Conference, was discussed both in the WTO Committee on Customs Valuation and in the WCO Policy Commission. In these discussions, the thrust and the approach in the proposal received support from a large number of delegations of developing countries. However, it was strongly opposed by the delegations from developed countries.

authorities, after carrying out necessary internal verification, have reasons to doubt the truth or accuracy "of any element of the import and export declaration or supporting document."

The reasons for the opposition of these delegations are summarised below.

- Their domestic legislations (confidentiality and secrecy laws) prevent their customs authorities from 'routinely' providing such information. The legislations of some countries even contain an outright prohibition on the provision of such information, except in criminal cases and in cases where there are allegations of fraud.
- The value data at the disposal of the exporting countries is often not reliable, and not subject to the same level of scrutiny as in the importing country. Some countries keep export value information only for statistical purposes. Sometimes data is also kept on a transaction-by-transaction basis.

Developing countries have argued that the difficulties encountered by the customs administrations of exporting countries while verifying the values declared by the exporter should not be exaggerated. The fiscal authorities, responsible for collecting value added tax (VAT) in these countries verify most export values when examining the requests of exporters for VAT credits or refunds. Coordination between customs administrations and VAT refund authorities through an information exchange system could facilitate the compliance with the obligations that would be imposed on the exporting countries.

F.   Preshipment inspection

Rules of the Agreement on Preshipment Inspection (PSI Agreement)

The rules that must be followed by countries using PSI services and those that export to such countries are prescribed in the WTO Agreement on Preshipment Inspection. The Agreement envisages that developing countries should use such services 'as long as they are needed' and till such time as their customs administrations are able to develop their own technical capacities to provide the services for which they rely on PSI companies.

Tabled Proposals	Points for consideration
1. The use of PSI services should be prohibited or phased out.	Over 30 developing or transition economies are using the services of preshipment inspection (PSI) companies for: The physical checking of the goods to be imported in the countries of export; Advice on the prices of the products to be imported; and Advice on tariff classification. Much of the evidence on the usefulness of PSI companies is anecdotal, and there is a wide gap between the views of analysts considering such services useful and those who do not, and who even maintain that such services should be prohibited. However, it appears that in many countries where the undervaluation of goods is widely prevalent and where it is not possible for customs to ascertain the true value of the imported goods, the use of such services seems to have resulted in the facilitation of trade, and a fuller collection of revenues due. The above considerations would have to be taken into account while examining further the proposal on the use of PSI services that has been tabled.

The practice followed in the past was to undertake inspections in the country from which the goods were to be exported prior to their shipment (hence the term 'preshipment inspection') in order to determine their value for customs purposes, and to check them physically. Before the Uruguay Round, many firms considered that the practices followed by PSI companies in inspecting goods for export in exporting countries constituted barriers to trade. Thus, the PSI Agreement lays down rules which the PSI companies are expected to follow while assessing whether the invoice price correctly reflects the value of the goods as well as during the physical inspections undertaken in exporting countries prior to the shipment of goods.

The technological developments that have taken place in recent years are increasingly making it possible for these companies to provide the details of their price verification and physical inspection services in the country of import ('destination country') instead of in the exporting country, through:

- The utilisation of cargo scanning equipment;
- Risk management databases; and
- Information technology (IT) solutions, such as trade community network systems, to facilitate the implementation of the 'single window' concept.

In providing such services, these companies often work in cooperation with customs authorities.

Thus, there is a gradual shift in the way services are being provided by PSI companies: instead of carrying out inspections and price verifications in the exporting country 'prior to the shipment of goods,' they are now undertaking such functions in the country of importation. From the strictly legal point of view, the provisions of the WTO Preshipment Agreement are not applicable when such services are provided in the country of importation after the goods have arrived, even if they are provided by a company which is registered as a preshipment inspection company.

II. Proposals relating to the techniques and modalities which customs could adopt to facilitate the release of goods

A. *Facilitating the release of goods through customs by adopting risk assessment and management techniques and other new innovative methods*

GATT Rules
In most of these areas, there are currently no specific WTO rules. The legal basis for the adoption of such rules is provided by the provisions of Art VIII which, inter alia, emphasise the need on the part of WTO members to take action for:

- *Minimising the incidence and complexity of import and export formalities, and*

- *Simplifying import and export documentation*

On almost all of these techniques and methods, the WCO and other international organisations e.g. UNECE or ISO, have adopted international standards.

Tabled Proposals	Points for consideration

Risk assessment and management

1. Customs should apply risk assessment and management techniques to expedite the clearance of goods through customs.

Risk management and assessment are management techniques that are widely used both in the private and public sector. In the public sector, the techniques are used by ministries and government departments for the assessment and examination of risks with regard to the achievement of the aims and objectives of the economic and social policies they propose to adopt.

The application of risk assessment and management techniques is not a rule-based process but is characterised by learning and experiment.

Consequently, if rules are adopted, they should provide sufficient discretionary authority to the senior management. Their aim should be only to encourage countries to apply such techniques, but leave the decision regarding how they should be applied to the management.

Traditionally, the practice in most customs administrations has been to allow the clearance of imported and exported goods only after the relevant documents are fully scrutinised, and all goods are physically checked, in order to ensure that they conform to the information provided by the importer/exporter regarding technical specifications, quality, quantity, and value.

However, risk assessment and management enables customs authorities to identify past transactions where there has been a high degree of compliance of customs rules in relation to such matters as declared value, tariff classification, and declaration of the origin of goods. The techniques could also be used to clearly identify importers who have a proven record of compliance, with no instance of the violation of customs rules to their credit.

By identifying such transactions, importers, and exporters, customs endeavour to classify them into different categories according to the risk that may exist for the non-compliance of rules. The most common practice is to classify imported products after an assessment of the risk of non-compliance into **high, low and medium** categories.

By using such categorisation, the customs determine the level of regulatory control that should be exercised at different levels of risk.

Imports falling into the **low risk** category are allowed in on the basis of declarations made by the importers and without any scrutiny of documentation or physical checking.

For imports falling in the **medium risk** category, customs may prescribe inspection on a selective basis. The selection of those transactions that are to be checked is made on the basis of criteria determined periodically by the higher management. The criteria are kept confidential in order to avoid the possibility of customs officials entering into collusive deals with traders for the avoidance of duties. This is particularly so in countries where customs related corruption is commonplace, and the practice of the undervaluation of imported goods widely prevalent.

For the remaining **high risk** categories, rigorous documentation control may be exercised, and a higher percentage of goods may undergo physical checking.

Case studies undertaken by the World Bank and the OECD regarding the experience with reform programmes have shown that in countries where information technology is well developed and its use widely prevalent especially among traders, customs can have easy access to the information needed to categorise transactions, importers, and exporters into difference risk categories. Thus, it becomes easier for them to allow the clearance of goods falling in the lower risk categories with only a limited scrutiny of documents, and without physical checking.

However, in countries where the practice of the undervaluation of goods by traders and other customs frauds are widely prevalent, the customs authorities are reluctant to rely entirely on the results of risk assessment systems in clearing goods. In such cases, they often tend to ignore the results of risk assessment and continue to classify a greater percentage of goods in the high risk categories (orange or red) because of fears that if they did otherwise, the revenues due would not be fully collected. Such practices are more prevalent in countries where, in the beginning of the year, the Ministry of Finance prescribes targets for the collection of revenue, and exercises vigilance on the progress that is being made in its collection.

Experience has also shown that the adoption of risk assessment measures is the most costly amongst the measures undertaken by countries to facilitate trade. This is so because of the expenditure incurred on infrastructure as well as training. Thus, the development of a well functioning and effective application of the system takes a number of years, and depends largely on the ability and willingness of countries to continue meeting the additional recurring expenditure from their annual budgets.

2. Countries should adopt the practice of designating authorised importers.

The adoption of risk management procedures also enables customs to adopt special or fast track procedures for the clearance of goods of those traders who have been able to establish a reputation for full compliance with customs rules and procedures. Such traders are referred to as 'authorised persons.' They are permitted to secure the release of goods on the basis of a minimum amount of information necessary to identify the goods. In certain cases, they may even obtain the clearance of goods at their own premises.

However, many countries are reluctant to adopt the system of 'authorised importers' as they fear that some firms may have to be included in the list of such importers because of their political connections. This can be so even though their past records may have proof that they have not shown full compliance with customs rules. The adoption of the system also presents practical problems: in many developing countries, imports are made by a large number of firms whose past records regarding their compliance with customs rules are not readily available.

3. Customs should increasingly rely on the system of post-audit.

In order to facilitate the early release of goods to be imported and exported, the risk management system envisages that customs should, where possible, rely on the system of post-audit to check the accuracy of the information provided in the documents rather than pre-check it prior to the release of goods. The selection of persons or companies which would be subjected to such audits is made on the basis of risk profiles. The special privileges extended to the 'authorised persons' (and their firms or companies) described above usually include the benefit of the post-audit. This is subject to their agreeing to have their accounts audited by customs after the release of goods. The objective of such post-audits is to check from the accounts and records of the companies whether the information they provided in the customs declaration regarding the value of their imported or exported goods, their origin and tariff classification, and the duty relief obtained under drawback/remission programmes was accurate or not.

The case studies referred to earlier show that although most of the countries covered have adopted a programme for post-audit, its generalised use has been limited because of resource constraints. Many countries do not have a sufficient number of people trained in undertaking such audits. The training of officials also poses practical problems: since the period of training is long, sending officials for training implies their absence from work for an extended period of time.

Moreover, in countries where corruption is widely prevalent, the senior management may be reluctant to rely on 'post- audits' because visits by auditors to the premises of the importing company may increase the possibilities for collusive deals with them.

4. Customs should adopt systems for providing advance rulings.	It considerably facilitates the business decision of firm or company regarding whether to import certain goods if there is a possibility of knowing before hand the exact duty that will have to be paid to customs. For this purpose, the laws of some countries provide that, if requested by a trader, customs should provide him/her with information in the form of a ruling on such matters as the tariff classification of the goods to be imported, and how their origin and value will be determined.
	Work on the preparation of such rulings requires coordination among different sections of the customs department. The general practice in countries that have adopted the practice for making such binding rulings is to establish a separate unit, staffed by experts in such areas as tariff classification, valuation, and the determination of the origin of goods. In deciding whether or not to adopt such a system, countries will have to take into consideration the administrative burden and financial costs needed to establish such units.

B. Other measures to facilitate the imports and exports of goods

Tabled Proposals	Points for consideration
1. Customs should be required to adopt systems for the pre-arrival clearance of goods.	The general practice of most customs administrations is to accept documentation after the goods have arrived. Increasingly, however, customs are encouraging importers to submit documents before the arrival of the goods in the port. The development of information technology (IT) facilitates the submission of documentation to customs before the arrival of goods at the ports of the importing country.
	Most developed countries and a few developing countries have now well-functioning systems for the pre-arrival clearance of goods. The system facilitates trade by reducing pressure on the regular staff responsible for examining documents after the arrival of goods.

However, the implementation of the system does, in most cases, require additional staff. Many developing countries, with resource-starved budgets, appear to be finding it difficult to find the funding needed for the adoption of the system of pre-arrival clearance.

2. Customs should establish 'one time shops'.	Even though customs is the primary agency responsible for the clearance of goods, it can release them only after importers have been able to get approval from other agencies responsible for ensuring that the imported goods conform to the technical regulations and requirements relating to their quality, safety, and conformity with health standards. The clearance of goods is often hindered because of the delays in obtaining approval from these agencies.

It is proposed that one of the ways to solve this problem is to ensure greater coordination among the various agencies, *inter alia*, through the establishment of 'one time shops.' The establishment of such 'one time shops' at all customs ports would, no doubt, greatly reduce the difficulties faced by traders in obtaining approvals from agencies situated in various ministries or government offices such as the Ministries of Health and Industry, and other national standard setting bodies. However, many developing countries may have to weigh the benefits of such 'one time shops' accruing to traders (because of reductions in clearance time) against the additional recurring costs they will have to incur in establishing them. |
| **3. Establishment of the single window clearance system should be encouraged.** | Most developed countries and some developing countries, in which the use of information technology (IT) among traders is well established, are facilitating greater coordination among agencies by adopting the 'single window' clearance system. Under this system, traders submit one single declaration containing all the data and information required by customs as well as the different agencies involved in the clearance of imported and exported goods.

The adoption of the 'single window' system by a particular country depends greatly on whether information technology is widely used among traders. For a large number of countries where the development of IT facilities are at a nascent stage, the adoption of the 'single window' concept, envisaging the electronic submission of a single document, is likely to be a long term goal in their present stage of development. |
| **4. Rules should be adopted to recognise the right of traders to secure the release of goods by providing collateral security where, *inter alia*:**

▦ There are differences between customs and the importers on the declared value of the imported goods, or on their tariff classification; and

▦ Goods are imported for exports after processing in the country. | As countries are already under an obligation under the Agreement on Customs Valuation to consider releasing goods on the basis of a security for the payment of duties provided by the importer in cases where there are differences between customs and the importer on the 'value' of the imported goods, the adoption of the proposals would only mean a broadening of this obligation to cover other differences between customs and traders on such matters as tariff classifications or the origin of goods. |

III. Transit trade and special problems of landlocked countries

GATT Rules

Countries through which goods imported or exported by landlocked countries (i.e. countries which are surrounded on all sides by other countries and do not have a sea coast) have to pass are known as transit countries.

Art V. contains rules governing transit trade.

Para 1 defines the term transit traffic to include goods, vessels and other means of transport. It clarifies that transit traffic is completed when the goods cross the frontier of the transit countries and enters the landlocked countries.

Para 2 of the Article provides the right of countries to the freedom of transit. It further clarifies that "there shall be freedom of transit through the territory of each country, via the routes most convenient for international transit, for traffic in transit to and from the territory of other countries". In order to ensure that countries are able to derive full benefits from the "right of transit," the rules further provide that "no distinction shall be made which is based on flags of vessels, the place of origin, departure, entry, exit or destination, or any circumstances relating to ownership of goods, of vessels and other means of transport".

It further affirms that "except in cases of failure to comply with applicable customs laws and regulations, such traffic coming and going to the territory of other contracting parties shall not be subject to unnecessary delays or restrictions and shall be exempt from customs duties and all forms of transit duties or other charges imposed on transit, except charges on transportation or those commensurate with administrative expenses entailed by transit or with the costs of services rendered".

Transit countries are also under obligations to ensure that transit charges and regulations are:

- *Reasonable having regard to the conditions of traffic; and*
- *Do not result in the collection of fees or the application of regulations or formalities to traffic in transit to and from any country, treatment that is less favourable than that it accords to traffic in transit to and from any other country.*

International Conventions

A number of Conventions that have been adopted for facilitating transit traffic and trade of landlocked countries complement these GATT rules. Important among them is the Customs Convention on the International Transport of Goods (commodity known as Transport International Router (TIR) Convention), Geneva (14 November 1975).

One of its main features is that the 'national association of transport operators' is responsible for the application of the procedures by transport operators. They issue the appropriate documents and provide a guarantee for the payment of customs duties and other taxes, in case where, because of the leakage of goods/or other reasons, the transport operators are required to pay them to the customs authorities of the transit countries.

From the point of view of the customs administrations, the main advantage of the system are:

- *Duties and taxes of risk during international transit movements are guaranteed up to US$ 50,000 (with a higher maximum for alcohol and tobacco), and*
- *Only registered transport operators are permitted to use TIR carnets, thus ensuring the reliability of the system.*

The TIR Convention has been a great success mainly in Europe. Though the system is being used by transport operators in Central Asia, the Caucasus and the Maghreb, and in some parts of the Middle East, its use in these countries has so far been modest. In June 1982, sixteen countries belonging to the Economic Community of West African States (ECOWAS) also established a system (commonly known as TRIE: Transit Routier Inter-Etats) which is similar to the International Convention. However, it is being ignored by transport operators in the membership countries: about 70% of transit procedures in the ECOWAS region stem from bilateral accords, and national regulations and procedures.

The main reason for the lack of success in the use of the Convention is the general absence of efficient and well functioning national associations of transport operators in most of these countries. Even in countries where effective and credible national associations exist, they are not in a position to set up the required system for guaranteeing payments of duties to customs of transit countries (in cases of the leakage of goods) due to the under development of the local financial infrastructure as well as the unwillingness of international insurance companies to provide cover given their perception of political and commercial risks.

Regional Agreements
A number of regional agreements on transit trade have been adopted in recent years. These include:

- *The Transit Routier Inter-Etats (TRIE) of ECOWAS, the one example beyond TIR of an agreement dedicated only to transit;*

- *The Association of Southeast Asian Nations (ASEAN) Framework Agreement on the Facilitation of Goods in Transit;*

- *The Greater Mekong Sub-region (GMS) Agreement for Facilitation of Cross Border Transport of Goods and People; and*

- *The Economic Cooperation Organisation's (ECO) Transit Transport Framework Agreement – formed by Afghanistan, Azerbaijan, Iran, Kazakhstan, Kyrgyzstan, Pakistan, Tajikistan, Turkey, Turkmenistan, and Uzbekistan; and*

- *The Common Market for Eastern and Southern Africa (COMESA) Agreement on a Single Administrative Document.*

However, these regional agreements tend to lay down broad goals and policy directions. Actual customs transit facilitation may be dependent on other existing agreements or procedures. A 2001 UNCTAD report points out "there has not been any shortage of measures and initiatives to improve facilitation of transit traffic. COMESA, ECA and SADC all have various measures that are in place to address transit facilitation. Unfortunately, the major problem has been poor implementation."

GATT Rules and Tabled Proposals	Points for consideration
1. It is, *inter alia*, suggested that countries should be required to apply the principle of non-discrimination to: ▓ Modes of transport used in transit; ▓ Carriers of goods in transit; ▓ The routes chosen; and ▓ The types of consignments in relation to transit procedures.	The difficulties that may be encountered while strictly applying the MFN principle to customs control procedures would also be relevant in the case of transit trade. The extent of documentary control and physical inspections could vary according to the level of risks regarding the non-compliance of transit rules. If the customs authorities find that because of collusive links among traders, there is a greater risk of goods being leaked during transit into domestic markets if they are transported by road, they may like to insist that imports originating in countries in which the risk of such leakage is high, must be ▓ Transported by rail and not by road or vice-versa, and ▓ Transported by a more direct route than that permitted to be used for transit from other countries.
2. It is suggested that countries should be required to extend to imported/exported goods in transit, treatment that is no less favourable than that accorded to domestic goods. Such obligation to extend "national treatment" should, however, be "without prejudice to the legitimate objectives relating to customs control and supervision of imported and exported goods in transit".	Since most national laws and regulations contain special provisions for the control of imported goods in transit to landlocked countries (to ensure that they are not leaked into the domestic market of the importing country without the payment of customs duties), there would be serious limitations in the application of the 'national treatment' rule to goods in transit. Fees charged for imported goods in transit to landlocked countries may also be higher than those charged for the transit of domestic goods which are transported without customs exercising any control or supervisions.
3. The proposals suggest that rules should be clarified to provide, *inter alia*: ▓ All fees and charges should be published; ▓ Fees which are not published should not be collected; ▓ There should be periodic reviews of fees and charges; and ▓ Provisions of Article VIII which require that fees and charges should not exceed the cost of the services rendered by customs should apply to transit trade.	The issues that would need examination with reference to the publication of fees and their levels would also be relevant while examining the issues relating to the fees charged in transit trade (**see Section B, Part I**).
4 Procedures relating to transit trade should be simplified. Promotion of regional transit agreements / arrangements and the use of international standards.	Efforts to simplify documentation and inspection requirements and other procedures applicable in transit trade have been made over the last few decades by almost all countries. This has been done by entering into agreements on a bilateral and regional basis. International conventions also provide models of procedures that should be applied to transit trade in order to keep documentation requirements and inspections to the minimum.

5. Rules should be adopted on sealing requirements.

The containers or rail wagons or vehicles in which goods are to be transported are 'sealed by customs' in order to ensure that these are not removed or added to during transit. The sealing requirements could cause delays in transit trade. It is suggested that rules relating to sealing should be reviewed, and appropriate guidelines be adopted.

The Kyoto Convention lays down detailed standards governing the methods to be used while applying customs seals (standards 10 and recommended practice 11) in its special Annex E. It also includes the 'minimum requirements' that the customs seals and fastenings must comply with (standards 16, 17 and 18 and Appendix).

---

6. Rules should be adopted to cover bonded transport regime guarantees.

International, regional or national customs guarantee system.

The customs administrations of transit countries require transport operators to provide a guarantee to cover the payment of customs duties and other taxes (such as value added tax) in case goods are removed from containers during transit, and introduced clandestinely into the domestic market. It is proposed that new rules aiming at 'more effective discipline on the level, nature and management of guarantees which are required from transit operators, including rules to ensure that they are not used as an instrument to raise revenue' should be adopted.

In practice, the customs authorities need considerable discretion in determining the level of the guarantee that should be imposed. If the transport operator meets certain 'criteria of reliability,' the amount of guarantee is reduced by the customs to as low as 30% of the estimated value of the goods in transit. On the other hand, in the case of high-risk goods, customs often demand a guarantee amount that is higher than the value of the goods in transit. Moreover, the amount may often be linked to the risk of non-compliance.

PART ONE

Background and Context

Chapter 1: Historical background of the inclusion of the subject of trade facilitation and the mandate for negotiations

Background

Under the procedures of the World Trade Organization (WTO), countries wishing to include a new WTO discipline of rules under the legal framework of the multilateral trading system must first secure the inclusion of the subject in the WTO's work programme for examination and analysis.

The objective of such a study programme is to examine whether it would be desirable and appropriate to apply the WTO's rule-based principles to the chosen subject. It is on the basis of the findings and conclusions of such studies that a decision is taken about whether or not negotiations should be initiated on the adoption of new rules.

Four new subjects – Trade and Investment, Trade and Competition Policy, Transparency in Government Procurement, and Trade Facilitation – were included for study and analysis in the work programme of the WTO at the first Ministerial Conference held in Singapore in 1996, a year after the establishment of the WTO. The inclusion of these subjects was resisted by many developing countries. Primarily due to their opposition, very little progress was made in the analytical work during the period between the first and the fourth Ministerial Conference held at Doha in 2001 for the launching of a new development Round of negotiations.

As a result, the Declaration launching the Round provided that, in all of the four 'new' areas, the study process should be continued, and that a decision regarding whether or not negotiations in these areas should take place would be dependent on an explicit consensus at the Fifth Ministerial Conference. This Conference, held at Cancun in 2003, failed. The failure was largely due to differences among member countries on whether the study process should be treated as completed, and negotiations in these four 'new' areas should be commenced. The failure of the Conference resulted in an interruption of the negotiations in all areas covered by the Round. However, the resulting deadlock was resolved at a meeting of the WTO General Council in Geneva in July 2004. The text adopted at that meeting has come to be known as the 'July Package' or 'July Framework,' and contains a compromise solution regarding the four 'new' subjects. It was agreed that negotiations would be confined to trade facilitation only, and the other three subjects would not be taken up at all during the present Round of negotiations.

This introductory chapter is divided into three sections:

- Section 1 describes the meaning of the term 'trade facilitation,' the measures covered by it, as well as the trade benefits of such measures to the country adopting them in the clearance of goods through customs.

- Section 2 explains that while most developing countries are aware of the importance of taking trade facilitation measures, it also highlights the fact that many countries have expressed serious doubts about the need for adopting new rules at the WTO since international organisations such as the WCO, UNECE and ISO have already been engaged in developing international standards and recommendations in this area. The chapter then goes on to explain the reasons why developing countries were reluctant in the past to adopt rules on trade facilitation under the WTO's legal framework.

- Section 3 explains how the frank and open discussions held during the period of study and analysis – i.e. from 1996 when the subject was included in the work programme of the WTO to the adoption of the July Package in 2004 – have resulted in removing many of the misgivings of developing counties. It describes the provisions that have been included in Annex D of the July Package which now provide a mandate for negotiations in this area to meet the main concerns of developing countries. These provisions also ensure that:

  - Developing countries are provided technical assistance for building up capacities for the application of the new rules that may be adopted, and
  - The extent and timing of the obligations they are required to accept under such rules are related to their implementation capabilities.

1. The term 'trade facilitation' and the benefits of adopting trade facilitation measures

1.1   Defining trade facilitation

There is no agreed definition of the term 'trade facilitation.' The term is used broadly in some analytical literature to include not only customs procedures but also a whole range of domestic policies, institutions, and infrastructure (transport and ports) associated with the movement of goods across borders.

Currently, a number of international organisations are working on various aspects of trade facilitation. Box 1 outlines the definitions of trade facilitation used by UNECE, OECD and APEC. The differences in the definitions generally reflect the emphasis each organisation places on the particular aspect of trade facilitation which falls under its purview.

Box 1: Definitions of trade facilitation adopted by selected international organisations

UNECE: "Comprehensive and integrated approach to reducing the complexity and costs of the trade transaction process, and ensuring that all these activities can take place in an efficient, transparent and predictable manner, based on intentionally accepted norms, standard and the best practices" (Draft document 3/13/2002).

OECD: "Simplification and standardization of procedures and associated information flows required to move goods internationally from seller to buyer and to pass payments in the other direction" (OECD, TD/TC/WP (2001) 21 attributed to John Raven).

APEC: "Trade Facilitation generally refers to the simplification, harmonization, use of new technologies and other measures to address procedural and administrative impediments to trade" (APEC Principles on Trade Facilitation 2002).

Source: Reproduced from the technical paper 'Business and the WTO Negotiations on Trade Facilitation', International Trade Centre UNCTAD/WTO (ITC), (Geneva, 2005).

In WTO discussions, the term has been used to denote work on the simplification and harmonisation of international trade procedures, including 'activities, practices and formalities related to the collection, presentation, communication and processing of data required for the movement of goods in international trade'.[7]

UNCTAD E-Commerce and Development Report 2001 (UNCTAD/SDTE/ECB/1), 20 Nov 2001, p. 180.

1.2   Benefits accruing from trade facilitation measures

Why is the inclusion of a discipline on trade facilitation considered to be of such importance? The answer to the question lies in the fact that, in most developing countries, the benefits of the trade liberalisation measures undertaken by them are being offset by serious delays in the clearance of goods by customs.

For example, the customs clearance of sea cargo takes an average 2.1 days in developed countries, and 4.8 days in East Asia and the Pacific. However, traders in Latin America and the Caribbean must wait up to 9 days, and those in Africa and South Asia up to 10 days.[8] Such delays increase transaction expenses, and lead to an increase in the cost of imported products. It is estimated that the increase in costs to importers as a result of the delays in clearance could vary between 5 and 15% of the cost of the imported products. Where imported products are used as an input in further production, they lead to increasing the costs of the final products. As a consequence, the rise in prices may make it difficult for processing firms to market their products in foreign markets. Delay in the clearance of goods – which constitutes an important component in production – also has disruptive consequences for trade since it adversely affects the delivery schedules of the final products.

Various estimates have been made of the benefits that would accrue to developing countries after the application of trade facilitation measures. One estimate suggests that enhanced capacity in global trade facilitation would increase world trade by 5-7%. Improving specific aspects of trade facilitation can also bring other large benefits. For example, if developing countries were able to reduce the time spent on the clearance of goods through customs by an average of one day, the savings in costs to importers would be around $240 billion annually.[9]

2.   The previous reluctance of developing countries to accept the WTO elaborating rules in the area of trade facilitation

2.1.   The recognition of the importance of trade facilitation by policy makers in developing countries

Given the benefits that would accrue to their trade after the adoption of uniform trade facilitation procedures, why were developing countries so reluctant in the past to launch negotiations on the development of new rules in this area in the WTO?

In this context, it is necessary to make a distinction between the need to take action for promoting trade facilitation at the national level, and the demand currently being made for the development of rules on trade facilitation at the WTO. Policy makers in most developing countries recognise that facilitating trade is in the best interest of their countries. Many of them are, in fact, taking steps to make the necessary improvements by, *inter alia*, minimising documentation requirements and reducing physical checking through the adoption of risk assessment systems. In carrying out such reforms, they are receiving technical and financial assistance from international organisations such as the World Bank and WCO as well as from other donor countries, on a bilateral basis.

---

8   World Bank, 'Global Economic Prospects 2004', (Washington D.C.) quoted in UN Millenium Project, Task Force on Trade, ' Trade for Development' (Earthscan, London, Sterling Va. 2005), p.188.

9   UN Millenium Project, Task Force on Trade 'Trade for Development' (Earthscan, London, Sterling Va. 2005), p.189, Box 9.1

However, the process has been time-consuming. Two of the many reasons for this delay include the following:

- Many developing countries currently lack the physical and human resources as well as the infrastructure necessary for creating the customs environment required for the adoption of the new and innovative methods commonly being used by developed countries. In many cases, the effective application of these methods would be possible only if the use of information technology were widely prevalent among traders in the country. In many least developed countries or economies at a lower stage of development, the use of such technology is at a nascent stage and it may take years for its use to spread among their business communities.

- The costs incurred during the modernisation and the reforms of customs are high. Even in cases where the initial expenditure for obtaining the required equipment (computers and software) and on building infrastructure is met from technical assistance funds, it is not certain that the resources needed for meeting the recurring expenditure on the continuing maintenance of the reform programme will be provided by their governments. While many governments may recognise that reforms in customs clearance time facilitates trade which contributes significantly to the development process, there may often be other, more urgent development-related priorities (e.g. education and health issues, HIV/AIDS and other diseases) facing them. In such a situation, customs reforms may get low priority in budget allocations.

2.2 The reluctance of developing countries in adopting rules on trade facilitation in the WTO context

Thus, while developing countries have always been aware of the importance of taking trade facilitation action at the national level, their main reluctance to adopt new rules in the WTO context has been because of:

(a) The existence of wide gaps/differences between the traditional approaches followed by many of these countries for the clearance of goods through customs;

(b) The fact that the new methods were aimed at establishing a 'paperless trade' based on the use of information technology similar to that existing in developed countries, and

(c) The extremely limited scope for the development of harmonised rules to be accepted for application by all countries on a binding basis.

In their view, it seemed illogical to require countries to harmonise their procedures at a time when there were wide differences in the customs related practices followed by each country. The theory and practice of the harmonisation of rules on an international basis assumes a degree of coherence and similarity in the basic rules followed by countries participating in the negotiations regarding the development of such rules. Moreover, the theory of harmonisation recognises that, where the differences in the domestic regulations of countries are 'legitimate and justifiable,' the case for the adoption of rules that have been harmonised on a multilateral basis might be weak or premature.

Box 2 explains how the differences in the level of tariffs, and in the percentage share of customs revenue in the total revenue of developing and least developed countries makes the adoption of harmonised customs rules difficult.

Box 2: Difficulties in the harmonisation of rules relating to the clearance of goods through customs and other conceptual issues

The techniques and methods currently being adopted by developed countries for the clearance of goods are greatly influenced by strides made in their economic development in the last few decades. This economic development has enabled them to widen their tax net and reduce their dependence on customs revenue in their total revenue collection. In many of these countries, the share of customs revenue is less than 2 – 3% of the total tax revenue.

At the same time, and as a result of their participation in the past rounds of multilateral trade negotiations, their average tariff rates applicable to imports of agricultural and non-agricultural products, with a few notable exceptions, have declined to an average level of 4%. Moreover, a substantial share of their imports enters on a duty free basis. The low tariff rates, and the fact that a large part of their imports enter duty free, have left no incentives for traders in these countries to indulge in practices like the undervaluation of goods aimed at keeping the incidence of customs duties on imported goods as low as possible.

This situation contrasts with the one still prevailing in many developing countries. Customs revenues still account for over 30% of the total revenue in a number of these countries. In some of them, it is as high as 60%. The average level of tariffs in these countries is also relatively high, around 12%.

Customs officials have two types of complementary functions. The first is to 'control the movement of goods' through customs ports; the second is to simultaneously ensure that the performance of the control function actually facilitates trade rather than unnecessarily slow it down and hinder it. Thus, the procedures adopted by a country reflect the balance between the emphasis it wishes to put either on the control functions of customs (aimed at securing the full collection of the revenues due and ensuring compliance with rules) or on its role as the facilitator of the speedy movement of goods through customs. The relatively small share of customs revenue in the total tax revenue, and the disappearance of incentives in the undervaluation of goods, have made developed countries re-orient their customs clearance procedures: they now put a greater emphasis on the trade facilitation functions of customs officials rather than on their control functions.

The high dependence of the governments of developing countries on customs revenues for meeting their budget expenditure makes them require their customs administrations to attach greater importance to their control functions, since due to high rates of tariffs, traders often resort to the practices of the undervaluation of imported goods. In drawing the balance between the control and trade facilitation functions, customs administrations tend to err on the side of exercising greater control.

Even in cases where documentation scrutiny and physical checking are made by applying risk assessment techniques, the customs administrations of developing countries are likely to allow the clearance of fewer consignments in the low-risk category as compared to that of developed countries. The lack of adequately trained personnel, and a chronic shortage of funds required for hiring new staff, prevents them further from adopting some of the new methods used by the customs administrations of developed countries. These new methods include clearing imported goods immediately upon arrival on the basis of the assessment made by the importer himself regarding the duties payable. The adoption of such methods in developed countries have been possible because the low level of tariffs have eliminated the incentives behind such practices as the undervaluation of goods.

Source: Vinod Rege, 'Theory and Practice of Harmonization of Rules on a Regional and International Basis – Its Relevance for the Work in WTO on Trade Facilitation,' Journal of World Trade, Vol. 36, No 4. (August 2002).

For these reasons, many developing countries believed that the WTO's legal framework was not suitable for adopting any new discipline on trade facilitation. Thus, so far, WTO Agreements have been confined to laying down broad principles, concepts, and standards. In trying to develop a WTO discipline in the area of trade facilitation, member countries will now, for the first time, be attempting to apply international norms to national laws and regulations that are mainly procedural in nature. In adopting such altered procedural laws, developing countries will need 'policy space' to tailor them to the specific trading realities and particular difficulties (including many customs malpractices and corruption among customs officials) that they might encounter while applying them.

Another concern of many developing countries was that the introduction of new disciplines at the WTO would also lead to the automatic application of WTO dispute settlement procedures. They felt that this would lead to unnecessary litigations as countries could start bringing cases regarding even minor procedural lapses for settlement in the WTO Secretariat.

Prior to the acceptance of the August 2004 July Package, many developing countries maintained that:

- Because work in the area of trade facilitation was also being undertaken by many other international organisations, it would be more desirable for the WTO to adopt an understanding/decision in the Round asking member countries to participate actively in the work being undertaken in the World Customs Organization (WCO) and other international organisations regarding the development of standards that would facilitate trade at the national level;

- The alternative could be to adopt rules at the WTO on selected issues that would be non-binding, and would only impose the obligation that countries 'make their best endeavours' to apply them at the national level;

- If such non-binding rules are adopted, the WTO's dispute settlement mechanism should not apply to these rules. However, it would be desirable to establish a separate mechanism for consultations, and for the consideration of complaints by a country other than the one about it not making its 'best efforts' to comply with the obligations;

- Developing countries would need technical and financial assistance for the modernisation and reform of their existing customs procedures. Such assistance would be considerable since customs reform programmes are expensive and involve sizeable capital expenditure for the development of information technology, the infrastructure for customs operations, and equipment for scanning imported goods etc.; and

- The provision of such technical assistance should not be linked to the acceptance of obligations under the WTO rules.

2.3 Views regarding the adoption of a trade facilitation discipline in the WTO context

While proposing the introduction of a new WTO discipline, a majority of developed countries and a few developing countries had argued that even though useful work was being done by international organisations such as WCO, UNECE and UNCTAD over the last few decades, it would be necessary for political reasons to complement their work by including a trade facilitation discipline in the legal framework of the WTO. The progress in making countries accept the standards developed by the above organisations has been slow. One reason for this is the low political clout of these organisations. The WTO, on the other hand, has gained political importance in most countries. The vital role of its legal framework has been recognised not only by governments, but also by the business community and the general public in many countries. Thus, the development of a new discipline at the WTO would galvanise the political will of developing countries to undertake reforms, and of developed countries to provide the financial and technical assistance needed for these reforms by developing countries.

3. The mandate for negotiations on trade facilitation as provided in the July Package of 2004

The mandate which Annex D of the 2004 July Package provides for the negotiations in trade facilitation seeks to meet most of the concerns of developing countries by meeting their two main demands that:

- The obligations they may undertake under the new rules shall be related to their technical capacity to implement them, and

- Developed countries should provide technical assistance both for their participation in the negotiations and for the implementation of the obligations they may assume in such negotiations.

3.1   The objective of the negotiations

The aim of the negotiations shall be to clarify and improve relevant aspects of:

- Article V relating to the freedom of transit;

- Article VIII on fees and formalities in connection with importation and exportation; and

- Article X providing for the publication and administration of regulations with a view to expediting the movement, release, and clearance of goods in transit.

Annex I at the end of this chapter contains the text of Articles V, VIII and X.

3.2   Special and differential treatment

In order to meet some concerns expressed by developing countries, the mandate provides that the results of the negotiations shall fully take into account the principle of Special and Differential treatment (S&D) for developing and least developed countries. Such treatment should:

- Extend beyond the traditional transitional periods for implementing commitments;

- Provide that the extent and timing of making the commitments shall be related to the implementation capacities of developing and least developed countries; and

- Not impose any obligations to undertake investment on infrastructure projects beyond their means.

3.3   Technical assistance for capacity building

The Decision also recognises that developing and least developed countries will need support and assistance for capacity building:

- During the course of negotiations, and

- For the implementation of the commitments resulting from the negotiations in accordance with their scope and nature.

As regards giving assistance to developing and least developed countries for the implementation of the commitments resulting from the negotiations, developed countries have agreed to make every effort to ensure that only that support and assistance which is directly related to the nature and scope of the commitments would be made available to developing countries. This would include support for infrastructure development. However, they have stated that their capacity to provide such support is not open-ended. The mandate provides that where such assistance for infrastructure development is not forthcoming, and where a developing or a least developed country continues to lack the necessary capacity, the implementation of the commitments will not be required.

The relevant provisions do not define the term 'commitment.' It is assumed that the term is used in the same way as it is used in the General Agreement on Trade in Services (GATS).

3.4   Developments in the negotiations since the adoption of the mandate

In accordance with the above mandate, the Negotiating Group on Trade Facilitation was established in October 2004. After intensive discussions on 40 submissions made by the participants regarding the clarification of various aspects of Articles V, VIII and X, and for the effective cooperation between customs and other authorities on trade facilitation and customs clearance, the Group has identified a number of specific 'trade facilitation measures' on which new rules may have to be adopted.

At the Hong Kong Ministerial Meeting, it was agreed that the 'Members should be mindful of the overall deadline for finishing the negotiations and the resulting need to move into focussed drafting mode early enough after the Sixth Ministerial Conference so as to allow for a timely conclusion of text-based negotiations on all aspects of the mandate' (Para 4, Annex E of the Declaration).

The Declaration also emphasises the need to pay special attention to the provision of technical assistance to developing and least developed countries, and states that 'all S&D treatment provisions be reviewed with a view to strengthening them and making them more precise, effective and operational' (Para 35 of the Declaration), and that 'special attention needs to be paid to support for technical assistance and capacity building' that 'reflects the trade facilitation needs and priorities of developing countries and LDCs' (Para 6, Annex E of the Declaration).

Towards this end, it calls on WTO members to 'continue and broaden on the process of identifying individual Member's trade facilitation needs and priorities, and the cost implications of possible measures' (Para 5, Annex E of the Declaration).

Annex II at the end of this chapter contains the texts of Annex D of the 2004 July Package, and of Annex E of the 2005 Hong Kong Ministerial Declaration.

ANNEX I

GATT Articles V, VIII and X

Article V
Freedom of Transit

1. Goods (including baggage), and also vessels and other means of transport, shall be deemed to be in transit across the territory of a contracting party when the passage across such territory, with or without trans-shipment, warehousing, breaking bulk, or change in the mode of transport, is only a portion of a complete journey beginning and terminating beyond the frontier of the contracting party across whose territory the traffic passes. Traffic of this nature is termed in this article "traffic in transit".

2. There shall be freedom of transit through the territory of each contracting party, via the routes most convenient for international transit, for traffic in transit to or from the territory of other contracting parties. No distinction shall be made which is based on the flag of vessels, the place of origin, departure, entry, exit or destination, or on any circumstances relating to the ownership of goods, of vessels or of other means of transport.

3. Any contracting party may require that traffic in transit through its territory be entered at the proper custom house, but, except in cases of failure to comply with applicable customs laws and regulations, such traffic coming from or going to the territory of other contracting parties shall not be subject to any unnecessary delays or restrictions and shall be exempt from customs duties and from all transit duties or other charges imposed in respect of transit, except charges for transportation or those commensurate with administrative expenses entailed by transit or with the cost of services rendered.

4. All charges and regulations imposed by contracting parties on traffic in transit to or from the territories of other contracting parties shall be reasonable, having regard to the conditions of the traffic.

5. With respect to all charges, regulations and formalities in connection with transit, each contracting party shall accord to traffic in transit to or from the territory of any other contracting party treatment no less favourable than the treatment accorded to traffic in transit to or from any third country.*

6. Each contracting party shall accord to products which have been in transit through the territory of any other contracting party treatment no less favourable than that which would have been accorded to such products had they been transported from their place of origin to their destination without going through the territory of such other contracting party. Any contracting party shall, however, be free to maintain its requirements of direct consignment existing on the date of this Agreement, in respect of any goods in regard to which such direct consignment is a requisite condition of eligibility for entry of the goods at preferential rates of duty or has relation to the contracting party's prescribed method of valuation for duty purposes.

7   The provisions of this Article shall not apply to the operation of aircraft in transit, but shall apply to air transit of goods (including baggage).

Article VIII
Fees and Formalities connected with Importation and Exportation*

1. (a) All fees and charges of whatever character (other than import and export duties and other than taxes within the purview of Article III) imposed by contracting parties on or in connection with importation or exportation shall be limited in amount to the approximate cost of services rendered and shall not represent an indirect protection to domestic products or a taxation of imports or exports for fiscal purposes.

   (b) The contracting parties recognise the need for reducing the number and diversity of fees and charges referred to in subparagraph (a).

   (c) The contracting parties also recognise the need for minimizing the incidence and complexity of import and export formalities and for decreasing and simplifying import and export documentation requirements.*

2. A contracting party shall, upon request by another contracting party or by the CONTRACTING PARTIES, review the operation of its laws and regulations in the light of the provisions of this Article.

3. No contracting party shall impose substantial penalties for minor breaches of customs regulations or procedural requirements. In particular, no penalty in respect of any omission or mistake in customs documentation which is easily rectifiable and obviously made without fraudulent intent or gross negligence shall be greater than necessary to serve merely as a warning.

4. The provisions of this Article shall extend to fees, charges, formalities and requirements imposed by governmental authorities in connection with importation and exportation, including those relating to:

   (a) consular transactions, such as consular invoices and certificates;
   (b) quantitative restrictions;
   (c) licensing;
   (d) exchange control;
   (e) statistical services;
   (f) documents, documentation and certification;
   (g) analysis and inspection; and
   (h) quarantine, sanitation and fumigation.

Article X
Publication and Administration of Trade Regulations

1. Laws, regulations, judicial decisions and administrative rulings of general application, made effective by any contracting party, pertaining to the classification or the valuation of products for customs purposes, or to rates of duty, taxes or other charges, or to requirements, restrictions or prohibitions on imports or exports or on the transfer of payments therefore, or affecting their sale, distribution, transportation, insurance, warehousing inspection, exhibition, processing, mixing or other use, shall be published promptly in such a manner as to enable governments and traders to become acquainted with them. Agreements affecting international trade policy which are in force between the government or a governmental agency of any contracting party and the government or governmental agency of any other

contracting party shall also be published. The provisions of this paragraph shall not require any contracting party to disclose confidential information which would impede law enforcement or otherwise be contrary to the public interest or would prejudice the legitimate commercial interests of particular enterprises, public or private.

2. No measure of general application taken by any contracting party effecting an advance in a rate of duty or other charge on imports under an established and uniform practice, or imposing a new or more burdensome requirement, restriction or prohibition on imports, or on the transfer of payments therefore, shall be enforced before such measure has been officially published.

3. (a)   Each contracting party shall administer in a uniform, impartial and reasonable manner all its laws, regulations, decisions and rulings of the kind described in paragraph 1 of this Article.

(b)   Each contracting party shall maintain, or institute as soon as practicable, judicial, arbitral or administrative tribunals or procedures for the purpose, *inter alia*, of the prompt review and correction of administrative action relating to customs matters. Such tribunals or procedures shall be independent of the agencies entrusted with administrative enforcement and their decisions shall be implemented by, and shall govern the practice of, such agencies unless an appeal is lodged with a court or tribunal of superior jurisdiction within the time prescribed for appeals to be lodged by importers; Provided that the central administration of such agency may take steps to obtain a review of the matter in another proceeding if there is good cause to believe that the decision is inconsistent with established principles of law or the actual facts.

(c)   The provisions of subparagraph (b) of this paragraph shall not require the elimination or substitution of procedures in force in the territory of a contracting party on the date of this Agreement which in fact provide for an objective and impartial review of administrative action even though such procedures are not fully or formally independent of the agencies entrusted with administrative enforcement. Any contracting party employing such procedures shall, upon request, furnish the CONTRACTING PARTIES with full information thereon in order that they may determine whether such procedures conform to the requirements of this subparagraph.

*Notes and Supplementary Provisions
Ad Article V
Paragraph 5

With regard to transportation charges, the principle laid down in paragraph 5 refers to like products being transported on the same route under like conditions.

Ad Article VIII

1. While Article VIII does not cover the use of multiple rates of exchange as such, paragraphs 1 and 4 condemn the use of exchange taxes or fees as a device for implementing multiple currency practices; if, however, a contracting party is using multiple currency exchange fees for balance of payments reasons with the approval of the International Monetary Fund, the provisions of paragraph 9 (a) of Article XV fully safeguard its position.

2. It would be consistent with paragraph 1 if, on the importation of products from the territory of a contracting party into the territory of another contracting party, the production of certificates of origin should only be required to the extent that is strictly indispensable.

ANNEX II

Doha Work Programme
Decision Adopted by the General Council on 1 August 2004
WT/L/579 (2 August 2004)
'The July Package'

Annex D
Modalities for Negotiations on Trade Facilitation

1. Negotiations shall aim to clarify and improve relevant aspects of Articles V, VIII and X of the GATT 1994 with a view to further expediting the movement, release and clearance of goods, including goods in transit.[10] Negotiations shall also aim at enhancing technical assistance and support for capacity building in this area. The negotiations shall further aim at provisions for effective cooperation between customs or any other appropriate authorities on trade facilitation and customs compliance issues.

2. The results of the negotiations shall take fully into account the principle of special and differential treatment for developing and least-developed countries. Members recognise that this principle should extend beyond the granting of traditional transition periods for implementing commitments. In particular, the extent and the timing of entering into commitments shall be related to the implementation capacities of developing and least-developed Members. It is further agreed that those Members would not be obliged to undertake investments in infrastructure projects beyond their means.

3. Least-developed country Members will only be required to undertake commitments to the extent consistent with their individual development, financial and trade needs or their administrative and institutional capabilities.

4. As an integral part of the negotiations, Members shall seek to identify their trade facilitation needs and priorities, particularly those of developing and least-developed countries, and shall also address the concerns of developing and least-developed countries related to cost implications of proposed measures.

5. It is recognised that the provision of technical assistance and support for capacity building is vital for developing and least-developed countries to enable them to fully participate in and benefit from the negotiations. Members, in particular developed countries, therefore commit themselves to adequately ensure such support and assistance during the negotiations.[11]

---

10 It is understood that this is without prejudice to the possible format of the final result of the negotiations and would allow consideration of various forms of outcomes.
11 In connection with this paragraph, Members note that paragraph 38 of the Doha Ministerial Declaration addresses relevant technical assistance and capacity building concerns of Members.

6. Support and assistance should also be provided to help developing and least-developed countries implement the commitments resulting from the negotiations, in accordance with their nature and scope. In this context, it is recognised that negotiations could lead to certain commitments whose implementation would require support for infrastructure development on the part of some Members. In these limited cases, developed-country Members will make every effort to ensure support and assistance directly related to the nature and scope of the commitments in order to allow implementation. It is understood, however, that in cases where required support and assistance for such infrastructure is not forthcoming, and where a developing or least-developed Member continues to lack the necessary capacity, implementation will not be required. While every effort will be made to ensure the necessary support and assistance, it is understood that the commitments by developed countries to provide such support are not open-ended.

7. Members agree to review the effectiveness of the support and assistance provided and its ability to support the implementation of the results of the negotiations.

8. In order to make technical assistance and capacity building more effective and operational and to ensure better coherence, Members shall invite relevant international organisations, including the IMF, OECD, UNCTAD, WCO and the World Bank to undertake a collaborative effort in this regard.

9. Due account shall be taken of the relevant work of the WCO and other relevant international organisations in this area.

10. Paragraphs 45-51 of the Doha Ministerial Declaration shall apply to these negotiations. At its first meeting after the July session of the General Council, the Trade Negotiations Committee shall establish a Negotiating Group on Trade Facilitation and appoint its Chair. The first meeting of the Negotiating Group shall agree on a work plan and schedule of meetings.

Ministerial Conference
Sixth Session
Hong Kong, 13–18 December 2005
WT/MIN(05)/DEC
(22 December 2005)

Trade facilitation negotiations

33. We recall and reaffirm the mandate and modalities for negotiations on Trade Facilitation contained in Annex D of the Decision adopted by the General Council on 1 August 2004. We note with appreciation the report of the Negotiating Group, attached in Annex E to this document, and the comments made by our delegations on that report as reflected in document TN/TF/M/11. We endorse the recommendations contained in paragraphs 3, 4, 5, 6 and 7 of the report.

Annex E
Trade Facilitation

Report by the Negotiating Group on Trade Facilitation to the TNC

1. Since its establishment on 12 October 2004, the Negotiating Group on Trade Facilitation met eleven times to carry out work under the mandate contained in Annex D of the Decision adopted by the General Council on 1 August 2004. The negotiations are benefiting from the fact that the mandate allows for the central development dimension of the Doha negotiations to be addressed directly through the widely acknowledged benefits of trade facilitation reforms for all WTO Members, the enhancement of trade facilitation capacity in developing countries and LDCs, and provisions on special and differential treatment (S&DT) that provide flexibility. Based on the Group's Work Plan (TN/TF/1), Members contributed to the agreed agenda of the Group, tabling 60 written submissions sponsored by more than 100 delegations. Members appreciate the transparent and inclusive manner in which the negotiations are being conducted.

2. Good progress has been made in all areas covered by the mandate, through both verbal and written contributions by Members. A considerable part of the Negotiating Group's meetings has been spent on addressing the negotiating objective of improving and clarifying relevant aspects of GATT Articles V, VIII and X, on which about 40 written submissions[12] have been tabled by Members representing the full spectrum of the WTO's Membership. Through discussions on these submissions and related questions and answers (JOB(05)/222), Members have advanced their understanding of the measures in question and are working towards common ground on many aspects of this part of the negotiating mandate. Many of these submissions also covered the negotiating objective of enhancing technical assistance and support for capacity building on trade facilitation, as well as the practical application of the principle of S&DT. The Group also discussed other valuable submissions dedicated to these issues.[13] Advances have also been made on the objective of arriving at provisions for effective cooperation between customs or any other appropriate authorities on trade facilitation and customs compliance issues, where two written proposals have been discussed.[14] Members have also made valuable contributions on the identification of trade facilitation needs and priorities, development aspects, cost implications and inter-agency cooperation.[15]

3. Valuable input has been provided by a number of Members in the form of national experience papers[16] describing national trade facilitation reform processes. In appreciation of the value to developing countries and LDCs of this aspect of the negotiations, the Negotiating Group recommends that Members be encouraged to continue this information sharing exercise.

4. Building on the progress made in the negotiations so far, and with a view to developing a set of multilateral commitments on all elements of the mandate, the Negotiating Group recommends that it continue to intensify its negotiations on the basis of Members' proposals, as reflected currently in document TN/TF/W/43/Rev.4, and any new proposals to be presented. Without prejudice to individual

---

12 TN/TF/W/6-W/15, W/17-W/26, W/28, W/30 W32, W/34-36, W/38-W/40, W/42, W/44-W/49, W/53, W/55, W/58, W/60-W/62, W/64-W/67, W/69, W/70.
13 TN/TF/W/33, W/41, W/56, W/63, W/73 and W/74.
14 TN/TF/W/57 and W/68.
15 TN/TF/W/29, W/33, W/41, W/62 and W/63.
16 TN/TF/W/48, W/50 , W/53, W/55, W/58, W/60, W/61, W/65, W/69 and W/75.

Member's positions on individual proposals, a list of (I) proposed measures to improve and clarify GATT Articles V, VIII and X; (II) proposed provisions for effective cooperation between customs and other authorities on trade facilitation and customs compliance; and (III) cross-cutting submissions is provided below to facilitate further negotiations. In carrying out this work and in tabling further proposals, Members should be mindful of the overall deadline for finishing the negotiations and the resulting need to move into focussed drafting mode early enough after the Sixth Ministerial Conference so as to allow for a timely conclusion of text-based negotiations on all aspects of the mandate.

5. Work needs to continue and broaden on the process of identifying individual Member's trade facilitation needs and priorities, and the cost implications of possible measures. The Negotiating Group recommends that relevant international organisations be invited to continue to assist Members in this process, recognizing the important contributions being made by them already, and be encouraged to continue and intensify their work more generally in support of the negotiations.

6. In light of the vital importance of technical assistance and capacity building to allow developing countries and LDCs to fully participate in and benefit from the negotiations, the Negotiating Group recommends that the commitments in Annex D's mandate in this area be reaffirmed, reinforced and made operational in a timely manner. To bring the negotiations to a successful conclusion, special attention needs to be paid to support for technical assistance and capacity building that will allow developing countries and LDCs to participate effectively in the negotiations, and to technical assistance and capacity building to implement the results of the negotiations that is precise, effective and operational, and reflects the trade facilitation needs and priorities of developing countries and LDCs. Recognizing the valuable assistance already being provided in this area, the Negotiating Group recommends that Members, in particular developed ones, continue to intensify their support in a comprehensive manner and on a long term and sustainable basis, backed by secure funding.

7. The Negotiating Group also recommends that it deepen and intensify its negotiations on the issue of S&DT, with a view to arriving at S&DT provisions that are precise, effective and operational and that allow for necessary flexibility in implementing the results of the negotiations. Reaffirming the linkages among the elements of Annex D, the Negotiating Group recommends that further negotiations on S&DT build on input presented by Members in the context of measures related to GATT Articles V, VIII and X and in their proposals of a cross-cutting nature on S&DT.

PROPOSED MEASURES TO IMPROVE AND CLARIFY GATT ARTICLES V, VIII, AND X

- Publication and Availability of Information
- Publication of Trade Regulations
- Publication of Penalty Provisions
- Notification of Trade Regulations
- Establishment of Enquiry Points/SNFP/Information Centres
- Other Measures to Enhance the Availability of Information
- Internet Publication of elements set out in Article X of GATT 1994 of specified information setting forth procedural sequence and other requirements for importing goods

TIME PERIODS BETWEEN PUBLICATION AND IMPLEMENTATION

- Interval between Publication and Entry into Force

CONSULTATION AND COMMENTS ON NEW AND AMENDED RULES

- Prior Consultation and Commenting on New and Amended Rules
- Information on Policy Objectives Sought

ADVANCE RULINGS

- Provision of Advance Rulings

APPEAL PROCEDURES

- Right of Appeal
- Release of Goods in Event of Appeal

OTHER MEASURES TO ENHANCE IMPARTIALITY AND NON-DISCRIMINATION

- Uniform Administration of Trade Regulations
- Maintenance and Reinforcement of Integrity and Ethical Conduct Among Officials
    Establishment of a Code of Conduct
    Computerised System to Reduce/Eliminate Discretion
    System of Penalties
    Technical Assistance to Create/Build up Capacities to Prevent and Control Customs Offences
    Appointment of Staff for Education and Training
    Coordination and Control Mechanisms

FEES AND CHARGES CONNECTED WITH IMPORTATION AND EXPORTATION

- General Disciplines on Fees and Charges Imposed on or in Connection with Importation and Exportation
    Specific Parameters for Fees/Charges
    Publication/Notification of Fees/Charges
    Prohibition of Collection of Unpublished Fees and Charges
    Periodic Review of Fees/Charges
    Automated Payment
- Reduction/Minimisation of the Number and Diversity of Fees/Charges

FORMALITIES CONNECTED WITH IMPORTATION AND EXPORTATION

- Disciplines on Formalities/Procedures and Data/Documentation Requirements Connected with Importation and Exportation
    Non-discrimination
    Periodic Review of Formalities and Requirements
    Reduction/Limitation of Formalities and Documentation Requirements
    Use of International Standards (Brazil)
    Uniform Customs Code
    Acceptance of Commercially Available Information and of Copies
    Automation

Single Window/One-time Submission
Elimination of Pre-Shipment Inspection
Phasing out Mandatory Use of Customs Brokers

CONSULARISATION

- Prohibition of Consular Transaction Requirement

BORDER AGENCY COOPERATION

- Coordination of Activities and Requirement of all Border Agencies

RELEASE AND CLEARANCE OF GOODS

- Expedited/Simplified Release and Clearance of Goods
    Pre-arrival Clearance
    Expedited Procedures for Express Shipments
    Risk Management /Analysis, Authorised Traders
    Post-Clearance Audit
    Separating Release from Clearance Procedures
    Other Measures to Simplify Customs Release and Clearance

- Establishment and Publication of Average Release and Clearance Times

TARIFF CLASSIFICATION

- Objective Criteria for Tariff Classification

MATTERS RELATED TO GOODS TRANSIT

- Strengthened Non-discrimination

- Disciplines on Fees and Charges
    Publication of Fees and Charges and Prohibition of Unpublished ones
    Periodic Review of Fees and Charges
    More effective Disciplines on Charges for Transit
    Periodic Exchange between Neighbouring Authorities

- Disciplines on Transit Formalities and Documentation Requirements
    (a) Periodic Review
    (b) Reduction/Simplification
    (c) Harmonisation/Standardisation
    (d) Promotion of Regional Transit Arrangements
    (e) Simplified and Preferential Clearance for Certain Goods
    (f)   Limitation of Inspections and Controls
    (g) Sealing
    (h) Cooperation and Coordination on Document Requirements
    (i)   Monitoring
    (j)   Bonded Transport Regime/Guarantees

- Improved Coordination and Cooperation
    (a) Amongst Authorities

(b) Between Authorities and the Private Sector

- Operationalisation and Clarification of Terms

PROPOSED PROVISIONS FOR EFFECTIVE COOPERATION BETWEEN CUSTOMS AND OTHER AUTHORITIES ON TRADE FACILITATION AND CUSTOMS COMPLIANCE

- Multilateral Mechanism for the Exchange and Handling of Information

CROSS-CUTTING SUBMISSIONS

Needs and Priorities Identification

- General tool to assess needs and priorities and current levels of trade facilitation
- Take result of assessment as one basis for establishing trade facilitation rules, arranging S&D treatment and providing technical assistance and capacity building support

Technical Assistance and Capacity Building

Technical Assistance and Capacity Building in the Course of the Negotiations

- Identification of Needs and Priorities
- Compilation of Needs and Priorities of Individual Members
- Support for Clarification and Educative Process Including Training

Technical Assistance and Capacity Building beyond the Negotiations Phase

- Implementation of the Outcome
- Coordination Mechanisms for Implementing Needs and Priorities as well as Commitments

Multiple-Areas

- Identification of Trade Facilitation Needs and Priorities of Members
- Cost Assessment
- Inter-Agency Cooperation
- Links and Inter-relationship between the Elements of Annex D
- Inventory of Trade Facilitation Measures
- Assessment of the Current Situation
- Timing and Sequencing of Measures

Chapter 2: Description of the trade facilitation work undertaken by selected international and regional organisations

General

A number of international organisations are currently engaged in work regarding the development of standards for and recommendations on the modernisation and reform of customs administrations, and on procedures for the clearance of goods through customs.

In this context, many countries have suggested that instead of developing a new set of rules on trade facilitation at the WTO, it would be more efficient and effective if a WTO understanding or decision were to be adopted requiring countries to make their 'best endeavours' to apply some – if not all – of the standards formulated by international standard setting organisations. Another proposal envisages that the approach adopted in the WTO Agreements on Technical Barriers to Trade (TBT) and Sanitary and Phytosanitary Measures (SPS) could be utilised under any other legal instrument that may be adopted on trade facilitation. The two Agreements require countries to base their technical regulations and sanitary and phytosanitary measures on international standards developed by international standard setting bodies. Likewise, the proposed WTO legal instrument on trade facilitation could require – or encourage – countries to adopt the standards that have been developed by other international organisations.

This chapter provides an overview of the work being done in this area by international organisations other than the WTO to further examine the suggestions cited above.

The international organisations working in the area of trade are listed below:

- The World Customs Organization (WCO);
- The UN Economic Commission for Europe (UNECE) and the United Nations Centre for Trade Facilitation and Electronic Business (UN/CEFACT);
- The International Maritime Organization (IMO);
- The International Civil Aviation Organization (ICAO);
- The Asia Pacific Economic Cooperation (APEC);
- The United Nations Conference on Trade and Development (UNCTAD);
- The World Bank;
- The International Monetary Fund (IMF); and
- The Commonwealth Secretariat.

1. The World Customs Organization (WCO)

There is a long history of cooperation between the WTO and the World Customs Organization. Under the WTO Agreements on Customs Valuation and Rules of Origin, technical committees have been established at the WTO to provide advice on technical issues relating to the day-to-day administration of their provisions. The latter Agreement further provides that the initial negotiations at the technical level on the development of a harmonised system on the rules of origin should take place in the WCO's technical committee, and the results of the negotiations should be brought to the WTO for further negotiations and acceptance.

The WCO specialises in technical work on all aspects of customs laws and procedures. The organisation currently has 168 member countries. Its meetings are regularly attended by officials from national customs administrations. The secretariat of the organisation is also almost entirely staffed by persons who have the necessary background as well as work experience in the national customs authorities of their countries.

The work of the organisation provides technical support to the work done by the WTO on customs related matters. The GATT rules lay down the broad principles and concepts on which customs laws and regulations should be based. The WCO complements these rules by adopting conventions which lay down standards and recommendations for securing their effective implementation at the national level. This informal division of work between the two organisations is further strengthened by provisions in the two WTO Agreements on Customs Valuation and on Rules of Origin, which formally recognise the role of the WCO in providing advisory opinions on technical issues.

For this purpose, the WCO has established technical committees of experts in the field, which provide advice and opinions on technical problems that may arise in the day-to-day administration of the customs valuation system, or in the application of the rules of origin. It is also open to the WTO Agreement Committee to request for an opinion of the technical committees on issues relating to the administration and application of the rules. The technical committees are expected to submit annual reports on their activities to the Agreement Committee. The Agreement on Rules of Origin also envisages that the negotiations on the development of a harmonised system of rules of origin should take place at the technical level in the WCO's Technical Committee, and the package developed by it should be brought to the WTO for further negotiations and acceptance.

From the point of view of the WTO's work on trade facilitation, the most relevant among the WCO Conventions is, perhaps, the 'International Convention on the Simplification and Harmonization of Customs Procedures,' also known as the 'Revised Kyoto Convention.' It was revised in 1999 to take into account the new and innovative methods based on Information Technology that have been adopted by many countries to facilitate the movement of goods through customs.

The Convention contains General Annexes and a number of Special Annexes. The General Annexes prescribe the 'standards' and 'transitional standards' which countries acceding to the Convention are expected to apply by incorporating them in their national laws and regulations relating to the customs procedures governing import, export, the transit of goods, customs control, and other matters such as the application of information technology, customs offences, appeals procedures, and relations with the business community. The Specific Annexes complement the General Annexes by laying down standards dealing with specific aspects of procedures: for example, they lay down standards regarding the temporary storage of goods, clearance for home use, re-importation into the same state, and relief from import duties and taxes.

One of the important features of the general and specific annexes is that they lay down elaborate guidelines for the application of the standards they prescribe. These guidelines explain the provisions; provide concrete examples on how the standards could be applied in practice; the difficulties and problems that may arise in their application; and how such difficulties could be met.

All countries acceding to the Convention have to accept all of the general annexes. However, the acceding countries are free to accept all, or only a few, of the specific annexes. In order to achieve a greater level of harmonisation of customs procedures and practices on a worldwide basis, countries are not allowed to make any reservations when accepting the general or specific annexes. Acceding countries are expected to implement the standards in the General Annex as well as those in the specific annexes, within a period of 36 months. A longer period of 60 months is available for the implementation of the transitional standards.

However, progress in the adoption of the Convention has been protracted. Of the 43 countries which have acceded to the Convention (40 countries are 'contracting parties') only six – China, Morocco, Sri Lanka, Uganda, Zambia and Zimbabwe – are developing countries (see **Table 1**).

Table 1: Contracting Parties to the International Convention on the Simplification and Harmonisation of Customs Procedures *(as amended)* **(Revised Kyoto Convention)**

ALGERIA	AUSTRALIA	AUSTRIA	BELGIUM	BULGARIA
CANADA	CHINA	CONGO	CROATIA	CZECH REPUBLIC
CYPRUS	DENMARK	EUROPEAN COMMUNITY	FINLAND	FRANCE
GERMANY	GREECE	HUNGARY	**INDIA**	IRELAND
ITALY	JAPAN	KOREA	LATVIA	LESOTHO
LITHUANIA	MOROCCO	NETHERLANDS	NEW ZEALAND	PAKISTAN
POLAND	PORTUGAL	SLOVAKIA	SLOVENIA	**SOUTH AFRICA**
SPAIN	SRI LANKA	SWEDEN	SWITZERLAND	**UGANDA**
UNITED KINGDOM	ZAMBIA	ZIMBABWE		

The reasons for the reluctance of developing countries to accede to the Convention may be attributed to two factors.

1. They consider that while they would like to begin applying the standards – particularly those relating to the adoption of methods such as risk assessment, the speedy clearance of the imports of authorised importers without full documentation scrutiny subject to post-auditing – their effective implementation will be a long term process. They would also need technical assistance to implement most of the standards. Thus, they would not be able to accept the obligations imposed by the Convention in the period immediately after becoming contracting parties.

2. Many of them appear to consider that since the issues relating to the acceptance of the obligations under the Convention are expected to be discussed in the present Round of negotiations, it may be desirable to wait till the conclusion of the Round before deciding on acceding to the Convention.

Box 3 lists other important conventions adopted by the WCO. These focus on assisting customs administrations in avoiding or solving problems in specific customs areas.

Box 3: WCO Conventions forming part of the 'Harmonised System' (HS)

General information

'The Harmonised Commodity Description and Coding System, generally referred to as 'Harmonised System' or simply 'HS', is a multipurpose international product nomenclature developed by the World Customs Organization (WCO). It comprises about 5,000 commodity groups, each identified by a six digit code, arranged in a legal and logical structure and is supported by well-defined rules to achieve uniform classification. The system is used by more than 177 countries and economies as a basis for their Customs tariffs and for the collection of international trade statistics. Over 98% of the merchandise in international trade is classified in terms of the HS.' [17]

There are a number of conventions on specific customs matters, including the following:

◆ Customs Conventions concerning facilities for the importation of goods for display or use at exhibitions, fairs, meetings or similar events.

◆ Customs Conventions on the temporary importation of packings.

◆ Customs Conventions on the temporary importation of professional equipment.

◆ Customs Conventions on the temporary importation of pedagogic material.

◆ Customs Conventions on the temporary importation of scientific equipment.

◆ Customs Conventions concerning welfare material for seafarers.

◆ Customs Conventions on the international transit of goods (ITI Convention).

◆ Customs Conventions on Containers (1972).[18]

◆ ATA Carnet, or the temporary admission of goods (ATA Convention).

2. UNECE and UN/CEFACT [19]

The UN Economic Commission for Europe (UNECE) is a UN agency that has been actively engaged in work on trade facilitation over the past 40 years. The UNECE encourages close collaboration between governments and private business to secure the interoperability for the exchange of information between the public and private sector through the United Nations Centre for Trade Facilitation and Electronic Business (UN/CEFACT), a United Nations body that has a global – not a regional – remit. The UN/CEFACT has developed a number of trade facilitation standards, recommendations and tools, *inter alia*:

◉ The UN Layout Key for Trade Documents, which is the foundation for EU's Single Administrative Document (SAD);

◉ UN/EDIFACT, the international standard for Electronic Data Interchange (EDI); and

◉ Numerous trade facilitation recommendations.

The UN Layout Key minimises the number of documents to be submitted by importers to customs and only requires a master document in which all the information needed for the clearance of goods by customs, and for approval by other agencies regarding the compliance of the goods with technical and health regulations, is provided.

---

17 Quoted from the WCO website (visited on 23 December 2005): http://www.wcoomd.org/ie/en/Conventions/conventions.html
18 The 1972 Convention on Containers is a UNECE convention administered with technical input from WCO.
19 The information in this section draws on information provided on the websites of UN/CEFACT and the UNECE. For more information on UN/CEFACT's work and recommendations on Trade Facilitation, see http://www.unece.org/cefact/about.htm

The UN/CEFACT coordinates its work with other international organisations, *inter alia*, the World Trade Organization (WTO), the World Customs Organization (WCO), the Organization for Economic Co-operation and Development (OECD), the United Nations Commission on International Trade Law (UNCITRAL) and the United Nations Conference on Trade and Development (UNCTAD), in the context of a Memorandum of Understanding for a Global Facilitation Partnership for Transport and Trade.

It also seeks to secure coherence in the development of Standards and Recommendations by co-operating with other interested parties, including international, intergovernmental and non-governmental organisations. In particular, for UN/CEFACT Standards, this coherence is accomplished by cooperating with the International Organization for Standardization (ISO), the International Electrotechnical Commission (IEC), the International Telecommunication Union (ITU), and selected non-governmental organisations (NGOs) in the context of the ISO/IEC/ITU/UNECE Memorandum of Understanding (MoU). These relationships were established in recognition of the fact that UN/CEFACT's work has broad applications in areas beyond global commerce and that the interoperability of applications and their ability to support multi-lingual environments are its key objectives.

3. IMO and ICAO

Other international organisations such as the International Maritime Organisation (IMO) and the International Civil Aviation Organization (ICAO) are also engaged in work on trade facilitation in the areas falling within their respective mandates. The IMO has adopted a Convention on the Facilitation of International Maritime Traffic (FAL). The ICAO has adopted a trade facilitation programme aimed at reducing paper work, standardising documentation, and simplifying procedures to minimise delays for both travellers and traders.

4. United Nations Conference on Trade and Development (UNCTAD), the World Bank, and the International Monetary Fund (IMF)

While the work of the international organisations described above puts greater emphasis on the development of international standards and recommendations, the work of UNCTAD, and of financial institutions such as the World Bank and IMF focuses on assisting countries in taking concrete measures for trade facilitation.[20]

For the last two decades, UNCTAD has been assisting countries in establishing 'trade points' which assist local industries, particularly small and medium-sized enterprises, in carrying out foreign trade transactions. National trade points are interconnected with one another electronically through UNCTAD's Global Trade Point Network (GTP Net). This network is equipped to link up with other global networks.

In 1985, UNCTAD also developed a customs software programme – the Automated System for Customs Data (ASYCUDA). The updated version of the system enables countries to adopt formats for customs declarations based on the UN Layout Key and, thus, have the information required for the handling of cargo

---

20 See also Chapter 4 on Technical Assistance and Capacity Building, particularly section 2.1 'Overview of the assistance currently being provided for trade facilitation'.

manifests and for the determination of duties to be paid readily available. The system can also be used for choosing consignments for physical inspection by using a selection criterion (including a random rate).

The World Bank is one of the largest providers of technical assistance in the area of trade facilitation. Most of its projects have comprehensive trade facilitation components, which aim at improving customs valuation, customs clearance and other related procedures and tariff reform.

The International Monetary Fund also provides assistance to developing countries on request. However, unlike the World Bank, it does not provide assistance for comprehensive reform programmes but concentrates on selected areas of customs administration, such as combating frauds and increasing the collection of revenues by adopting risk management and other techniques.

5. The Commonwealth Secretariat

Under its mandate to help countries improve their export competitiveness by meeting international standards in customs and trade facilitation, the Commonwealth Secretariat provides short-term technical assistance to developing and least developed countries for trade facilitation.

6. APEC[21] and other Regional cooperation Arrangements

Twenty-one member countries of the Asia-Pacific Economic Cooperation (APEC) have identified trade facilitation as one of the key areas of work on a priority basis. Its work programme aims at assisting countries to adopt the WTO Convention on the Harmonised System of Customs Classification (HSCC), and the Kyoto Convention standards relating to, *inter alia*, the transparency of customs procedures such as risk assessment, permission to submit documents prior to import, the speedy clearance of imports by authorised persons and of express consignments, and appeals procedures. It has also developed a draft non-binding code on trade facilitation for adoption by its member countries.

Regional Cooperation Arrangements in Asia (ASEAN), Africa (COMESA, ECA, ECOWAS and SADC) and in Latin America (MERCOSUR) are also putting increased emphasis on customs reform and other trade facilitation measures.

---

21   APEC's 21 Member Economies are: Australia; Brunei Darussalam; Canada; Chile; People's Republic of China; Hong Kong, China; Indonesia; Japan; Republic of Korea; Malaysia; Mexico; New Zealand; Papua New Guinea; Peru; The Republic of the Philippines; The Russian Federation; Singapore; Chinese Taipei; Thailand; United States of America; Viet Nam (see the website of APEC, visited on 22 November 2005, http://www.apec.org).

PART TWO

Legal Forms, Codification and the
Modalities for the Negotiations

Chapter 3: Legal forms for the codification of the rules and modalities for negotiations on rule making

General

It is normal practice for countries participating in trade negotiations to decide on the 'legal framework that should be adopted for the codification of the results of the negotiations' and on the 'modalities and techniques' that could be used in the actual conduct of negotiations, once the issues on which new rules are to be adopted have been identified.

I. CODIFICATION FORMS USED UNDER THE WTO'S LEGAL FRAMEWORK – PRESENT WTO PRACTICE

Under WTO law and practice, the following types of instruments are used for the codification of the results of the negotiations:

* Understandings
* Decisions
* Codes
* Multilateral Agreements and
* Plurilateral Agreements.

To facilitate the consideration of the legal form that could be used for incorporating the results of the negotiations on trade facilitation, the practices currently in use are described below in their historical context.

1. Understandings

'Understandings' are generally utilised where the aim of the negotiations is to clarify the existing rules. Six Understandings were adopted in the Uruguay Round for the clarification of the provisions of GATT. Some examples are: the Understanding on the Clarification of the Rules of Article II (b) on 'other duties and charges,' and the Understanding Clarifying the Provisions of Article XXIV on regional trade arrangements relating to the length of time within which the process of dismantling tariff and other barriers must be completed.

2. Decisions

'Decisions' are made when the results of the negotiations – in addition to clarifying the rules – provide for the imposition of additional obligations and/or lay down the procedures to be followed during their implementation. For instance, in the Uruguay Round of negotiations, a Decision was adopted in the area of customs, clarifying the rules of the Agreement on Customs Valuation which require customs to determine the dutiable value of imported goods on the basis of the value declared by the importer. The Decision now permits customs authorities to deviate from this basic rule and reject such a value if they have doubts regarding its truth and accuracy, and re-determine it on the basis of other methods provided under the Agreement.

3. Codes, multilateral and plurilateral agreements: developments from the Tokyo Round to the Uruguay Round — A historical perspective

In the first few years of its existence, GATT relied mainly on 'Understandings' and 'Decisions' for the clarification of its rules. The practice of utilizing separate agreements for the clarification of and elaboration on the provisions of GATT Articles started in the Kennedy Round, when the Agreement on Anti-dumping Practice was adopted. This practice was continued in the Tokyo Round, and new agreements clarifying various GATT articles – such as those relating to the valuation of goods for customs purposes; the application of licensing procedures; the use of subsidies, and the application of countervailing duties – were adopted in the Round. The Round also resulted in the adoption of an agreement in the area of technical regulations, on which GATT's legal framework did not previously contain any specific rules.

These agreements were comprehensive instruments, which spelt out the procedures for the application of the rules at the national level in detail. They also provided for the continuous examination and review of the operation of the Agreements by a committee consisting of countries that had become their members.

In the Uruguay Round, all the agreements negotiated in the Tokyo Round were reviewed and improved. A new agreement was also added to the list – the Agreement on Sanitary and Phytosanitary Measures.

However, the Uruguay Round made an important change in the membership status of the agreements. In the Tokyo Round, it had been tacitly accepted that GATT member countries would have a choice about whether they would like to become members. The agreement became operational when a 'critical mass of countries' became members. The result was that, in most cases, only the developed countries, and a few developing countries with the capacity to accept the additional obligations, chose to become members. To encourage developing countries (that had chosen not to become members) to join the agreements, the rules of these agreements permitted non-member countries to attend the meetings of the committees established for the surveillance of their operation as observers.

Observer countries had the same rights as members to participate in the discussions. The committees also made continuous efforts to expand their membership by arranging meetings for discussions on the steps that could be taken to eliminate the difficulties of developing countries in acceding to the agreements.

The situation changed dramatically during the last phase of the negotiations in the Uruguay Round, when it was agreed that the provisions of the Punta del Este Declaration launching the Round (which provided that the negotiations and their results were one single undertaking) envisaged that all countries that had acceded to GATT automatically became members of agreements negotiated in the Round. By applying this principle, the Marrakech Agreement establishing the WTO divided the agreements that were revised or negotiated in the Uruguay Round into two categories: Multilateral and Plurilateral. Membership of multilateral agreements was to be obligatory for all WTO member countries. However, the WTO members had a right to decide whether or not to become members in the case of plurilateral agreements. Apart from these two Agreements, all other WTO agreements are currently multilateral.

The earlier Tokyo Round agreements, which have now been replaced by revised versions adopted during the Uruguay Round, are often referred to in analytical literature as 'codes.' The use of the term appears to have been derived from the fact that only those countries that had chosen to become members of the Agreement were bound by their obligations. A GATT member country which had not become a member of a particular Agreement was not under any legal obligation to abide by its provisions; however, it was encouraged to follow its rules in order to prepare for membership.

Of significance here is that a decision adopted before the conclusion of the Tokyo Round had clarified that the MFN rule of GATT required member countries to extend the benefits of the Agreements to non-member countries even though they were not required to abide by the obligations they imposed. In practice, this implied that a member country of the Agreement on, for example, Subsidies and Countervailing Measures, could not discriminate between member and non-member countries, or apply different investigation procedures while examining petitions for the levying of countervailing measures to member and non-member countries.

The main advantage of a 'code' was that it permitted countries that were not ready to join, to stay out. However, the advantages provided by the Tokyo Round codes to non-member countries which could benefit from the rights thus created, is no longer available. The Marrakech Agreement establishing the WTO now provides that agreements with limited membership (i.e. plurilateral agreements) should not create rights in favour of non-members (Article II: 3).[22] This provision is intended to prevent non-members from taking advantage of the plurilateral agreements as 'free riders.'

II. A MULTILATERAL AGREEMENT ON TRADE FACILITATION?

It is also necessary to examine what kind of form will be most suitable for the codification of the results of the negotiations in the area of trade facilitation. Any decision regarding this matter will have to keep in mind the following features of the results likely to emerge from the negotiations:

- The results will cover the clarification of a number of provisions of Articles V, VIII and X;
- The legal instrument would have to provide a mechanism for:
  - Ensuring that developing and least developed countries are not required to accept obligations for which they do not have the technical capacities to implement, and
  - Granting technical assistance to these countries (which do not currently have such capacities) for gradually building up the required capacities for the implementation of the rules and of the commitments which they may assume;
- Surveillance of the progress made in the acceptance of the obligations and for the consideration of complaints of non-compliance.

These possible features of the results suggest that 'Understandings' or 'Decisions' may not be suitable codifying instruments. As noted in the last section, the term 'Understanding' is mainly used for the clarification of existing rules; the term 'Decision' suggests the imposition of additional obligations, generally of a procedural nature, in addition to the clarification of rules. Both terms seem appropriate only for the clarification of a limited number of rules, and do not generally contain any provisions regarding the surveillance of their operation. Thus, the most appropriate form seems to be 'Agreement.'

---

22 The relevant paragraph reads as follows: 'The Plurilateral Trade Agreements do not create either obligations or rights for Members that have not accepted them'.

If, after taking into account these factors, it is decided to adopt the term 'Agreement' as the form for the codification of the results of the negotiations, the question that arises is whether such agreements should be plurilateral or multilateral.

It appears that the plurilateral agreement may not be acceptable both to countries that are proponents of the adoption of new rules in trade facilitation, as well as to many developing countries who may decide upon not acceding to it. Any such development would go against the general objective of wanting the clarification of the existing rules, or for the adoption of new ones. Despite fears about the difficulties of accepting the obligations such agreements may impose in the foreseeable future, there is no doubt that most developing countries consider that, in the long run, the technical assistance made available to them following the adoption of the agreement would assist them in improving their customs clearance procedures which are currently increasing the costs of imported and exported goods for traders unnecessarily.

The adoption of a plurilateral agreement would result in the exclusion of non-member countries from receiving technical assistance. On the other hand, a multilateral agreement would ensure that all countries are able to secure such assistance within the constraints imposed by the total availability of financial resources among the donors. Thus, it is the multilateral rather than the plurilateral agreement that seems to be the more desirable option.

1. Approaches in other WTO Agreements

In order to meet the requirements of the mandate for the negotiations contained in Annex D of the 2004 Council Decision, and in Annex E of the 2005 Hong Kong Ministerial Declaration, as well as to accommodate some of the concerns that are currently being expressed by developing countries, the proposed Agreement would have to aim at avoiding the unnecessary duplication of the work being done by other international organisations, particularly by the WCO.

It may be possible to achieve these aims by utilising the approaches used in some of the WTO Agreements. If the approach adopted in the Agreements on TBT and SPS as well as in the Agreements on Customs Valuation and on Rules of Origin for cooperation with international organisations is suitably adapted to ensure a cooperative relationship between the WTO and organisations such as the WCO (as well as other international organisations working on customs matters), the unnecessary duplication of work can be avoided.

2. The approach of the TBT and SPS Agreements

The TBT and SPS Agreements require WTO member countries to base their technical regulations and SPS measures on the international standards developed by international standard setting bodies. The obligation to use such standards is binding, except in situations specifically mentioned in the two Agreements. The TBT Agreement does not specify by name which international standard setting bodies fall under the scope of the Agreement and its obligation on members to comply with such standards. However, it is generally assumed that the standards to be used are those developed by the International Organization for Standardization (ISO), the International Electrotechnical Commission (IEC), the International Telecommunication Union (ITU), and the Codex Alimentarius Commission (CAC). The SPS Agreement, on the other hand, specifies the international standard setting bodies whose standards are to be utilised. These bodies are: the Codex Alimentarius Commission (CAC), the World Organization for Animal Health (i.e. the *Office International des Epizooties*' or OIE), and the International Plant Protection Organization (IPPO).

3. The approach of the Agreements on Customs Valuation and Rules of Origin

The SPS and TBT Agreements do not lay down any norms or guidelines on how international standards should be formulated. The WTO negotiators of these agreements were keen on ensuring the autonomy and independence of these organisations in the procedures followed while developing standards.

However, in negotiating the Agreement on Customs Valuation and the Agreement on Rules of Origin, the WTO negotiators did not adopt such a 'hands off' approach. The two Agreements contain provisions requiring the WCO to establish Technical Committees for the examination of the 'specific problems that may arise in the day-to day-administration' of their provisions. These committees are also expected to provide advice to the WTO Agreement Committees on 'technical matters' relating to the implementation of the rules in each agreement.

The Agreement on Rules of Origin goes further, and envisages the cooperation between WTO and WCO in the formulation of new rules. In particular, it provides that negotiations on the development of a harmonised system of origin should, in the first instance, take place at the technical level in the WCO Technical Committee. The current negotiations at the WTO are largely based on the package developed by the WCO, and are confined to providing policy guidelines and finding compromises in areas where serious differences had arisen in the discussions at the technical level in the WCO.

III. THE MODALITIES FOR NEGOTIATIONS ON RULE MAKING ON MEASURES IDENTIFIED BY THE NEGOTIATING GROUP

1. The division of measures into two categories

The discussions that have taken place since trade facilitation was included in the agenda for negotiations in the Negotiating Group have been able to identify the measures on which new rules could be made. If the approaches used in the Agreements described above are to be appropriately used for the codification of the results of the negotiations in the area of trade facilitation, it may be desirable to divide the 'measures that have been identified' as necessary to improve and clarify GATT Articles V, VIII and X (Annex E of the Hong Kong Ministries Declaration) into the following two categories:

- Category I: Measures which primarily raise trade policy issues, and

- Category II: Measures dealing with methods and techniques that customs should apply in the day-to-day administration of customs procedures.

Box 4 lists measures which fall under category I; those falling under category II are listed in Box 5.

Box 4: Category I: Measures that primarily raise trade policy issues

PUBLICATION AND AVAILABILITY OF INFORMATION

- ◆ Publication of Trade Regulations
- ◆ Publication of Penalty Provisions
- ◆ Internet Publication
    - of elements set out in Article X of GATT 1994
    - of specified information setting forth procedural sequence and other requirements for importing goods
- ◆ Notification of Trade Regulations
- ◆ Establishment of Enquiry Points/SNFP/Information Centres
- ◆ Other Measures to Enhance the Availability of Information

---

TIME PERIODS BETWEEN PUBLICATION AND IMPLEMENTATION

◆ Interval between Publication and Entry into Force

CONSULTATION AND COMMENTS ON NEW AND AMENDED RULES

◆ Prior Consultation and Commenting on New and Amended Rules

◆ Information on Policy Objectives Sought

ADVANCE RULINGS

◆ Provision of Advance Rulings

APPEAL PROCEDURES

◆ Right of Appeal

◆ Release of Goods in Event of Appeal

OTHER MEASURES TO ENHANCE IMPARTIALITY AND NON-DISCRIMINATION

◆ Uniform Administration of Trade Regulations

FEES AND CHARGES CONNECTED WITH IMPORTATION AND EXPORTATION

◆ General Disciplines on Fees and Charges Imposed on or in Connection with Importation and Exportation
  - Specific Parameters for Fees/Charges
  - Publication/Notification of Fees/Charges
  - Prohibition of Collection of Unpublished Fees and Charges
  - Periodic Review of Fees/Charges
  - Automated Payment

◆ Reduction/Minimisation of the Number and Diversity of Fees/Charges

FORMALITIES CONNECTED WITH IMPORTATION AND EXPORTATION

◆ Disciplines on Formalities/Procedures and Data/Documentation Requirements Connected with Importation and Exportation
  - Non-discrimination
  - Periodic Review of Formalities and Requirements
  - Reduction/Limitation of Formalities and Documentation Requirements
  - Use of International Standards
  - Elimination of Pre-Shipment Inspection
  - Phasing out Mandatory Use of Customs Brokers

CONSULARISATION

◆ Prohibition of Consular Transaction Requirement

BORDER AGENCY COOPERATION

◆ Coordination of Activities and Requirement of all Border Agencies

MATTERS RELATED TO GOODS TRANSIT

◆ Strengthened Non-discrimination

◆ Disciplines on Fees and Charges
  - Publication of Fees and Charges and Prohibition of Unpublished ones
  - Periodic Review of Fees and Charges

- More effective Disciplines on Charges for Transit
- Periodic Exchange between Neighbouring Authorities

◆ Disciplines on Transit Formalities and Documentation Requirements
- Periodic Review
- Reduction/Simplification
- Harmonisation/Standardisation
- Promotion of Regional Transit Arrangements

Box 5: Category II: Methods and techniques which customs should apply in the day-to-day administration of customs procedures

FORMALITIES CONNECTED WITH IMPORTATION AND EXPORTATION

◆ Uniform Customs Code

◆ Acceptance of Commercially Available Information and of Copies

◆ Automation

◆ Single Window/One-time Submission

RELEASE AND CLEARANCE OF GOODS

◆ Expedited/Simplified Release and Clearance of Goods
- Pre-arrival Clearance
- Expedited Procedures for Express Shipments
- Risk Management /Analysis, Authorised Traders
- Post-Clearance Audit
- Separating Release from Clearance Procedures
- Other Measures to Simplify Customs Release and Clearance

◆ Establishment and Publication of Average Release and Clearance Times

TARIFF CLASSIFICATION

◆ Objective Criteria for Tariff Classification

MATTERS RELATED TO GOODS TRANSIT
- Simplified and Preferential Clearance for Certain Goods
- Limitation of Inspections and Controls
- Sealing
- Cooperation and Coordination on Document Requirements
- Monitoring

OTHER MEASURES TO ENHANCE IMPARTIALITY AND NON-DISCRIMINATION

◆ Maintenance and Reinforcement of Integrity and Ethical Conduct Among Officials
- Establishment of a Code of Conduct
- Computerised System to Reduce/Eliminate Discretion
- System of Penalties
- Technical Assistance to Create/Build up Capacities to Prevent and Control Customs Offences
- Appointment of Staff for Education and Training
- Coordination and Control Mechanisms

1.1 Measures raising trade policy issues

Category I comprises mainly of proposals that raise trade policy issues such as publication obligations, the application of the non-discrimination principle; the clarification of rules relating to the level of fees, and the right of appeal against the decisions of customs authorities. On almost all these issues, the relevant GATT Articles V, VIII, and X lay down broad principles and rules which WTO member countries are under obligation to follow at the national level. These articles cover broad ground: for instance, rules governing the level of fees and their publication apply to all types of fees charged at the border (e.g. import and export licence fees, and inspection fees for ensuring that the imported goods meet with the prescribed sanitary regulations and technical standards). The basic purpose of clarifying and improving these broad rules in relation to the above-mentioned measures is to make it easier for customs administrations and other border agencies to ensure that the following elements are complied with:

- Transparency as an essential element of a regulatory business environment;
- Consistency and predictability that help remove uncertainly in trade operations;
- Non-discrimination as a guarantee of impartial and uniform administration of border related trade regulations and procedures; and
- Due process, i.e. devise an appropriate mechanism to review and correct administrative activities.

These trade policy measures on which the new rules would be adopted fall clearly within the competence of the WTO. Moreover, the trade diplomats who normally participate in WTO meetings have the expertise required for participation in the discussions and negotiations on these issues. Thus, the negotiations on the adoption of rules governing these measures would have to take place in the WTO.

1.2 Measures dealing with the methods and techniques used by customs on which standards have been adopted by the WCO and other international standardisation organisations

The position of the proposals in Category II (which call upon customs to apply new and innovative methods/ techniques in the clearance of goods on a daily basis) is considerably different from those in Category I. Rules that ask for the use of new methods and techniques (such as the adoption of risk management and the systems of authorised importers and post-clearance audit) do not raise any major trade policy issues.

Currently, there are no specific rules governing these measures in GATT. The proposals for the development of rules in GATT requiring countries to use these innovative methods have been tabled to operationalise the provisions of sub paragraph (c) of Art VIII which, *inter alia*, call upon member countries 'to minimise the incidence and complexity of import and export formalities' and 'to decrease and simplify import and export documentation.'

However, in the last few decades, work on the development of standards and recommendations regarding almost all the measures relating to the techniques and methods which customs follow in the clearance of goods, has been undertaken primarily by WCO and other international organisations such as UNECE and UN/CEFACT. The WCO in particular, has developed the revised Kyoto Convention which contains standards and guidelines for the application of almost all the measures listed under Category I in Box 5. These standards are being applied in 44 countries which have acceded to the Convention (see **Annex I** for a list of contracting parties). A few other countries are applying all, or some, of the standards in the Convention on a *de facto* basis.

IV. NEGOTIATING OPTIONS

1. The obligation of WTO members to apply the revised Kyoto Convention

In discussions in the Negotiating Group, some delegations had proposed that, instead of trying to develop new rules in the WTO in relation to such measures, the desirable course would be to require WTO member countries to accede to the revised Kyoto Convention by incorporating suitable provisions in the proposed Agreement.

The Convention imposes a binding obligation on its members to apply standards in its General Annex, with a longer minimum implementation period wherever necessary. It allows countries to choose which of the special annexes it should accede to, and permits them to make reservations based on their individual capacity.

A practical difficulty that arises in adopting this approach is that the Convention contains standards that apply not only to the techniques and methods used in customs clearance but also to some trade policy issues (such as the level of fees and appeals procedures). These issues fall clearly under the WTO's mandate and, thus, become the legitimate rationale for developing new rules in the WTO to address such trade concerns adequately and effectively.

2. The imposition of obligations to apply standards selected by the Negotiating Group

In this context, the most appropriate course for the Negotiating Group may be to first identify the international organisations that are engaged in developing standards on measures listed under Category II: i.e. regarding the techniques and methods used by customs administrations in the clearance of goods. Box 6 lists a number of intergovernmental organisations that are currently engaged in the work on trade facilitation.

Box 6: Intergovernmental organisations (international and regional) actively involved in the work on trade facilitation

- The World Customs Organization (WCO)
- The UN Economic Commission for Europe (UNECE)
- The United Nations Centre for Trade Facilitation and Electronic Business (UN/CEFACT)
- The International Organization for Standardization (ISO)
- The International Maritime Organization (IMO)
- The International Civil Aviation Organization (ICAO)
- The Asia-Pacific Economic Cooperation (APEC)
- UNCTAD
- The World Bank
- The International Monetary Fund (IMF)
- The Commonwealth Secretariat

Of the organisations listed above, UNCTAD, the World Bank, the IMF and the Commonwealth Secretariat do not prepare standards in the area of trade facilitation. Their work is to focus on providing technical assistance to developing countries. As noted earlier, the main organisation that has developed standards or recommendations dealing with different aspects of customs administration is WCO. In addition, UN/CEFACT has developed standards, *inter alia*, for the UN Layout Key (the single document for submission to customs) and for Electronic Data Interchange.

The standards adopted by IMO and ICAO in the area of trade facilitation cover areas which fall within their specialised mandates. APEC is a regional organisation whose work aims at assisting countries in accepting the Kyoto and other Conventions developed by the WCO. It has also developed a draft non-binding Code on Trade Facilitation.

From the above overview of the work being done at the international level on preparing standards regarding customs related issues, it is evident the main organisations responsible for developing such standards are:

- The WCO, and
- UNECE and UN/CEFACT.

If it is agreed that it would be desirable and appropriate for the Agreement to provide that its member countries should apply the standards developed by these organisations (instead of rewriting them in WTO negotiations), what should be the extent of the obligation to apply such standards? Should the obligation apply to all standards that have been developed until now as well as to those that may be developed in the future? The TBT and SPS Agreements impose such open ended obligations in the area of technical regulations, and sanitary and phytosanitary measures. The result is that countries are required to use these international standards in their mandatory regulations, even though they may not have participated at all in the negotiations leading to the adoption of these standards or, where their representatives were present, they had even voted against the adoption of these standards.

Taking this into account, it would be desirable for the modalities to provide that the obligation to apply standards developed by WCO, UNECE, UN/CEFACT and other specified organisations shall apply only to those standards in respect of which it is agreed in the negotiations that they are suitable for application, and are listed at an appropriate place in the Agreement.

3. Special sessions for the identification of those standards on which obligations should apply under the proposed Agreement

Negotiations for the identification of such standards in respect of which the Agreement could impose obligations on countries to apply them at the national level should take place in 'special sessions' organised by the Negotiating Group dedicated to the examination of a selected standard or standards. Sufficient advance notice should be given for such meetings in order to ensure attendance by customs experts from developing and least developed countries.

3.1. The cost of the participation of customs experts to be met by the WTO from its technical assistance funds

In addition, workshops at the technical level to brief delegations from developing and least developed countries on the standard or standards that will be examined at the session, should be arranged two or three days beforehand, in cooperation with WCO or other concerned organisations in order to ensure the informed and effective participation of these delegations in the discussions. The travel costs and subsistence allowance of officials (who may need such assistance) for attending the workshop and the subsequent dedicated session of the Negotiating Group should be met by the WTO from its technical assistance funds.

The practice of holding workshops prior to the meetings of the technical committees and the payment of travel and subsistence allowance to participants through the technical assistance funds is being increasingly followed by standard setting bodies like Codex Alimentarius and OIME to improve the participation of developing countries in the technical level discussions on the formulation of standards. The WTO Committee on Sanitary and Phytosanitary measures has recognised that such measures are an important step in this direction. It is necessary and desirable for the WTO also to adopt these practices, particularly in cases where trade diplomats do not have the required expertise in technical issues.

4. The advantage of linking standards developed by the WCO and other international organisations to WTO rules

The main advantages of requiring or encouraging countries to apply standards adopted by WCO, UNECE, UN/CEFACT and, where relevant, by other international organisations are the following:

- The standards adopted by these organisations are not as prescriptive as the WTO rules;
- The standards adopted by these bodies are complemented by guidelines on how they should be applied;
- The formulation of such standards also requires the active participation of representatives of the trading and business community. The WCO and other organisations permit open and active participation by all interested stakeholders in the work on the formulation of customs related standards. In contrast, under the WTO rules, participation is confined only to the representatives of governments.
- Experience has shown that standards have to be kept under continuous review, taking into account technological developments that have taken place since their adoption. For example, rapid developments in Information Technology require the constant review of technical standards. Thus, the WCO applied IT Guidelines to the General Annex of the Revised Kyoto Convention in 1999. These Guidelines were updated in 2002 and in 2004 in order to keep up with progress in this field. Another example is the WCO Customs Data Model which contains standardised maximum data elements for the use of customs and other border procedures. This is an important component of the 'single window' clearance concept, developed by the UNECE. The WCO is constantly reviewing its Data Model in close cooperation with the public and private sector stakeholders, taking into account the UN Layout Key, to ensure interoperability.

5. Standards needing review to be referred back to the WCO and other international organisations

There could be cases in which, after examination at the dedicated session, the Negotiating Group finds that the standard adopted by the WCO or other international organisations needs reviewing. Such a review may be found necessary, *inter alia*:

- When it is found that the standard has failed to take into account certain aspects, or

- When the majority of developing countries have not been able to participate in the technical level discussions in the relevant organisation during the formulation of the standard.

It is expected that such cases are likely to be few, as these standards have been adopted by the WCO and in UNECE after discussions and negotiations lasting over a number of years in which customs experts from many countries participated. In these (few) cases, the modalities for negotiations should provide for referring the standards/recommendations back to the organisation which had formulated them in the first instance, for review at the technical level, taking into account the proposals tabled in the Negotiating Group and the views expressed in the discussions. In remitting the standard for review, the WTO shall indicate the period within which the results of the review will be communicated to the Negotiating Group.

In order to ensure that customs experts from all countries, particularly developing countries, participate in the work on the review of standards by the WCO, the modalities should provide that all countries should make their best endeavours to participate in such technical-level work. Moreover, in order to ensure the effective participation of developing countries, consideration should be given to the adoption of measures similar to those described above to ensure the participation of developing and least developed countries in the dedicated sessions of the WTO Negotiating Group, e.g. holding workshops for experts from developing countries on the subject, and meeting the travel costs of the delegations from developing and least developed countries for attending such meetings.[23]

The financial resources required for this purpose could be made available by the WTO to WCO. Such a decision would be consistent with the commitment already assumed by developed countries to make financial resources available to developing countries for their effective participation in the negotiations.

---

23 For more detailed information on the measures that are being taken by international standard setting bodies to ensure the effective participation of developing countries in international standardisation activities, see Vinod Rege and Shyam Gujadhur, *Influencing and Meeting International Standards*, Volume Two, published jointly by the Commonwealth Secretariat and the International Trade Centre (ITC) (UNCTAD/WTO) in 2004.

Chapter 4: Technical assistance and capacity building

General

An important feature of the mandate for the negotiations on trade facilitation is the explicit commitment made by developed countries to provide technical assistance to developing and least developed countries to build capacity:

- During the course of the negotiations, for their improved participation in technical work on the development of rules; and

- After the completion of the negotiations, for the implementation of the results and commitments they have made.

Further, the mandate also recognises that the negotiations could lead to certain commitments whose implementation would require 'support for infrastructure development' by some developing and least developed countries. Developed countries have agreed to make every effort in this 'limited number of cases' to ensure support and assistance directly related to the nature and scope of the commitment for the purpose of implementation. However, they have stated that their capacity to provide such support is not unlimited.

The Hong Kong Ministerial Declaration, adopted in December 2005, urges developed countries to 'reinforce and operationalise their commitments' regarding the assistance and support to be provided to developing and least developed countries both for their effective participation in the negotiations, as well as for the implementation of the commitments they may be assuming in the negotiations. It also calls on developed countries to ensure that the assistance provided for the latter purpose should be 'precise, effective and operational,' and 'reflect the trade facilitation needs and priorities' of both developing and least developed countries.

This chapter is divided into two sections.

Section 1 describes the assistance that is currently being provided for the improved and effective participation of developing countries in the negotiations on trade facilitation. This is followed by a description of the assistance such countries will need in the final phase of the negotiations.

Section 2 contains an overview of the assistance that is currently being provided by international organisations and donor countries to reform and modernise customs clearance procedures. It also identifies the positive aspects as well as the weaknesses of the technical assistance being provided. It goes on to describe the institutional framework, including the establishment of a separate dedicated Fund that may have to be created by developed countries to oversee the implementation of the obligation they have assumed, i.e. to provide technical assistance to developing countries to build technical capacities for compliance with the rules of the proposed Agreement, and of the commitments they may assume in the negotiations.

1. Assistance for improved and effective participation in the negotiations

1.1 The role of multilateral organisations

Assistance for the improved participation of developing countries in the WTO negotiations on trade facilitation is currently being provided in specialised workshops or seminars by the following:

- The WTO Secretariat;
- Multilateral organisations dealing with trade issues, such as UNCTAD, ITC, OECD, and the Commonwealth Secretariat; and
- International financial institutions, such as the World Bank and the IMF.

The subject of trade facilitation has usually been an important agenda item in the workshops organised by the above organisations, for the specific purpose of briefing participants regarding developments in the negotiations in the Doha Round. The participants in such workshops are generally visiting officials from capitals who are responsible for the work on trade facilitation; Geneva-based officials responsible for their country's participation in the negotiations on the subject at the WTO; and representatives of trade and business associations of the participating countries. In some workshops, the discussions are based on case studies undertaken in developing countries regarding their experience of adopting trade facilitation measures at the national level.

1.2 The role of non-governmental organisations

A number of non-governmental organisations (NGOs) are also working actively to promote the benefits of trade facilitation. Prominent among these organisations is the UK-based SITPRO and the India-based CUTS International. The Boksburg Group – named after the venue where the first meeting of the Group took place in 2003 – established by SITPRO and the Commonwealth Business Council for work in the area of trade facilitation, comprises public (trade and customs) and private sector representatives mainly from developing countries.

The workshops and seminars arranged by these inter-governmental and non-governmental organisations have played a positive role both in dispelling many of the doubts and concerns of developing countries regarding the proposals on the adoption of new WTO rules on trade facilitation, and in appreciating the potential benefits that would accrue from the adoption of such rules. There is now a general recognition that if, under the proposed Agreement on Trade Facilitation, the responsive assistance required to meet the specific needs of each developing country for building up technical capacity for the implementation of its rules is assured, developing countries as a group would be in a win-win situation in the long run. The elimination of delays in the clearance of goods and an increase in the speed of payments would attract foreign investment, and assist companies in the avoidance of over-stocking to compensate for delays.

1.3 Coalitions of developing countries

Geneva-based delegations have established 'coalitions' for consultations among themselves on the approaches and strategies they could adopt in the discussions and negotiations at the WTO. The first coalition to come into existence was the 'Colorado Group.'[24] Its members are delegations from countries that initially proposed that the subject should be taken up for negotiation at the WTO. The other Group, known as the 'Core Group'[25] consists of delegations of countries that would like to see that any new rules adopted are responsive to the needs of developing countries, and do not require them to accept obligations which they do not have the technical capacity to implement.

1.4 Future assistance

One of the major problems encountered by the delegations of developing countries in effectively participating in trade facilitation discussions and negotiations at the WTO arises from their lack of expertise in the customs related field. These problems are likely to be enhanced as the negotiations enter the substantive phase and become more technical. Thus, it is necessary that all countries are represented by customs experts, especially in discussions on subjects requiring expertise in customs related matters including customs administration, and with experience in the application of risk management techniques, the selection and designation of 'authorised traders,' and 'post-clearance audits.'

To facilitate the participation of customs experts in negotiations on these subjects, it may be desirable to adopt a three-pronged approach. This will involve:

The identification of subjects in the negotiations in which participation at the expert level is necessary;
The arrangement of sessions of the Negotiating Group dedicated to negotiations on these subjects; and
An undertaking by the WTO to cover the travel expenses and subsistence allowance of experts visiting Geneva from its technical assistance funds in order to facilitate maximum attendance from developing and least developed countries.[26]

2. The provision of technical assistance to build capacity for the compliance of rules and the meeting of commitments undertaken in the negotiations

2.1 Overview of the assistance currently being provided for trade facilitation

Before discussing the institutional framework to be adopted for the provision of technical assistance for building technical capacity in developing countries for the application of the rules of the proposed Agreement on Trade Facilitation, it is necessary to note that there has been, in the last few years, a substantial increase in trade related assistance provided by donor countries as well as by multilateral financial institutions such as the World Bank and the IMF.

According to the WTO/OECD 2005 report, the assistance provided to help developing countries participate more effectively in international trade has increased by nearly 50% since the launching of the Doha Round

---

24 Australia, Canada, Chile, Columbia, Costa Rica, EC, Hong Kong China, Hungary, Japan, Korea, Morocco, New Zealand, Norway, Paraguay, Singapore, Switzerland and the U.S.A.

25 Bangladesh, Botswana, Cuba, Egypt, India, Indonesia, Jamaica, Kenya, Malaysia, Mauritius, Nigeria Philippines, Rwanda, Tanzania, Trinidad & Tobago, Uganda, Venezuela, Zambia and Zimbabwe.

26 It is relevant to note that this idea is not new. The international standard setting bodies, such as Codex Alimentarius Commission and OIE, have been bearing the cost of travel and subsistence allowance of delegations from developing countries, in order to ensure their participation in standardisation activities, in accordance with the provisions of the relevant WTO Agreements.

of negotiations in 2001. The trade facilitation component in such trade related assistance has also increased significantly. For instance, during 2001 to 2004, the assistance provided by developed countries for 'improvements in customs clearance and other related procedures, customs valuation, and tariff reform' rose nearly threefold: from US$ 105 million to US$ 372 million.[27] The rise in the assistance provided by the World Bank is more pronounced. During 1996 to 2003, the trade facilitation component in the World Bank's projects amounted to US$ 305 million. From 2004 to 2006, the amount spent – and projected to be spent – is expected to be around US$ 1.918 million.[28]

The number of countries receiving assistance from the World Bank has also increased. During the years 1996 to 2003, projects in 34 countries had a trade facilitation component. This number has risen to 60 in the projects approved or planned for the years 2004 to 2006.

2.2 The nature and type of assistance provided by international organisations

In addition to the World Bank, there are a number of other international organisations currently providing technical assistance to developing countries. Box 7 provides a synoptic picture of the nature and type of assistance being provided by different organisations.

Box 7: Agencies providing technical assistance in the area of trade facilitation

1. INTERNATIONAL ORGANISATIONS
The World Bank.
Among international organisations, the World Bank is probably the largest provider of technical assistance. Its customs reform activities are part of a broader reform programme aimed at facilitating trade, mobilizing general revenues, enhancing public finance management, and providing support to infrastructure. The 'Customs components' in such programmes try to cover all aspects of customs administrations, such as the legislative environment, customs procedures management, (including the use of information technology), and human resource development (e.g. recruitment procedures, training, and the salaries of customs officials). The content, priorities, and sequencing of activities are determined on the basis of intensive pre-project and diagnostic work.

During 1982-2005, 117 of the Bank's projects had a customs component. The bilateral donor agencies often collaborate with the Bank by contributing financial resources for the implementation of customs reform projects. The actual implementation of the reform programme may be assigned to a private consulting firm by the Bank and the co-operating donor agency. The firm is selected by inviting tenders.

IMF
The international monetary fund (IMF) has also had a long tradition of supporting customs reform programmes. It makes diagnostic assessments available, and assists governments in the preparation and implementation of reform strategies by providing long term resident technical assistants.

WCO
The WCO has, so far, focussed on providing assistance to encourage countries to reform their customs clearance systems with a view to preparing for accession to its revised Kyoto Convention.

---

27   See the Doha Development Agenda Trade Capacity Building Database (TCBDB), established jointly by OECD and WTO.
28   See the World Bank website, which provides information on Trade Facilitation, referred to and quoted by J. Michael Finger and
       John S. Wilson, 'Trade Facilitation, Implementation, the Doha Development Agenda', (World Bank), 12 April 2006 (draft).

UNCTAD
UNCTAD makes available its ASYCUDA software system, developed to enable developing (and other) countries handle most customs transactions.

WTO
The assistance provided by the WTO mostly targets developing countries, which have not acceded to its Agreement on Customs Valuation, in applying its rules in determining value for customs purposes.

COMMONWEALTH SECRETARIAT
The Commonwealth Secretariat provides practical and policy guidance to its member countries to help them address the bottlenecks to efficient trade; analysis of customs, trade and logistics-related problems which inhibit export competitiveness and advice on effective strategies to create a more business-friendly environment.

2. BILATERAL GOVERNMENTAL ASSISTANCE
Trade facilitation is a high priority in the assistance programmes of a number of donor countries. These programmes have made experts available to provide advice (on a short and long term basis) regarding the adoption of new methods in the clearance of goods through customs.

3. ASSISTANCE BY PRIVATE COMPANIES
A number of private sector consulting and other firms (e.g. Crown Agents Société General de Surveillance) are active in providing assistance in the area of facilitation. The costs of their services are often met by donor countries from their technical assistance funds.

Source: Michael Engelschalk and Tuan Minh Le, 'Two Decades of World Bank Lending for Customs Reforms,' in Customs Modernization Handbook, 2004.

The assistance provided by multilateral organisations and donor countries on a bilateral basis generally takes the following forms:

- Comprehensive programmes, and
- Partial or area-specific programmes.

2.2.1 Comprehensive programmes

Under the comprehensive programmes, the reform process covers all aspects of customs procedures. Such reform and modernisation programmes may involve fundamental changes in policy for the recruitment of customs officials, the dismissal of 'corrupt' officials, the upward revision of salaries (to remove incentives for corruption), the training of officials, as well as the adoption of detailed, coherent and well-sequenced procedures for the clearance of goods with the use of information technology. The aim of such programmes is twofold: to increase the revenue collected, and to minimise the time taken for the clearance of goods.

However, such reform programmes are time-consuming and costly. So far, the technical assistance required for this purpose has been provided mainly by the World Bank – often in the context of its civil service reform projects, its export promotion revenue mobilisation, or its trade and transport facilitation programme. Many bilateral donors (financial agencies) have also collaborated with the World Bank in the implementation of some of these comprehensive programmes by providing financial resources. Often, the Bank and the cooperating donor agency assign the responsibility for carrying out the reform programmes to a private consulting firm with expertise in the area.

Case studies undertaken by the World Bank, OECD, and other organisations provide a mixed picture of the success of these reform programmes in the countries that have adopted them. In Peru, Turkey, and Morocco, the programmes are generally considered to have succeeded in reducing the time required for the clearance of goods as well as increasing the revenue collected. However, in other countries the success achieved has been modest. In some countries, it is even doubtful whether the reforms introduced will be maintained after the technical assistance programme has ended, and the foreign consultants have left.

2.2.2   Partial or area-specific programmes

Customs administrations in a number of countries have, on the whole, relied on an 'area-specific approach' because of the difficulties encountered while preparing 'comprehensive programmes' and while obtaining the necessary funding from international financial institutions. The general objective seems to have been to 'fix some urgent problems without modifying the overall functioning of customs operations.' Such reform initiatives have absorbed substantial domestic and external resources. Examples are:

- The adoption of valuation systems in accordance with the WTO's Agreement on Customs Valuation;
- The adoption of special import regimes for certain types of imports and exports; and
- The introduction of advanced information technology.

Some of these partial reform initiatives have been successful. However, most observers agree that such initiatives display a poor record in terms of sustainable improvement in the overall efficiency and effectiveness of customs operations.

Another limitation of the assistance provided on a partial or area-specific basis is that there is a lack of coordination among international and bilateral institutions providing advice. Customs advisers coming from a variety of organisations are frequently unaware of other advice given on the subjects they are called upon to consider. Such advice is often repetitive, contradictory, or inconsistent, thus ensuring that it is ignored, or poorly applied. Moreover, rather than being demand-driven, these capacity building projects are often driven by the donors' own agenda which may include geopolitical elements, as well as extraneous reasons such as spending budgeted money to secure allocations for the next year.

The lesson to be learnt from this past experience of providing technical assistance on a partial or area specific basis is that, before seeking technical assistance, the country must undertake intensive preparatory work drawing out a programme identifying the areas where such assistance is needed. This can be done by using the diagnostic tools developed by such organisations as the World Bank, WCO and, more recently, the WTO. In undertaking such a diagnostic exercise, it is important to bear in mind that customs administration is not an exact science: a flexible approach may have to be adopted with the diagnostic analysis tailored to suit the environment in which the concerned customs authorities work, and the specific objectives they wish to achieve. It is also necessary to ensure that the programme provides for proper sequencing, and for meeting the recurring expenditure needed for the continuing implementation of the reform after the technical assistance programme is completed.

Experience has also shown that reform programmes often fail because of the lack of cooperation by customs staff. Thus, it is necessary for senior customs officials to inform the staff of the advantages of the reform before adopting the programme to secure their support.

2.3 Suggested institutional framework for ensuring greater coordination among aid-giving agencies and for improving the effectiveness of the assistance provided

Any examination of the institutional framework to be adopted for the provision of technical assistance in the area of trade facilitation needs to take into account the general consensus that is emerging among the Finance and Development Ministers of various countries about expanding 'Aid for Trade.' This consensus has been made amply clear in the discussions in various international fora (including the Development Committee of the World Bank and the IMF). As a result, the Declaration adopted by the Trade Ministers at the Hong Kong Ministerial meeting called upon the Director General of the WTO to create a 'task force' to examine how 'Aid for Trade' could be made operational, and how it could effectively contribute to the development dimension of the Doha Development Round by, *inter alia*, assisting developing countries in building the supply capacity and trade related infrastructure needed for implementing WTO Agreements, and for expanding trade in general. The decision on the institutional framework that may have to be adopted for the provision of technical assistance in the area of trade facilitation would be greatly influenced by the recommendations of the Task Force report on this issue.[29]

Widely differing views are currently being expressed in academic circles, international financial institutions, international trade organisations, donor countries and developing countries about how the greatly expanded 'Aid for Trade' could be provided effectively, and how predictability, country ownership, and coherence could be ensured while providing such assistance. These views take two forms:

- Continue utilising the existing mechanism, and
- Establish a new global Trade Facility and/or specific dedicated Funds.

2.3.1 Continuation of the existing mechanism

The main mechanism for providing trade policy related aid today is the Integrated Framework (IF) which emerged from the 1996 WTO Singapore Ministerial Conference as a part of the WTO Action Plan for least developed countries. Its aim was to boost their participation in the World Trading System. The first few years of its operation were disappointing. It improved after the first evaluation report submitted in 2000: a new governance structure was installed and a Trust Fund created to integrate trade policies into the national plans of the least developed countries. However, in its present form, the IF is a mechanism for relatively small projects, and does not include infrastructure or supply side components.[30]

The question of whether the IF process can be enhanced and strengthened to provide aid for trade – which is expected to increase by nearly 50% of the present level to $40 billion by 2010 – was examined at the request of the IMF and the World Bank by the Ambassadors of Rwanda and Sweden to the WTO who coordinated the discussions of the various Groups in Geneva. Their report suggested the creation of three pillars for the effective disbursement of expanded aid by, *inter alia*:

- Enhancing the in-country trade development agenda through the adoption of programmes providing technical assistance for capacity building on the basis of the needs identified by Diagnostic Trade Integration Studies (DTIS);

---

29 See para 57 of the Hong Kong Ministerial Declaration.
30 See AITIC, Agency for International Trade Information and Cooperation, Background Note, Aid for Trade, Moving Target, April 2005, pages 6 and 7.

- Establishing a multilateral fund to respond to prioritizing trade diagnostic needs; and

- Creating a separate multilateral fund to address the specific adjustment needs arising from the Doha Round (not only preference erosion but also other adjustment issues, including the loss of tax revenue).

However, the report recognised that donors with a strong presence in the recipient country may prefer to provide funding bilaterally, by using their own processes instead of contributing to the Funds.[31]

The proposals for the establishment of pillars consisting of a separate additional fund to undertake trade diagnostic studies on a priority basis was not supported by the staff of the World Bank and the IMF, including by the Development Committee of the two institutions. These institutions have also expressed serious misgivings about the need to establish a 'dedicated fund' to assist countries in meeting the adjustment costs of the Doha Round, including those arising from the erosion of preferential margins. In their view, the mechanisms currently in existence (the IMF's Trade Integration Mechanism (TIM) and the World Bank's Structural Adjustment Lending), as well as the channels established by donor countries to provide assistance for this purpose are adequate for meeting the demands of developing countries for such assistance.

Moreover, these mechanisms enable the World Bank and the IMF to provide assistance for meeting adjustment costs 'as a part of an overall package of domestic policy reforms and economic planning.' The two institutions consider it both unrealistic and inappropriate to provide assistance for meeting adjustment costs in isolation. Given this situation, the establishment of a separate dedicated fund to meet adjustment costs could only lead to the further bureaucratisation of the administration of aid. This is especially so if such a fund was to be administered through interagency cooperation: it would run the risk of the politicisation of aid administration.[32]

2.3.2 Establishment of a Global Trade Facility

While international financial institutions and the donor countries generally appear to be against the establishment of a global fund to channel aid for trade – or funds dedicated for providing assistance in particular areas – there is support at the academic and the political levels for the establishment of such a fund in developing countries.

The report on 'Aid for Trade' prepared for the Commonwealth Secretariat by Joseph E. Stiglitz and Andrew Charlton, takes a middle view. It proposes that 'dedicated funds' for aid for trade – donated through specific binding commitments in the final Doha Agreements and subsequently enforceable within the WTO – should be allocated to a special facility, the Global Trade Facility (GTF), to be established by the World Bank for providing aid for trade.

Further, the two economists have recommended that the management of such a Facility should be firmly concentrated within the World Bank, and the cumbersome process of being managed by six institutions – as is the case of the Integrated Framework – should be avoided. They also suggest that because the GTF

---

31   See the 'Aid for Trade' Initiative – Options to Enhance Support, Non-paper, 20 July 2005, Annex I in the 'Doha Development Round and Aid for Trade', Development Committee (Joint Ministerial Committee of the Board of Governors of the Bank and the Fund on the Transfer of Real Resources to Developing Countries), D.C. 2005 – 0016, September 12, 2005.

32   Supra, Report of the Development Committee.

would be the result of an agreement negotiated at the WTO, one of its aims should be to enforce the commitment assumed by developed countries. The Governance structure of the GTF should, therefore, be different from that of the World Bank in which voting is dominated by developed countries. The Facility should be managed by a Board consisting of 24 countries, with 8 seats reserved for low-income countries, 8 for middle-income countries, and 8 for developed countries. Seats should be rotated periodically amongst members. A 'supermajority' of 60% should be necessary for major decisions.[33]

2.4   Rationale for the establishment of a separate Trade Facilitation Fund or Facility

Against this background, the institutional framework to be adopted for the provision of technical assistance in the area of trade facilitation would have to be discussed and negotiated after taking into account the above views on the various aspects of aid for trade.

There appears to be a strong case for the establishment of a separate dedicated Fund or Facility for the provision of assistance in the area of trade facilitation. This is for two reasons:

● Developing countries have agreed to accept new and additional disciplines in this area only if the assistance required by them to build technical capacities for the application of the rules, and for the implementation of the commitments they may assume, is made available to them, and

● Developed countries have already made a commitment to provide assistance for the above purposes, including the assistance needed for related infrastructural development.

The establishment of a separate fund would help ensure that developed and developing countries fulfil their commitments.

In fact, these considerations appear to have influenced the Group of African, Caribbean and Pacific (ACP) countries to propose the establishment of a special Trade Facilitation Technical Assistance and Capacity-Building Fund to the Negotiating Group on Trade Facilitation. The proposal envisages that the required resources should be contributed by bilateral and multilateral donors, and should be managed by an 'inter-agency coordinating mechanism' consisting of the relevant international, regional, and sub-regional organisations such as, but not limited to, UNCTAD, UNECE, UNECA, WTO, WCO, the World Bank (see **Annex I** for extracts from the proposal relating to the establishment of the Fund).[34]

If such a fund or facility is to be established, besides taking into account the views that are being expressed in the general debate described above on the subject of 'aid for trade,' some of the issues which will have to be addressed in the negotiations will include the following:

● Would such a fund be a stand-alone one, as for example the Standards and Trade Development Facility which has been established at the WTO? Would it be a part (pillar or window) of the Integrated Framework? Or, would it be some new Global Facility especially established to provide aid for trade?

● If such a facility or fund were to be established, what would be its size? How would it be managed? Where would it be established?

---

33   Joseph E. Stiglitz and Andrew Charlton, 'Aid for Trade, A report for the Commonwealth Secretariat,' March 2006, pages 23-24.
34   Communication from Mauritius on behalf of the ACP Group, WTO document TN/TF/W/73, 10 November 2005.

- How would such a fund relate to the assistance provided on a bilateral basis? What purpose/s would justify the availability of resources from the Fund?

These issues are discussed briefly in the following paragraphs.

2.4.1   A 'standalone' Fund or a separate pillar within the existing or future Facility

The main advantage of a separate Fund, whether it is a 'standalone' one or a part of the existing facility, is that it would earmark clearly the resources required for providing assistance in the area of trade facilitation as well as ease their disbursement. However, so far, international financial institutions and donor countries have been hesitant to support the establishment of such a fund for two reasons:

The establishment of the fund may unnecessarily bureaucratise the process of granting aid; and
Its establishment may require them to change their existing systems for the provision of assistance. Since they are already providing a significant amount of assistance in the area of trade facilitation, they would prefer to disburse such aid through already existing procedures even after the proposed Agreement is adopted.

Thus, these objections would apply equally if such a fund was to be established as a separate window, or as a pillar of the Integrated Framework, or be a stand-alone one.

From the point of view of developing countries as a group, the Integrated Framework provides further serious limitations. The assistance under the programme is directed entirely to the least developed countries. The staffs of the World Bank and the IMF have suggested that country eligibility could be extended to cover other relatively less developed countries that also qualify for international development assistance (IDA) at concessional rates of interest. Though the adoption of the IDA-only criteria could increase the number of developing countries eligible for assistance to 81 (See Annex II), this would, nevertheless, exclude a large number of other developing countries and transitional economies. Of relevance here is that case studies on the experience of providing assistance suggest that the developing countries which have benefited most from the assistance given for reform and improvements in custom procedures are those at a higher stage of development.

2.4.2.   The Trade Facilitation Fund: size, management, structure, and location

If a Trade Facilitation Fund were to be established, the following issues need to be kept in mind:

- The initial size of the Fund would have to be negotiated by taking into account the approximate assessment of needs being made by the World Bank, WCO, and other organisations;

- The Fund should be managed by an inter-agency committee. In determining the management structure of the fund, ways to avoid the problems and difficulties typical of management by interagency committees would need careful consideration;

- In order to ensure that the programme is recipient driven and focuses on providing assistance that is need-based, the management structure should provide for the establishment of an Advisory Board, consisting of representatives of both donor and recipient countries. This has been suggested by Joseph Stiglitz and Andrew Charlton in their report on 'Aid for Trade' prepared for the Commonwealth Secretariat (March 2006).

- As regards the membership and management of the Fund:
  - The size and membership of the Advisory Body should ensure the balanced representation of both donor and recipient countries;
  - At least half of the members appointed should have the background and experience of working in customs administration; and
  - The agencies responsible for the management of the Fund (WTO, WCO, ITC, UNCTAD, UNECE, World Bank and the IMF) should be ex-officio members of the Advisory Board.

- How regional organisations such as the Asia-Pacific Economic Cooperation (APEC) which is actively engaged in providing assistance in this area, and other international organisations such as the Commonwealth Secretariat are associated with the work of the Advisory Board, should be given due consideration; and

- Since the Fund would be the result of a contractual obligation assumed by developed countries under the proposed Agreement on Trade Facilitation to provide technical assistance to developing countries, it should be located in the WTO. This should be so despite its management by an inter-agency committee.

2.4.3   The relationship of the Fund to bilateral assistance or assistance provided by international financial institutions

As developed countries and international financial institutions are likely to be unwilling to change their existing practices for providing assistance in the area of trade facilitation, the procedures should provide that, while pledging resources, they should indicate clearly the amount of resources:

- Devoted to providing assistance on a bilateral basis, and

- As a direct contribution to the Fund.

Further, the procedures should provide that at least [x] % of the resources must be earmarked for disbursement through the Fund. The exact percentage could be agreed in the negotiations. Such a requirement is considered necessary because:

- For political and other reasons, donor countries often focus their aid to those countries with which they have close historical ties. This often makes giving aid to other countries a low priority.

- When aid giving countries do not have friendly political relations with a particular country, it is often excluded by law from the list of countries to which aid can be given. However, if aid giving countries were required to contribute some proportion of their resources to the Fund, the disbursement of aid on an equitable basis could be greatly facilitated.

2.4.4   The Fund's resources — the purpose of the assistance

The resources from the Fund shall be available to provide assistance for:

- The preparation of diagnostic studies to identify needs, and the preparation of project documents; and

- The implementation of capacity building projects, *inter alia*, for:
  - The application of the rules of GATT Articles V, VIII and X, and the new rules that may be adopted under the proposed Agreement on Trade Facilitation; and
  - The implementation of the commitments that may be assumed by the countries during the course of the negotiations for the adoption of the Agreement.

Since very few countries have undertaken studies (with the use of the diagnostic tools developed by the WCO, the World Bank, and the WTO) to identify their technical assistance needs in the area of trade facilitation, it is likely that the Fund's initial focus will be on assisting in the preparation of studies diagnosing such needs and, subsequently, on creating project documents.

Of relevance here is that the mandate for negotiations recognises that these could lead to certain commitments whose implementation would require support for infrastructural development. Developed countries have undertaken to provide such assistance but have also stated that their undertaking cannot be open ended. Given this mandate, the assistance provided from the resources of the Fund would have to be limited to that infrastructural development which is directly related to the application of its rules, and to the implementation of the commitments.

In most cases, such assistance would focus on the introduction and adoption of information technology by customs, and of new and innovative methods (such as the application of risk management techniques in the physical checking of imported goods, and in the scrutiny of documents). The adoption of such technology in customs clearance procedures is expensive, with the software itself involving large amounts of expenditure. (Information about off-the-shelf software currently available for use by the customs is provided in **Annex III**).

Besides the cost of such software being high, the cost of adapting it to local conditions is even higher, and could vary from US$ 2.5 million to US$ 5 million. The UNTCAD makes its ASYCUDA software available to developing countries on a 'no cost basis,' and is currently in use in over 60 countries. However, these countries have to pay UNCTAD implementation costs on a cost recovery basis, with a mark up ranging between 13 to 15%. These implementation costs, including those on the adaptation of the software to local conditions, are high: for instance, in Lebanon they amounted to US$ 9 million and in Bolivia to US$ 3.8 million.

The above issues will have to be kept in mind while determining both the size of the Fund and the types of assistance provided for infrastructural development. However, it should be clearly recognised that the assistance provided from the Fund for infrastructural development would be limited to that which is directly needed for the application of the rules of the Agreement, and for the implementation of the commitment.

As has been noted earlier, the term trade facilitation is often used very broadly to include the development of the infrastructure of ports, airports, and warehousing facilities and even, for the development of roads for internal traffic in some countries where these are not in existence. This is particularly so in transit countries. However, the assistance needed for all these purposes would have to continue to be provided, as is currently being done, by the World Bank, and/or bilateral donors, or from the Global Trade Facility that may be established under 'Aid for Trade' Programme, and not from the proposed Trade Facilitation Fund.

2.4.5   The terms and conditions under which the assistance should be provided

Consideration should be given regarding how the assistance from the Fund, and that given on a bilateral basis, should be provided in the form of grants or as loans repayable on soft terms.

Experience has shown that some assistance receiving countries have not been able to maintain the reform programme after the technical assistance project is completed because of their inability to meet the recurring expenditure needed to continue it from their own budgets. To avoid such a situation, the provision of assistance from the Fund should be made conditional on the recipient country agreeing to contribute a certain percentage of the expenditure on a project (say 5% in the case of least developed countries, and

10% in the case of others), and undertaking to meet the recurring costs afterwards from its own budgets. The imposition of such conditions may also result in the creation of a feeling of 'ownership' of the reform programme in the government of the recipient country.

2.5   Mentoring and Twinning (M&T) arrangements

To ensure transparency in the assistance given, and to provide a greater degree of choice in deciding on the agencies or donor countries from which a country could obtain assistance, it may be necessary to establish a complementary mechanism under the umbrella of the Trade Facilitation Fund that would facilitate the exchange of information between the country needing the assistance and the country or agency with the necessary technical competence to provide such assistance. Such a mechanism could take the form of a Mentoring and Twinning arrangement.

The dictionary meaning of the term 'mentor' is 'experienced and trusted adviser.' 'Twinning' is a process by which 'similar bodies or agencies' are brought together. Thus, the term 'Mentoring and Twinning Arrangement' may be applied to an agreement under which a country with the technical capacity to provide assistance in a particular field agrees to do so to countries in need of it.

Under such arrangements, the international organisation establishing the agreement plays the role of the coordinator and catalyst. It brings together 'mentor' countries capable of providing the advice, and 'twins' them with countries needing the assistance. The actual areas of assistance, and the accompanying terms and conditions, are left to be negotiated on a bilateral (or a plurilateral) basis between the interested mentor country and the country or countries wishing to obtain the assistance. There are many advantages in such arrangements:

● Countries may have the opportunity to select the mentor country they consider best equipped to provide the type of assistance they need.

● Countries may have the opportunity to seek assistance from other developing countries if they feel that the assistance provided by them is likely to be more responsive to their needs because of the similarities in their trading environments.

● Because the assistance would be obtained through bilateral agreements, the probability of the mentoring and twinning countries developing a long term and continuing relationship of mutual cooperation becomes much higher. This would be of great help should problems arise in the period following the completion of the assistance project.

The use of a mentoring and twinning arrangement for providing assistance to developing countries is not new. It has been tested with some success in the last few years by international standard setting bodies, particularly by the ISO and the Codex Alimentarius Commission in certain areas. However, the emphasis of these organisations is currently on providing assistance through such arrangements for the establishment of secretariat facilities (including chairing) to the technical committees, and in arranging training for standardisation issues.

2.5.1   Broad outline of the M&T Arrangement for trade facilitation

For the purpose of further examination and discussion, the broad features of the mentoring and twinning (M&T) arrangement that could be adopted for providing technical assistance in the area of trade facilitation under the auspices of the WTO arc provided in Box 8.

Box 8: Broad features of the M&T Arrangement

◆ All WTO members shall automatically become members of the arrangement.

◆ Immediately on its coming into operation, members would be requested to notify the Facilitator appointed under the M&T Arrangement about:
  - Whether they would wish to act as mentors for providing assistance, and,
  - The specific areas in which they may be able to provide assistance.

◆ Immediately on receipt of a request for assistance from a country, the Facilitator shall advise the requesting country about mentoring countries and/or multilateral organisations able to provide assistance in the specific areas required.

◆ On hearing from the requesting country, the Facilitator shall immediately forward its request (letter) to the chosen mentoring country/countries and/or multilateral organisation.

◆ Further negotiations regarding the terms and conditions of technical assistance would take place bilaterally or plurilaterally among the interested parties, i.e. the mentoring and requesting (twinning) countries and/or concerned multilateral organisations. If requested by the parties, the Facilitator shall provide assistance in preparing the project document.

◆ To ensure transparency, in cases where the mentoring country/multilateral organisation offering assistance agrees to meet the cost of assistance from funds earmarked by it for providing technical assistance, the project document shall be notified to the M&T arrangement and to the Working Group responsible for the management of the Trade Facilitation Fund, jointly by the country seeking the assistance and the country/international organisation providing the assistance.

◆ In all other cases, where funding is sought from the Trade Facilitation Fund, the application for funds (accompanied by the project document) shall be made jointly by the country seeking the assistance and the country/multilateral organisation which has agreed to provide the assistance.

2.5.2   M&T arrangements can facilitate south-south cooperation

One of the main advantages of the M&T mechanism is that it could provide opportunities for cooperation on a south-south basis in providing technical assistance. Because of similarities in the environment and practices among developing countries, there is increasing recognition that, in certain trade related areas, the assistance provided by experts or consulting firms from developing countries to other developing countries is likely to be more responsive to their needs than if such assistance were to be provided by developed countries.

Thus, in 'Meeting and Influencing Standards,' a workshop organised jointly by the Commonwealth Secretariat and the International Trade Centre (ITC) in 2005, participants were nearly unanimous in believing that, given the similarity of processes and methods used in production, and consequently of product standards used, it might be desirable for developing countries to seek technical assistance from other developing countries for participation in the work of international standards-setting bodies on the formulation of standards.[35]

---

35   For a detailed description of mentoring and twinning arrangements used in providing assistance to developing countries in the area of standards, see Vinod Rege and Shyam Gujadhur, *Influencing and Meeting International Standards*, Volume One, published jointly by the Commonwealth Secretariat and the International Trade Centre (ITC) in 2004, pp. 74-76.

In customs matters also, a Workshop on Trade Facilitation (arranged in Montreaux, Switzerland by the Commonwealth Secretariat at the request of the Geneva Group of Commonwealth Developing Countries in 2001) recommended that the potential benefits of south-south cooperation in providing assistance could be examined further. Case studies undertaken as a part of the preparatory work for the workshop about the measures taken for the reform of customs procedures indicated that some Commonwealth developing countries possessed the technical capacity to provide assistance to other developing countries. These included Singapore, Malaysia, and India in Asia, and Barbados in the Caribbean.

2.5.3 Recognition by a joint OECD-UNDP Forum of 'trilateral' development cooperation

One of the problems encountered by 'mentor' developing countries is that they are sometimes unable to meet the entire costs of providing assistance to other developing and least developed countries from the limited resources earmarked for such purposes by their governments. In this context, a Forum organised jointly by the Development Committee of OECD and UNDP in February 2005, recommended that one way of making this possible is for the international community to enter into 'trilateral development cooperation arrangements.' In such arrangements, an international financial institution or organisation, or a bilateral donor agency, agrees to provide the financial resources required to pay for a developing country's experts or consultancy firms to provide assistance to other developing and least developed countries.

The effectiveness of such assistance provided by mentor developing countries was evident in a Workshop (for senior customs officials from the Commonwealth developing countries in Asia, Africa, and the Caribbean) on the Agreement on Customs Valuation arranged in Mumbai by the Commonwealth Secretariat in cooperation with the WTO.

While the Commonwealth Secretariat provided the funds for the Workshop, the Indian customs authorities were responsible for providing technical support, including 'on-the-spot training' at the customs port. An evaluation of the Workshop has shown that the participating officials found the training very useful mainly because of similarities in the trading realities between India and their countries as, for instance, in the tendency on the part of traders to undervalue imported goods. Thus, the methods used to deal with such and other malpractices were also found to be appropriate.

There is some evidence to show that some donor agencies are increasingly relying on such trilateral arrangements while providing assistance in trade and other fields. For example, a German aid-providing agency relies on Brazilian standards institutions in providing assistance to developing countries in Latin America in the area of technical regulations and SPS measures. Similarly, assistance to Russia for HIV/AIDS issues is being provided by the UK's Department for International Development (DFID), under a trilateral arrangement between DFID, Russia, and Brazil.[36]

The establishment of mentoring and twinning arrangements at the WTO under the umbrella of the TF Facility would help in the negotiation of such trilateral arrangements and thus, enable the international community to make the best use of available expertise in the field of trade facilitation.

---

36 CUTS, 'Trilateral Development Cooperation: An Emerging Trend', Economics and Environment, No. 1, 2005.

91

2.6   Technical assistance versus actual technical capacity

The experience of multilateral organisations and donor countries giving technical assistance during the last two decades for the reform and modernisation of customs procedures – both on a comprehensive and area-specific basis – shows that there have been very few success stories. Thus, it becomes necessary to ensure that the grant of assistance does not lead to the assumption that a country receiving assistance would, in all cases, be able to comply with the rules of the Agreement, or be able to abide by the commitments it has assumed. Various factors such as the unwillingness of customs officials to cooperate and support the reform procedures, or the inability of foreign experts to relate their expertise and experience to the situation in the country receiving their assistance, or the lack of financial resources to meet the recurring expenditure after the technical assistance funds dry up, have resulted in the reforms not having significant positive effects.

These issues are discussed further in the next chapter.

ANNEXES I-III

ANNEX I[37]

A.   ESTABLISHING AN INTER-AGENCY COORDINATING MECHANISM FOR TRADE FACILITATION TA&CB

We emphasise the need to strengthen existing trade facilitation-related TA&CB programmes and the need for closer collaboration and enhanced coordination among relevant international, regional and sub-regional organisations (such as, but not limited to, UNCTAD, UNECE, UNECA, WTO, WCO, World Bank) in the delivery of trade facilitation-related TA&CB support to ACP countries and other developing and least-developed countries.

In this respect, there should be an operational inter-agency coordinating mechanism set up for the provision of TA&CB to developing countries *during and after the negotiations* to help them design and undertake trade facilitation-related projects or programmes identified as part of their trade facilitation negotiations needs or priorities.

This mechanism should be a *trade facilitation TA&CB "one-stop shop" or "single window" facility* (to be participated in by bilateral and multilateral donors or agencies with experience in trade facilitation) for the expeditious processing, allocation, and evaluation of funding for TA&CB requests from developing countries in connection with specific projects or programmes in the key areas for trade facilitation TA&CB described below.

B.   KEY AREAS FOR FUNDING OF TRADE FACILITATION TA & CB

Pursuant to Annex D, there are three (3) key areas where trade facilitation-related TA&CB need to be supported and to which the inter-agency coordinating mechanism described above should endeavour to source and allocate supportive funding. These are:

---

37   This Annex is an extract from the proposal submitted by the ACP Group to the WTO Negotiating Group on Trade Facilitation, TN/TF/W/73, pages 3-5.

(i)   Support for the identification of trade facilitation negotiating needs and priorities of developing and least-developed countries (Paragraph 4, Annex D);

(ii) Support and assistance during the trade facilitation negotiations (Paragraph 5, Annex D); and

(iii) Support and assistance to help developing and least-developed countries implement the commitments resulting from the negotiations, in accordance with their nature and scope (Paragraph 6, Annex D).

In order to efficiently source and allocate TA&CB support for developing countries in the three areas listed above, a special *Trade Facilitation Technical Assistance and Capacity-Building Fund* needs to be established. This fund shall be managed by the inter-agency coordinating mechanism described previously, and contributions thereto shall be sourced from bilateral and multilateral donors. Developing countries requiring trade facilitation TA&CB support in the course of or after the trade facilitation negotiations, may submit their TA&CB proposals and requests to the inter-agency coordinating mechanism, which will then expeditiously process and allocate such TA&CB support funded through this special fund.

Consistent with the provisions of Annex D, the negotiation and implementation of new trade facilitation rules by developing and least-developed countries should be subject to the prior provision of effective and sufficient TA&CB targeted at building and enhancing the capacity of these countries to effectively negotiate and implement such new rules. Among the trade facilitation-related TA&CB projects, programmes, or activities for which support and assistance could be provided through the inter-agency coordinating mechanism and special fund described above would be, *inter alia*, the following:

(i)   Support for the identification of trade facilitation negotiating needs and priorities
   ◆   National inter-agency trade facilitation needs and priorities assessment projects which ACP and other developing countries need in order to enable them to build a complete and comprehensive picture of their domestic trade facilitation needs and priorities for purposes of the trade facilitation negotiations.

(ii) Trade facilitation negotiations support
   ◆   The development of a human and technical resource base relevant to the trade facilitation negotiations in ACP and other developing countries through trade facilitation negotiations training projects and programmes to be undertaken at the national level for the benefit of, and to be participated in by, developing countries' trade negotiators, customs officials, and other relevant domestic stakeholders in trade facilitation;
   ◆   Ways and means through which ACP and other developing countries' negotiating capacity could be enhanced including, *inter alia*, financial support for the direct participation by their capital-based customs officials in the on-going trade facilitation negotiations;
   ◆   Facilities for direct and specific trade facilitation negotiations-related policy and legal research and analytical support for developing-country delegations;
   ◆   Subject to the need to preserve development policy space and flexibility, the identification of trade facilitation-relevant physical and policy infrastructure needed to enable ACP and other developing countries to fully maximise the benefits of trade facilitation and to effectively comply with any new trade facilitation rules, including policies or measures needed to upgrade and streamline existing customs administration, transparency, and procedures consistent with individual developing countries' needs or conditions;

(iii) Trade facilitation commitments implementation support
- The acquisition or transfer of appropriate trade facilitation-related equipment, technologies, systems or methodologies that could be adopted or adapted by developing countries as they deem necessary;
- Identification and implementation of ways and means appropriate to developing countries through which traffic in transit could be secured and its transit facilitated;
- Subject to the need to preserve development policy space and flexibility, implementation of trade facilitation-relevant physical and policy infrastructure that will be needed by ACP and other developing countries to fully maximise the benefits of trade facilitation and to effectively comply with any new trade facilitation rules or commitments;
- Support for regional trade facilitation initiatives and programmes in ACP and other developing countries;
- Enhancement of ACP and other developing countries' human and technical resource base in trade facilitation through, *inter alia*, continuing skills exchange, training, scholarships, and information exchange in trade facilitation-related matters among WTO Members' customs and trade agencies.

ANNEX II[38]

BREAKDOWN OF LDCs AND IDA ONLY COUNTRIES BY REGION

Countries	Category	Countries	Category	Countries	Category
Africa (39)		Mozambique	LDC	**Europe and Central Asia (10)**	
Angola	LDC	Niger	LDC	Albania	IDA only
Benin	LDC	Rwanda	LDC	Armenia	IDA only
Burkina Faso	LDC	São Tomé and Príncipe	LDC	Georgia	IDA only
Burundi	LDC	Senegal	LDC	Kyrgyz Republic	IDA only
Cape Verde	LDC	Sierra Leone	LDC	Moldova	IDA only
Cameroon	IDA only	Somalia	LDC	Tajikistan	IDA only
CAR	LDC	Sudan	LDC		
Chad	LDC	Tanzania	LDC	**Middle East and North Africa (2)**	
Comoros	LDC	Togo	LDC	Djibouti	LDC
Congo (Rep. of)	IDA only	Uganda	LDC	Yemen, Rep. of	LDC
Congo (Democratic Rep of)	LDC	Zambia	LDC		
Cote d'Ivoire	IDA only			**Latin America and the Caribbean (9)**	
Ethiopia	LDC	**East Asia (13)**		Guyana	IDA only
Eritrea	LDC	Cambodia	LDC	Haiti	LDC
The Gambia	LDC	Kiribati	LDC	Honduras	IDA only
Ghana	IDA only	Lao, P.D.R.	LDC	Nicaragua	IDA only
Guinea	LDC	Mongolia	IDA only		
Guinea-Bissau	LDC	Myanmar	LDC	**South Asia (8)**	
Kenya	IDA only	Samoa	LDC	Afghanistan	LDC
Lesotho	LDC	Solomon Islands	LDC	Bangladesh	LDC
Liberia	LDC	Timor-Leste	LDC	Bhutan	LDC
Madagascar	LDC	Tonga	IDA only	Maldives	LDC
Malawi	LDC	Vanuatu	LDC	Nepal	LDC
Mali	LDC	Vietnam	IDA only	Sri Lanka	IDA only
Mauritania	LDC				

---

38 'Doha Development Agenda and Aid for Trade', Development Committee, World Bank and IMF (DC2005-0016), 12 September 2005 ('Annex III'), page 41.

ANNEX III[39]

Synoptic picture of the 'off-the-shelf' customs software available in the market

N. B. The synoptic information does not describe special features of the software

Name of the software	Agencies responsible for the development of the software and its main features	Countries using the software at present
ASYCUDA World	Developed by UNCTAD in 1999. Latest version, "World" allows customs administration to handle most customs transactions. The software is made available at no cost, which means countries do not pay for software development costs. However, countries pay UNCTAD for systems implementation, on a cost recovery basis with a mark-up of between 13 to 15%. These implementation costs, including those of the hardware facilities, could be high. In Lebanon such costs amounted to US$ 9 million; in Bolivia US$ 3.8 million and in Philippines US$ 28 million	Over 60 countries are reported to be using ASYCUDA. The figure includes earlier versions which were geared mainly to the implementation of the WTO Customs Valuation Agreement.
Trade and management systems (TIMS)	Developed by Crown Agents, a UK consultancy firm. The software package aims at supporting the efficient day-to-day operation of the modern customs administration.	Mozambique and Angola. A partial roll out has been undertaken, among other countries, in Bulgaria and Kosovo.
The Solutions Informatiques Français (SOFIX)	First developed by French customs. However, the software is no longer supported by it, and the work on the development of the software SOFX is currently being undertaken by the consultancy firm Solutions Informatiques Francais (SIF). Provides support for all customs activities.	Argentina, Paraguay and the French Polynesia.
Trade Information Management System (TATIS)	The system is marketed, delivered, and supported by TATIS, business partners of Hewlett Packard, Pricewaterhouse Coopers and Societé General de Surveillance. Provides support for all customs activities.	Not available.
Micro Clear	The system has been developed by Inspection and Control Services. Provides support for all customs activities.	Current or previous releases of the software – partial or full solution – are working in China, Dubai, Kuwait, the United States, and India.
P.C. Trade	New Zealand Statistics Department: Designed to produce trade statistics, relying on ASYCUDA generated import data.	It is widely used in the island states of the Pacific such as Tonga, French Polynesia, Vanuatu and Guam.

---

39   The box draws on information provided in Luc De Wulf and Gerard McLinden, 'The Role of Information Technology in Customs Modernisation', pp. 285-310, in Luc De Wulf and Jose B. Sokol (eds.), 'Customs Modernization Handbook', (World Bank, 2004).

Name of the software	Agencies responsible for the development of the software and its main features	Countries using the software at present
ALICE	The European Union is currently developing ALICE as part of its customs and fiscal office programme.	Being tested in Bosnia and Herzegovina. It is possible that ALICE will become a choice for further accession countries.
Danish Customs Administration Solution	Developed by Danish Customs Administration in conjunction with Bull SA.	Being introduced in Cyprus.

Chapter 5: The Extension of Special and Differential (S&D) Treatment to developing countries in accepting obligations under the Agreement

1. General

The last two chapters dealt with the description of the modalities that could be adopted for the negotiations on rules and the institutional framework to be adopted at the WTO to provide technical assistance to developing and least developed countries for building technical capacities for the implementation of the rules of the Agreements and of the commitments they may assume. This chapter examines the provisions on Special and Differential (S&D) treatment that may have to be incorporated in the Agreement to ensure that countries are not required to apply rules for which they do not have the technical competence. It emphasises that the mere fact of a country having been provided technical assistance should not lead to the assumption that it has acquired the required capacity to implement the relevant rules. The final decision to abide by the rules on a binding basis should be left to the country to decide. The chapter also describes the mechanism that could be adopted for reviewing the progress made by the countries receiving assistance in actually assuming binding commitments to apply the rules.

The mandate in Annex D of the 2004 General Council Decision requires that S&D treatment 'should extend beyond' merely providing transitional periods – the main method used so far in WTO Agreements. Annex E in the Hong Kong Declaration calls on the Negotiating Group to intensify its negotiations on S&D treatment, with a view to arriving at S&D provisions that are precise, operational, and that allow the necessary flexibility in implementing the results of the negotiations.

2. The past experience of extending S&D treatment through transitional periods

When a new WTO trade Agreement is adopted, it is accepted practice under the WTO system to provide a period of one/two years for its implementation at the national level. This period is intended to give time to countries that have accepted the Agreement to adopt legislation, establish institutional systems, and make arrangements for the training of officials regarding the application of the rules at the national level.

However, most WTO Agreements provide longer preparatory periods to developing countries. In addition, periods even longer than those provided to developing countries may be provided to least developed countries. Some Agreements provide still longer periods for certain specified areas[40] as compared to those provided for the general application of the rules.

---

40   A good illustration of how the method of transitional periods can be used to provide S&D treatment to developing countries and LDCs that is responsive to their needs is provided by the Agreement on Trade Related Aspects of Intellectual Property (TRIPS). The Agreement provides a transitional period of 5 years (from 1 January 1995 when the Agreement became operational), to 1 January 2000) to developing countries for the implementation of the Agreement. A longer period up to 2011 was provided for LDCs. In addition, special transitional periods for the acceptance of obligations in relation to patents for pharmaceutical products have been provided under the Agreement. For developing countries, this period expired on 1 January 2005. For the least developed countries, the initial longer period provided under the Agreement was later extended until 1 January 2016. As the period for the application of all the rules of the Agreement was also subsequently extended, the transitional periods for bringing national legislations relating to patents for pharmaceutical products and in other areas, is now the same.

Taking advantage of the transitional periods provided under these Agreements, developing countries were not under any obligations to apply the rules during the validity of the period. The obligation to apply the rules arose only on the termination of the transitional period. Because of this, many developing countries postponed taking action at the national level both for adopting the required legislation and for training officials till almost the end of the transitional period. This resulted in situations where countries accepted obligations without building the institutional and technical capacities for the application of the rules. In some cases, this even resulted in requests for the extension of the transitional period.

This past experience of the extension of S&D treatment after the transitional period is over has resulted in the mandate for negotiations in the area of trade facilitation incorporating provisions in which:

- S&D treatment should extend beyond the already granted transitional period;

- Technical assistance should be provided to developing and least developed countries to assist them in preparing themselves for the application of the rules of the proposed Agreement, and for the implementation of any commitments which they may assume in the negotiations;

- The extent and timing of the acceptance of commitments shall be related to the implementation capacities of developing and least developed countries; and

- Least developed countries will only be required to undertake those commitments which are consistent with their individual development, their financial and trade needs, and their administrative or institutional capacities.

3. Using the GATS scheduling technique as a complement to transitional periods

These specific provisions suggest that, in addition to one standard transitional period, techniques that take into account the capacities of individual developing countries to implement the rules would have to be adopted while extending S&D treatment to them. It may be possible to achieve these aims by combining the transitional period technique with the scheduling techniques used for recording the commitment assumed under the General Agreement on Trade in Services (GATS). This combination for the implementation of the rules of the Agreement on Trade Facilitation would enable developing countries to decide on the level and nature of the obligation they wish to undertake on a rule-by-rule basis.

The flexibility to use the scheduling technique in undertaking obligations should be available only to developing countries. The developed countries would be expected to accept the obligations set out in the Agreement on a binding basis from the day it becomes operational. However, developing countries which consider that they can accept on a binding basis all the obligations which the Agreement imposes from the time it becomes effective, should also be free to decide on not taking advantage of the scheduling technique.

All developing countries, except those which accept the Agreement on a fully binding basis, would have a separate schedule. The schedule of each country would be divided into two parts.

- **Part I** of the schedule would list all those rules which do not ordinarily pose serious problems to developing and least developed countries regarding their acceptance. Rules raising trade policy issues, and which have been classified under Category I (Box 4, Chapter 3) above, would be listed in this part. Most of these rules aim at adding more specificity and precision to the obligations which GATT Articles V, VIII and X impose. Since all countries are currently bound by the basic obligations imposed by these articles, it may be possible for them to accept, at the national level, the additional obligations which the new rules of the Agreement may impose after it is adopted at the conclusion of the Round, within a period of the one/two years provided.

However, there could be a few rules in this first part which some countries, particularly least developed countries, could accept only after they have been given time to prepare themselves for the obligations involved. A short transitional period, of perhaps five/seven years beginning from the date of the adoption of the Agreement, should be made available to them.

- The rules that may be adopted regarding the techniques and modalities required to be followed by custom administrations in the clearance of goods, and which have been classified under Category II (Box 5, Chapter 3), would be listed in **Part II** of the schedule. Currently, there are no WTO rules regarding most of these techniques and modalities. The international norms or standards which do exist have been developed by international organisations like the WCO and UNECE, and only a few developing countries are applying them on a de jure basis. The technical capacities currently available in these countries for the application of these standards and norms vary greatly from country to country. The capacity of a country to effectively apply any new rules that may be adopted in the course of the present ongoing negotiations will also depend on the existence of information technology infrastructure and its widespread use by its business community. Thus, many countries may need assistance for the development of such infrastructure.

  For the measures listed in Part II of the schedule, the longer maximum transitional period of e.g. 15 years may have to be provided for the acceptance of obligations on a binding basis by all countries.

For the rules listed in Part I and II of the schedule, it shall be open to developing countries to choose the level of obligation they wish to assume during the specified transition period, and to lay down conditions to ensure that they are not required to accept obligations for which they do not have the technical capacity. The choices that developing and least developed countries could exercise while accepting obligations on a rule-by-rule basis would, *inter alia*, include the following:

- Undertake no obligation to apply the rule;
- Undertake to apply the rule after a specific number of years;
- Make the application of the rule conditional on the provision of technical assistance, and indicate the type and nature of assistance required; and
- Commit to applying the rule on a binding basis.

The final decision regarding which rules should be included in Part I (for which a shorter transitional period will be available for compliance) and in Part II (for which a longer transitional period will be available for compliance) would have to be decided through negotiations which take into account the criteria used in classifying the rules into the two categories mentioned above as well as such factors as:

- The degree of difficulty that may be faced by developing countries in accepting the rule, and
- The resources and capacity required for implementation.

An example of such a schedule is provided in **Annex II** at the end of this chapter.

Every schedule would be based on self-assessment made by the concerned country regarding the nature and type of obligation it is prepared to assume, and of its technical assistance needs. Every country would be required to submit its schedule to the WTO within the period of one/two years that is provided between the date of adoption of the Agreement and the date of its becoming operational. This will ensure that the negotiations about securing technical assistance from international agencies or donor countries are completed, and most of the assistance needed is made available to the country before the Agreement becomes operational.

The WTO Secretariat would be expected to prepare a consolidated document, listing all schedules, and publish it on the concerned country's website in the WTO Internet portal. The commitments assumed in the schedule shall be subject to periodic reviews – perhaps once in two years – in the Committee on Trade Facilitation. The purpose of such reviews will be to assess the effectiveness of the technical assistance provided under the Agreement in facilitating the implementation of the rules. Such reviews will also help in finding out whether it is possible for countries that have not undertaken fully binding commitments to improve the level of commitments they have assumed under the schedules.

4. Comparison of the above proposals with those tabled by other delegations

Amongst the proposals tabled on S&D treatment, perhaps the most comprehensive other ones are the two following:

- TN/TF/W/142 on the 'Implementation Mechanism for Special and Differential Treatment (S&D) and Technical Assistance and Capacity Building (TACB) Support', submitted by the Core Group of Developing Countries on Trade Facilitation (CGDCTF) – Bangladesh, Botswana, Cuba, Egypt, India, Indonesia, Jamaica, Kenya, Malaysia, Mauritius, Namibia, Nepal, Nigeria, Philippines, Rwanda, Tanzania, Trinidad & Tobago, Uganda, Venezuela, Zambia, and Zimbabwe; and

- TN/TF/W/137 on the 'Implementation Mechanism of Trade Facilitation Commitments including Key Elements for Technical Assistance,' submitted by Armenia, Canada, Chile, China, Dominican Republic, Ecuador, the European Communities, Georgia, Guatemala, Honduras, Japan, Kyrgyz Republic, Mexico, Moldova, Nicaragua, Pakistan, Paraguay, Peru, Sri Lanka, Switzerland, and Uruguay.

Both proposals envisage that during the period that would be available between the adoption of the Agreement at the conclusion of the Round and its coming into operation, developing, least developed, and low income countries in transition should – on the basis of self-assessment – notify the WTO Secretariat of those obligations whose implementation would require either transitional periods or technical assistance for capacity building.

However, there are differences in the two proposals, both in substance and nuance. The proposal submitted by the Core Group is briefly described in the following paragraphs.

The proposal envisages that developed countries would accept all the obligations of the Agreement from the date it enters into force. As regards developing, least developed and low-income countries in transition, special and differential treatment would be provided on the basis of the nature of the obligations. These would be divided into two categories.

- Category 1 would include those obligations which developing, least developed, and low-income countries in transition would have to implement from the date the Agreement enters into force. The first of such obligations would be agreed upon in the negotiations. However, it may be possible for these countries to avail of a transitional period to prepare themselves for the implementation of such obligations. Such a transitional period would have to be determined in the negotiations, and would not exceed [X] years.

- Category 2 would include all the obligations not included in Category 1. It is quite possible that in respect of some of the obligations in this category, developing, least developed and low income countries in transition may require technical assistance for capacity building. Countries needing such assistance would be expected to prepare capacity building plans, and to notify them to the WTO Secretariat before the Agreement enters into force. The transitional period required for the acquisition of implementation capacity should be specified in these plans. Thus, the transitional periods so required could vary from country to country.

At the end of the implementation period, each country would be expected to assess whether the assistance provided has resulted in the acquisition of the required capacity. If the capacity building plans provide for their involvement, both the donor country and the implementing agency should be associated in making such an assessment. When such an assessment is able to conclude that the country receiving the assistance has acquired the necessary capacity, it shall notify the WTO Committee on Trade Facilitation. After such notification, the country would be under obligation to apply the measure or rule.

It is envisaged that, in practice, there would only be a few cases in which the assistance- receiving country – after assessment and evaluation – comes to the conclusion that 'capacity has yet to be entirely acquired.' In such cases, the assistance receiving country and the donor country should bring the matter to the notice of the Trade Facilitation Technical Assistance and Capacity Building Support Unit (TFTACBSU). After reviewing the matter, the Unit could make appropriate recommendations.

The proposals further envisage that for some of the obligations falling under category 2, the Agreement may not impose a binding requirement to apply the rules. It may only require countries to make their best endeavours to implement them (taking into account their individual capacity) as soon as possible after the Agreement enters into force. Moreover, it would also be open to developing, least developed, and low income countries in transition to request technical assistance for capacity building from developed countries and/or international financial institutions in order to fulfil such obligations.

5. The advantage of the scheduling technique over the techniques suggested in the tabled proposals

Even though there are a number of common elements in the two proposals tabled by the delegations (described above) and the approach suggested in the Handbook, there are some important differences. For instance, the scheduling technique would provide a structured framework to a developing or least developed country to decide, on a rule-by-rule basis, for the level of obligation it wishes to undertake during the course of the transitional period, after taking into account its technical capacity for implementation. The experience gained during the application of the relevant rules would also make for a learning process and, thus, assist countries in improving the nature and the level of obligations being gradually undertaken by them, the ultimate goal being their accepting fully all binding obligations by the end of the transitional period of 15 years.

These two proposals are also based on the assumption that the verification exercise – undertaken on a bilateral (or trilateral) basis when the project is about to be completed – will, in most cases, result in an agreement that the capacity to accept a binding commitment to apply the relevant rules has been developed.

However, past experience has shown that even when reform programmes are adopted after a careful identification of the needs of a country, they have often failed to achieve the desired results, or have met with only partial success. This is so because of a number of extraneous factors.

These considerations have made World Bank economists like Michael Finger and John S. Wilson – with much experience in the administration and disbursement of aid for development – to point out that in practice it is often difficult to separate the benefits achieved in the area of trade facilitation from the improvements in the domestic business environment and the progress made in the development of infrastructure of the aid receiving country. This makes it necessary to exercise extreme caution in making direct links between the receipt of assistance for capacity building on the one hand, and the acceptance of a binding obligation to implement them on the other.

In the view of the above mentioned economists, the WTO approach of requiring countries to undertake commitments is suitable mainly for securing the removal of trade restrictions by requiring binding commitments. By doing so, countries agree not to increase tariffs over bound rates, or not to re-impose non-tariff barriers that have been removed. However, in the area of trade facilitation, the emphasis is not on the removal of restrictions but on encouraging countries to develop infrastructure, institutions, and practices for the application of new and innovative methods such as risk assessment and management, and the adoption of the systems of authorised importers and post-audit. The experience of development banks and agencies in providing assistance for such developmental purpose shows that 'what works at one place and a time may not work in another.' In this context, any attempt to apply the WTO approach of imposing legal obligations by drawing a rigid balance between the receipt of assistance on the one hand, and a binding commitment to apply the rules on the other, will constitute 'nihilism' as it completely ignores the lessons that can be drawn from the experience of development agencies while providing aid.[41]

6. Some tentative ideas on the multilateral mechanism that could be created for review and evaluation

The above factors suggest that it would be necessary to leave the aid receiving country to itself assess whether or not the necessary capacity has been developed and whether it is ready to accept obligations to apply the relevant rules on a binding basis. Consultations arranged on a multilateral basis should examine those cases in which the aid receiving country considers that the assistance provided has not resulted in the full development of the required capacity for implementation.

Also, any multilateral mechanism that may be established in the WTO for the review and evaluation of how far the aid provided is contributing towards building implementation capacities would have to draw a balance between the WTO approach of imposing binding obligations, and the difficulties of applying such an approach in areas where the capacity to implement rules and commitments is dependent on many development related extraneous factors. It may be possible to draw such a balance by ensuring that the same principles as are applied to reviews undertaken, on a country-by-country basis, by the WTO's Trade Policy Review Mechanism (TPRM) of developments in trade policy are also applied to reviews undertaken in the area of trade facilitation. These reviews are carried out against the background of the 'wider economic and developmental needs, policies and objectives of the Member concerned' as well as the

---

41   J. Michael Finger and John S. Wilson, 'Trade Facilitation, Implementation, the Doha Development Agenda', (World Bank), 12 April 2006 (draft).

external environment it faces.[42] However, it is clearly understood that such reviews should not be used as 'a basis for the enforcement of specific obligations under the Agreements or for dispute settlement procedures, or to impose new policy commitments on Members.'[43]

As in the case of TPRM, it would be necessary to provide that the objective of the periodic reviews undertaken (under the provisions of the Agreement on Trade Facilitation) would be to examine the progress made in the application of the rules of the Agreement, and how far the technical assistance provided has contributed to the building up of implementation capacity 'against the background of the development and economic policies of the country concerned.'

6.1   Objectives and principles

A broad outline of the multilateral mechanism that could be established for the review and evaluation of the technical assistance provided in the area of trade facilitation, taking into account the principles described above, is provided below.

- The Committee on Trade Facilitation (CTF) shall be responsible for the surveillance of:
    - Compliance by developed countries of the commitments made by them to provide technical assistance;
    - The progress made by developing countries in building up capacities for the application of rules and commitments listed in their schedules (i.e. for which they have not been able to accept binding obligations regarding implementation earlier); and

- The procedures adopted by the CTF for undertaking such reviews should provide that the developing or least developed country receiving the technical assistance shall itself be responsible for determining whether it has acquired the required capacity for the implementation of the rules of the Agreement. In cases where the country considers that the technical assistance provided has not resulted in the full acquisition of the capacity to implement the rules, the reviews should consider the provision of a more appropriate type of assistance to deal with those external factors that have prevented the full acquisition of capacity.

6.2   Relationship with the country reviews undertaken by the TPR Mechanism

- The procedures adopted for review (under the Trade Policy Review Mechanism) shall be modified to require developing and least developed countries consulting under the mechanism to include a special section on the measures they are undertaking for the reform of their customs and other trade related procedures aimed at facilitating trade in their report;

- Reports prepared by the Secretariat on the trade policy developments of the consulting country shall also include a section on trade facilitation. They shall provide an assessment of the steps being undertaken by the country for facilitating trade, and how far (if any) the assistance provided is being found useful by the country in building the technical capacity to implement the relevant rules;

- The relevant extracts from the above reports, together with the extracts from the Report of the TPRB relating to the discussions on trade facilitation, shall be forwarded by the WTO Secretariat to the Committee on Trade Facilitation for discussion in the review sessions.

---

42   See the Agreement Establishing the WTO, Annex 3 A 'Objectives', para (ii) on the Trade Policy Review Mechanism.
43   *Ibid*, Para (i).

6.3　Periodic review by the Committee on Trade Facilitation

- The Committee shall hold a special session to review the progress made in the implementation of the provisions of the Agreement every two/three years;

- The basis for such a review would be provided by the consolidated document containing the 'schedules of commitments' of individual countries. The main objective of the review would be to examine whether each country can improve the level of obligations it has accepted and whether it can undertake more binding obligations;

- For this purpose, developing and least developed countries will be required to submit reports on the progress they have made in the implementation of the Agreement. These reports would also include their views on how far the assistance being provided has enabled them to improve the level of the obligations they have accepted under their schedule of commitments;

- Extracts from country reports as well as from the reports made by the Secretariat about countries which have consulted under the TPRM programme during the preceding two-year period shall be used as the basis for the consultations;

- Developed countries, international organisations, and financial institutions shall be required to submit information regarding the assistance that is being provided by them on a country-to-country basis to the WTO Secretariat. This will enable the Secretariat to prepare its consolidated report on all the assistance being provided in the area of trade facilitation during the review period. The report should also contain an assessment of how developed countries are complying with the obligation they have assumed to provide technical assistance.

6.4　Recommendations by the CFT

On the basis of such review, the Committee shall make appropriate recommendations regarding the steps that could be taken by donor countries and international institutions to provide:

- Assistance to developing and least developed countries which need assistance but have not been able to and obtain it, and

- Additional assistance to those countries which have received assistance but have not been able to fully acquire the required capacity needed to implement the relevant rules. The CFT shall also examine the practical difficulties which developing and (especially) least developed countries may be encountering while applying the rules of the Agreement, and whether any modifications or improvements are necessary in order to facilitate their application.

ANNEX I

The findings and conclusions of case studies undertaken by the World Bank and OECD regarding the experience of developing countries introducing and implementing trade facilitation measures

Case studies undertaken by the World Bank and the OECD regarding the experience of developing countries introducing and implementing trade facilitation measures cover countries at various stages of development.[44] In almost all countries, technical assistance by international institutions and/or bilateral donors was provided for the reform of customs procedures and for improving efficiency in all aspects of customs related work. The assistance provided covered such areas as:

- The adoption of new legislation and regulations;

- The adoption of the institutional framework needed for the introduction and implementation of risk assessment and management systems, audit based controls, and special procedures for authorised traders;

- The training of officials for the implementation of the new procedures; and

- The provision of equipment (e.g. computers and scanning equipment).

The main findings of the case studies are summarised below.

General findings

- In some countries, the reform programme was dominated and driven by foreign consultants. An extreme case was Mozambique, where the entire responsibility for the management of the customs administration was given to a foreign consulting firm for a period of five years, with the authority to recruit new officials and train them in new methods of customs management. Such drastic steps were considered necessary because of the high level of corruption amongst the customs officials and their general lack of background knowledge and experience.

- Although it is unlikely that such drastic measures as in the case of Mozambique will be repeated again, experience shows that the chances of any reform programme continuing successfully after the departure of foreign experts are better if they have been able to secure the cooperation of the local customs officials and developed feelings for the 'ownership' of the programme among them. As the Mozambique case study makes clear, the sustainability of the programme depends greatly on how far the customs administration is itself able, after the termination of the technical assistance project, to effectively perform the tasks once performed by foreign experts.[45] The case study of the Philippines warns that if they fail to obtain staff support for the reform programme, it could become, like many other undertakings in the country's history, 'another missed opportunity'.[46]

---

44 Luc de Wulf and José B. Sokol (eds.), *Customs Modernization Initiatives – Case Studies*, (World Bank, Washington D.C.,2004) contains case studies on customs reforms undertaken by Bolivia, Ghana, Morocco, Mozambique, Peru, Philippines, Turkey and Uganda. The OECD Trade Policy Working Paper No.12 (22 February 2005) contains case studies of Mozambique, Angola, Pakistan and Peru.

45 Anthony Mwangi, Case study on Mozambique, in Luc de Wulf and José B. Sokol, *Customs Modernization Initiatives - Case Studies*, (World Bank, Washington D.C., 2004), p. 63.

46 *Ibid.*,Guillermo L. Parayano Jr., Case study on the Philippines, p. 100.

- In most cases, the government of countries receiving assistance for introducing and implementing trade facilitation measures did not allocate any additional funds. The customs department was expected to absorb all the expenses that could not be met from the technical assistance funds from their normal administrative operational costs.[47] Unless the governments are also ready to make some funds available to the customs department for the continued implementation of the reform programme, its success may be adversely affected. This becomes imperative since the technical assistance funds get reduced on the completion of the programme.

- The chances of the success of a reform programme are more assured if it has the full support of the government; particularly of the Minister and senior officials of the Ministry responsible for customs administration and its senior management.

- Case studies show that the pace of implementation of reform programmes may be adversely affected by changes in a government following elections, especially if the new government does not give as much priority to customs reform as the outgoing one. Also, the chances of reform programmes succeeding are better if they are introduced at a time when the economy is flourishing. Experience shows that a slow down in economic activity and the consequent reduction in imports may also discourage customs from introducing new and innovative methods (such as risk management) fearing a loss in revenue.

- Some countries – such as Chile, Peru, and Latvia – in which the undervaluation of goods and other customs related corruption were not widely prevalent, have been able to introduce facilitation measures with minimum change. Also, these countries had relatively friendly trade policy measures already in place.

- Many least developed countries and others at a lower stage of development have made less progress in custom reform, and are finding it difficult to introduce trade facilitation measures such as risk assessment and management, the system of authorised traders, and a reliance on post-audit.[48] For some of these countries, it is not even possible to comply fully with the rules of the WTO Agreement on Customs Valuation even though they are under an obligation to apply its rules. This is because of the widely prevalent practice of the undervaluation of imported goods among their traders. For instance, the case study on Uganda points out that of the total imports, nearly 30 to 50% of the invoice prices are undervalued by traders. This requires customs to raise invoice prices in order to determine the correct dutiable value. As customs have not so far been able to develop the database required for price comparison purposes, the dutiable value is often determined on the basis of reference prices or other information available with customs – a practice frowned upon by the Agreement.[49] The case study on Pakistan states that the 'progress towards full implementation of the WTO Agreement on Customs Valuation has been slow and incomplete' because of customs officials fearing a loss in revenue occurring as a result of the widely prevalent practice of the undervaluation of imported goods.[50]

---

47   OECD, Trade Policy Working Paper No. 8, p. 8.
48   *Ibid.*, p. 8.
49   Luc de Wulf, Case study on Uganda, pp. 121-123.
50   OECD, Trade Policy Working Paper No. 8.

ANNEX II

ILLUSTRATIVE SCHEDULE OF THE COMMITMENTS OF A DEVELOPING COUNTRY

	No Obligations	Commitment to accept binding obligations if technical assistance is provided (details of the specific assistance required are attached in the Annex)	Commitments to apply the rule after a specific number of years	Binding Obligations
PART I	Rules on Measures that raise trade policy issues for which a transitional period of six years would be provided in the Agreement to ensure compliance on a binding basis			
Internet Publication				
Advance rulings				
Appeals procedures				
Establishment of enquiry points				
Fees and charges imposed for importation and exportation				
PART II	Rules on measures relating to the techniques and modalities which should be applied in the day-to-day administration of customs procedures for which a transitional period of 15 years would be provided in the Agreement to ensure compliance on a binding basis			
Application of risk management techniques				
Authorised importers				
Post-clearance audit				
Pre-arrival clearance of goods				
Establishment of a 'one time shop'				
Establishment of a single window clearance system				
Release of goods on the basis of security payments				
Special procedures for the clearance of goods, including express shipments				
Advanced rulings				
Level of guarantees to be provided by transport operators in transit trade				
Sealing of goods in transit by customs				

Chapter 6: Dispute settlement

1. Trade Facilitation and the WTO dispute settlement procedures

Should the WTO dispute settlement procedures also be applicable to the settlement of the differences and disputes that may arise during the implementation of the provisions of the proposed Agreement on Trade Facilitation? Many developing countries appear to consider that these provisions should not be applicable for at least the first 10-15 years after the proposed Agreement on Trade Facilitation becomes effective.

The reasons for the general reluctance of these developing countries to make the WTO dispute settlement procedures applicable to the settlement of disputes under the proposed Agreement on Trade Facilitation are two.

First, they consider that the primary objective of the Agreement is to gradually prepare the least developed and other countries at a middle or lower stage of development to accept the obligations which the Agreement may impose, by providing them the needed technical assistance to build up the required implementation capacities. Thus, it is envisaged that, in the first 10 to 15 years, many developing countries may not accept binding obligations, but only make their best endeavours to apply most of its rules. Least developed countries may even be exempted from applying most, if not all, of its rules in the period immediately after the adoption of the Agreement.

Thus, the Agreement would result in the creation of 'soft laws' as distinct from the 'hard laws' otherwise created under most WTO Agreements.[51] In interpreting hard law, the reviewing authorities (Panels or Appellate Bodies) go by the literal meaning of the terms used while determining whether the measures under disputes have resulted in the non-compliance of rules or a breach of obligations by the respondent country. In the case of a soft law, the reviewing authorities have not only to interpret the rules on the basis of the terms used but also have to examine whether the non-compliance by the country against whom complaint is made is due to such factors as the lack of technical capacity or the financial resources required for the implementation of rules.

Second, one of the main features of the WTO dispute settlement procedures (which distinguishes it from provisions of settlement of disputes used in such organisations as the WCO), is that it provides for sanctions. If a country breaches its obligations under the WTO rules and fails to withdraw the infringing measure – or modify it to bring it in conformity with WTO law – the Dispute Settlement Body can authorise the complaining party to take counter measures that would affect the trade of that country. Because many of the rules of the Agreement would be – at least in the initial period 10 to 15 years – of a non-binding nature (merely requiring countries to make their best endeavours to comply), the general view of developing countries is that the procedures adopted for the settlement of differences and disputes should lay emphasis not on their settlement through judicial adjudication but through consultations and conciliation. Moreover, where a country is found to have failed in complying with the rules, the aim should be to find out how it could be assisted to build up the capacity to implement them, and not on imposing sanctions coercing it to comply.

---

51   It should be noted that some of these Agreements also contain provisions which create soft law, by requiring countries to make 'best endeavours'.

2. The legality of excluding an Agreement from the WTO's Dispute Settlement Understanding

Before turning to discussions regarding the nature and type of procedures (relying on consultations and conciliation rather than on sanctions) that could be established for the settlement of disputes under the proposed Agreement, it is necessary to ask whether, under WTO jurisprudence, it is permissible to exclude an Agreement from the purview of the Dispute Settlement Understanding (DSU) which lays down all procedures to be followed while settling disputes brought to the WTO. Prima-facie, it would appear that the answer to this question lies in the affirmative. The Understanding provides that its provisions shall apply 'only to multilateral and plurilateral agreements listed in the Appendix.'[52] These provisions suggest that while negotiating new Agreements, member countries could provide that the common dispute settlement procedures established under the DSU, shall not apply to the settlement of disputes relating to the application of its rules.

Moreover, it is also open to countries to provide in an Agreement that certain types of disputes would be excluded from the purview of the WTO's dispute settlement procedures. For instance, the Agreement on Subsidies and Countervailing Measures provides that all disputes relating to non-actionable subsidies should be settled by the Committee on Subsidies and Countervailing Measures, and not by the WTO's dispute settlement procedures.[53]

Thus, it seems clear that the WTO legal system provides sufficient flexibility to countries in the negotiations to agree on the type of dispute settlement system they wish to include under the proposed Agreement. For instance, instead of the WTO system, they could provide for a completely separate set of procedures for the settlement of disputes. Alternatively, they could choose to apply the WTO system in certain types of disputes but in other cases, authorise disputes to be settled by the Agreement Committees through especially formulated procedures.

3. A 'two-track approach' — a special system for dispute settlement under the proposed Agreement?

In this context, one suggestion offered is that it may be possible to adopt a 'two-track' approach for dispute settlement under the proposed Agreement:

- The Committee on Trade Facilitation which would be established under the Agreement would be responsible for the consideration of complaints regarding the non-compliance of its provisions by using a 'two track approach.'

- The Committee shall, if requested, authorise the complaining country to invoke the WTO dispute settlement procedures if:
    - In the case of a complaint against a *developed* country; and
    - In the case of a complaint against a *developing* country, after a preliminary examination it has reasons to believe that it is in breach of those obligations which it has accepted under the Agreement on a binding basis and/or of the obligations under GATT Article V, VIII and X.

---

52   Article 1.1, Coverage and Application: Understanding on Rules and Procedures Governing the Settlement of Disputes.
53   Article 9 of the Agreement on Subsidies and Countervailing Measures.

In all other cases, the Committee shall aim at settling disputes through conciliation. Where the Committee finds that failure to comply with the rules of the Agreement, or to abide by commitments, is due to the lack of technical competence on the part of the 'defendant' (the party against which the complaint is made), it shall examine all the circumstances of the case and make appropriate recommendations for the provision of the required technical assistance.

3.1   The responsibility of the Committee

The responsibility for the application of the two-track approach in settling disputes would rest with the Committee on Trade Facilitation (CTF).

As a first step, the Committee should encourage the parties to settle their differences through bilateral or multilateral consultations. Where no agreement is reached in the consultations, it shall be open to the complaining country to request the Committee to refer the matter for settlement to the WTO dispute settlement procedures. As suggested above, such a request would be made only in those cases where the country against which the complaint is made is a developed country, or where the allegedly contravening developing country has accepted fully binding obligations under the Agreement but is now in breach of them.

The decision of the Committee on this issue shall be final, and binding on all parties.

3.2   Special procedures: The Establishment of a 'Standing Group of Experts'

All cases that are not referred for settlement to the WTO dispute settlement procedures shall be settled under the special dispute settlement procedures established under the Agreement on Trade Facilitation. These procedures should emphasise that disputes should be settled through consultations and conciliation. To assist the committee in its conciliatory work, a Standing Group of Experts could be established for giving advice on legal and technical issues. This Standing Group could consist of three to five members, with the Committee ensuring that at least two of the five have expertise and experience in customs matters, and have previously been members of customs tribunals.

3.3   Consideration of the report of the Standing Group of Experts by the Committee

The Committee shall, after examining both the facts and the legal issues involved, make appropriate recommendations after taking into account wherever relevant, the advice offered by the Standing Group of Experts. If it concludes that the failure to comply with the rules was due to either the lack of infrastructure or of technical capacity, the Committee should examine how the assistance required could be provided, and make appropriate arrangements for the provision of the same .

3.4   Procedures for securing compliance with the Committee's recommendations

The recommendations made by the Committee for securing compliance with all rules shall be binding on the country which is found to be at fault. However, unlike the WTO dispute settlement procedures, the Committee's new procedures would not provide for the right of the aggrieved country/countries to request the authorisation of retaliatory action against the country at fault (i.e. when it has failed to comply with the recommendations within the stipulated time).

The absence of provisions regarding the authorisation of retaliatory action should not be understood as implying that the procedures will not be at all effective in securing compliance with the recommendations made by the Committee. It is important to note that most Governments make earnest efforts to abide by the obligations which international rules impose. The experience of the application of the WTO dispute settlement procedures shows that there is a general willingness to abide by the rulings of the Appellate Body. The only exceptions could be a few cases in which there could be apprehensions that, although from the legal point of view the rulings were justified, public opinion is against changes being made in national laws. The main motivation for the implementation of the panels' or Appellate Body's rulings is the political will to abide by them and not, necessarily, the possibility of threat or retaliatory action by the aggrieved party.

3.5 Review of the procedures after ten years

The special procedures that would be established under the Agreement could be reviewed after a period of 15 years to find out whether the WTO's dispute settlement procedures could be made applicable.

3.6 Concluding observations

It should be emphasised that the main purpose of the procedures suggested above is to prevent dispute settlement procedures being applied to those developing countries which do not have the technical capacity to implement the rules. Many developed countries already recognise that it would be futile to insist on the application of the WTO dispute settlement system to complaints brought against such countries. In discussions of the General Council in 2003, the EU stated that it had to be ensured that 'no country could be brought before the DSU system because it was too poor to implement its commitments. That concept could surely be translated into WTO terms. Basically, this would mean to provide assistance to support and speed up the implementation' (G/C/M/69 (paragraph 1.56) and 70 (paragraph 4.21)).

A similar view was expressed by the United States of America. In the US view, it would be a shame to undergo a full formal dispute settlement procedure, only to find out that another Member's problem in implementing trade facilitation reforms simply reflected a failure of international assistance agencies to provide the necessary help at the right time and place (G/C/M/70 (paragraph 4.58)) (G/C/M/70 (paragraph 4.58)).

However, while ensuring that WTO rules relating to dispute settlement should not apply in the above cases, the proposal envisages that these procedures should apply to cases of complaints of non-compliance by developed countries. This would enable developing countries to bring in complaints, for instance, of the non-compliance of commitments which they may assume under the Agreement for the provision of technical assistance. The Committee could also authorise complaints against developing countries being taken to the WTO Dispute Settlement Body when they are about the breach of either the obligations which they have accepted on a binding basis under the Agreement, or of the obligations under GATT Articles V, VIII and X. Such provisions are considered necessary, as with the increasing south-south trade, many disputes about the application of the rules of the Agreement are likely to arise among developing countries.

Chapter 7: The 'Single Undertaking' concept and the continuation of the negotiations after the conclusion of the Round. A possible structure of the Agreement on Trade Facilitation

General

It may be recalled that the negotiations on Trade Facilitation commenced nearly three years after the negotiations in other areas took place in the Doha Round. It is quite possible that, because of this late start as also because of the complexities of the issues that still need to be addressed, negotiations in a few areas may have to be continued after the Agreement on Trade Facilitation is adopted at the end of the Round. The 'single undertaking' concept – i.e. that the negotiations should be treated as a 'package' and completed at the same time – included in the Agreement should not prevent the continuation of the negotiations if they are considered necessary in a few areas of trade facilitation after the conclusion of the Round.

A synoptic picture of the structure of the agreement that would emerge from the negotiations if the suggestions made in the previous chapter are taken into account is provided at the end of this chapter.

The 'Single Undertaking' concept and the continuation of the negotiations after the conclusion of the Round

The Doha Ministerial Declaration stipulates that 'the conduct, conclusion and entry into force of the outcome of the negotiations shall be treated as parts of a single undertaking.'[54] Thus, the 'single undertaking' principle implies that the negotiations on the Agreement on Trade Facilitation would have to be completed at the same time as the negotiations on other subjects of the Doha Round.

Past experience of the application of the single undertaking principle shows that while adopting legal instruments covering all subject areas included in the agenda for negotiations, it may be possible for WTO member countries to agree that, on certain identified issues covered by the Agreement or Agreements, negotiations may be continued after the completion of the Round.

For example, in the Uruguay Round it was agreed that the negotiations on certain 'unfinished business' in the General Agreement on Trade in Services (GATS) should continue after the Round and be completed within specified periods. A two-pronged approach was adopted for this purpose. In relation to the inclusion of GATS provisions on 'Emergency Safeguard Measures' and Government Procurement of Services, the Agreement provided that the negotiations should commence immediately after it became operational, and be completed by a target date.[55]

In certain other areas – financial services, basic telecommunications, maritime services, and the movement of natural persons – the negotiations on the liberalisation of trade were continued after the termination of the Round, through separate Decisions adopted at its end and completed within a specified time period.[56]

---

54   See paragraph 47 of the Doha Ministerial Declaration, (WT/MIN(01)/DEC/1).
55   See Article X and XIII of GATS.
56   See related Decisions listed in the Results of the Uruguay Round of Multilateral Trade Negotiations.

The substantive negotiations on Trade Facilitation commenced after the 1 August 2004 Decision, while the negotiations in other areas of the Doha Round (such as the liberalisation of trade in agriculture as well as non-agricultural products and services) began in 2001. Given this late start, and taking into account the complexity of the issues that would have to be addressed in the process of adopting new rules, it may become necessary to continue the negotiations on a few, clearly defined (and limited) areas after the Agreement on Trade Facilitation is adopted at the conclusion of the Round. Past experience of the Single Undertaking concept shows that it is possible to agree on continuing the negotiations in limited areas after the adoption of the Agreement on Trade Facilitation.

2. Structure of the Agreement

Regarding the structure of the new Agreement on Trade Facilitation, it is envisaged that, as in other WTO Agreements, it should consist of a 'Preamble' followed by other parts containing the substantive rules and provisions relating to the institutional arrangements for the surveillance of the operation of the Agreement.

2.1. Preamble

The preamble defining the aims and objectives of the Agreement could, *inter alia*, include a recognition of the necessity of:

* Applying the procedures for the clearance of goods in a transparent and predictable manner;

* Simplifying and minimising the complexity of such procedures;

* Clarifying the provisions of GATT Articles V, VIII and X, taking into account that customs administrations in developing and least developed countries may have to exercise a greater degree of control in the clearance of goods (than the customs administrations in developed countries) due to the high proportion of customs revenue in the total revenue, and the wide prevalence among the traders of these countries of the undervaluation of imported goods and other customs related malpractices;

* Ensuring a greater degree of coordination between customs administrations and other agencies, such as national standards institutions and Ministries of Industry, Food, and Health whose approvals are required before the clearance of goods;

* Ensuring that developing and least developed countries are not required to accept the obligation to apply those rules of the Agreement for which they lack technical implementation capacity;

* Providing developing and least developed countries with technical assistance to build up capacity for the implementation of the rules of the Agreement, of the specific commitments they may have undertaken, and for the development of infrastructure required for their implementation;

* Recognising that just because technical assistance has been provided should not lead to the assumption that the recipient country has been able to develop the required technical capacity;

* Providing a consultative mechanism for the speedy, effective, and equitable resolution of disputes arising under the Agreement after taking into account the differing technical capacities of countries to apply such rules in the period immediately following the ratification of the Agreement; and

* Recognising that the rules of the Agreement shall not prevent a country from adopting any measures it may consider necessary for national security reasons and to prevent customs related malpractices and frauds.

2.2. The four parts of the Agreement

A synoptic picture of the four possible parts the Agreement (or the pillars on which the structure of the Agreement could be based) is provided here.

PART 1	PART 2	PART 3	PART 4
Rules on measures raising trade policy issues	Rules relating to the techniques and methods that customs should apply in the clearance of goods	Rules governing the provision of technical assistance	Rules relating to the establishment of a Committee on Trade Facilitation and other final provisions as well as the settlement of disputes
The rules would include: ▪ Publication obligations; ▪ The level of fees; ▪ The prohibition of consular formalities; and ▪ The application of the Non- Discrimination Principle. Providing S&D Treatment to developing countries over a transitional period of six years.	The rules would include: ▪ The application of risk management techniques; ▪ The designation of authorised traders; ▪ Reliance on post- audit; and ▪ The establishment of the 'single window' clearance system. The desirability of countries to apply the standards developed by the WCO and other international organisations to be examined in the special sessions of the Negotiating Group. S&D Treatment to be extended on the basis of a 'GATS-like' schedule during the transitional period.	The rules would provide for: ▪ The establishment of a Trade Facilitation Fund/Facility at the WTO; and ▪ The establishment of Mentoring and Twinning Arrangements (M&T). Notification to the Management of the Fund/Facility about assistance provided on a bilateral basis. Review of the progress made in the provision of technical assistance, and in the preparation for the acceptance of the obligations by recipient countries.	The rules would provide for: ▪ The establishment of a Committee on Trade Facilitation for: ▪ The surveillance of the operation of the Agreement; ▪ The settlement of disputes; and ▪ Overseeing the conduct of the negotiations in a limited number of listed areas, and for completing them in a reasonable period of time.

It is envisaged that the Agreement could be adopted by completing the negotiations on the measures listed in Part 1 (rules raising trade policy issues), Part 3 (rules governing the provision of technical assistance) and Part 4 (rules relating to the establishment of the Committee on Trade Facilitation and other final provisions, as well as the settlement of disputes). However, if found necessary, the Agreement may have to provide for the continuation of the negotiations for a further specified agreed short period on measures listed in Part 2 (rules relating to techniques and methods which customs should apply in the clearance of goods). The continuation of the negotiations may be found necessary as it is proposed that special dedicated sessions of the Negotiating Group, attended by customs experts from developing countries, would have to arranged to identify which of the standards developed by international organisations relating to these measures could be brought under the purview of the Agreement, and an obligation imposed on member countries to make their best endeavours to apply them.

PART THREE

Trade Policy Issues

Chapter 8: Publication obligations

1. Applicable regulations

1.1 The Provisions of Article X of GATT 1994

Article X imposes an obligation on member countries to publish all 'laws, regulations, judicial decisions and administrative rulings of general application … in such a manner as to enable governments and traders to become acquainted with them.' It then lists the areas in which the obligation applies. In the area of customs, the obligation applies to:

- The classification or valuation of products for customs purposes;
- Rates of duty, taxes and other charges;
- Requirements, restrictions or prohibitions of imports; and
- The transfer of payments thereof.

Moreover, countries are under obligation to administer 'all such laws, regulations decisions and rulings in a uniform, impartial and reasonable manner.'

1.2 Provisions of the Agreements on Customs Valuation and Preshipment Inspection

In all customs related matters, the provisions of Article X regarding the publication of laws and regulations are complemented by the provisions of the Agreement on Customs Valuation and the Agreement on Preshipment Inspection. Article 12 of the Customs Valuation Agreement stipulates that all laws, regulations, judicial decisions and administrative rulings of general application giving effect to the Agreement, shall be published in conformity with Article X of GATT 1994 by the concerned country of importation. Likewise, the Agreement on Preshipment Inspection requires exporting countries using the services of Preshipment Inspection companies (PSI) not to enforce laws relating to preshipment inspection (or amend such laws and regulations) before they (including changes, if any) have been officially published.

2. The proposals and their objectives

2.1 General

The areas covered in the proposals that have been tabled in the Negotiating Group on Trade Facilitation include:

- The publication of trade regulations;
- The publication of standard clearance time;
- The publication of plans for reform;
- Internet publication;
- The interval between publication and entry into force;
- The right of other countries to comment on the proposed new regulations or amendments; and
- The establishment of enquiry points/offices.

A synoptic summary of the proposals regarding the clarification of the provisions of Article X is contained in Box 9.

Box 9: A clarification of the provisions of Article X

Publication and Availability of Information:

Publication:

1. Members shall publish promptly all laws, regulations, judicial decisions and administrative rulings of general application relating to or affecting trade in goods in such a manner provided for in Article X of GATT 1994 as to enable governments[57] and traders to become acquainted with them. The information to be published shall include:

(a) Procedures of border agencies (including port, airport, and other entry point procedures and relevant forms and documents);

(b) Rate of duties and taxes imposed on or in connection with importation or exportation (including applied tariff rates);

(c) Decisions and examples of customs classification;

(d) Import and export restrictions;

(e) Fees and charges imposed on or in connection with importation or exportation;

(f) Penalty provisions against breaches of import and export formalities;

(g) Appeal procedures; and

(h) Agreements with any country or countries relating to the above issues.

Availability:

2. Members shall ensure that the information referred to in paragraph 1 is made available to governments and traders in a non-discriminatory and convenient manner via an officially designated source notified to [the WTO Secretariat or a newly established body], including official gazette, official journal and whenever practicable, official website.

Outline of major trade related procedures:

3. Members shall, whenever practicable, provide documents regarding the outline of major trade-related procedures [in English, French or Spanish] and make publication and notification of them in a manner provided for in paragraph 2. (Japan, Mongolia and Switzerland, TN/TF/W/114).

◆ (i) *"All relevant laws, regulations, administrative guidelines, decisions and rulings of or having general application;"* (ii) *"Information on customs and other border-related agency processes (including port, airport and other entry-point procedures and relevant forms and documents);"* (iii) *"Conditions for different forms of customs treatment;"* (iv) *"Appeal procedures (including standard times and conditions for appeal);"* (v) *"All fees and charges applicable to import, export and transit procedures and requirements;"* (vi) *"Agreements with any other country or countries relating to the above issues;"* (vii) *"Customs' and other government agencies' management plans relating to the implementation of WTO commitments. This could include standard processing times or relevant reform and modernisation programmes;"* (viii) *"All significant amendments to the above"* (European Communities, TN/TF/W/6). The EC also proposes a requirement to make this information "easily available". See also a related EC-Australia proposal in TN/TF/W/23 as reflected in section G:2.

◆ *"... the laws, regulations, judicial decisions, administrative rulings as defined in Article X.1 of the GATT, and advance rulings of general application and a binding nature, as well as any agreements with other Member or Members relating to the relevant regulations or laws;"* including the requirement *"to make any exceptions, derogations or changes"* to those items *"readily available"* (Korea, TN/TF/W/7).

---

57 The term 'governments' is deemed to include the competent authorities of any Separate Customs Territory Member and the European Communities.

- ◆ (i) *"All trade-related laws and regulations (including trade-related treaties and agreements)"*; (ii) *"Procedures and administrative rules of border agencies (including documentation formats)"*; (iii) *"Applied tariffs rates"*; (iv) *"Decisions and examples of customs classification"*, (v) *"Fees and charges imposed on or in connection with importation or exportation"*; (vi) *"Details of preshipment inspection activities"*; (vii) *"Details of export inspection for safety standards, etc.;* (viii) *"Standard processing period for major trade procedures"*; with relevant governments and traders also being able to obtain information from the competent authorities on the *"legitimate purpose or objective"* for *"imposing trade-related restrictions"* as well as the *"reasons for any delay in cases where trade-related procedures take longer than the standard processing period"* (Japan, Mongolia, Chinese Taipei, Pakistan and Peru, TN/TF/W/8 and Corr.1). See also the proposal's input on publishing decisions against appeals contained in section E:1.

- ◆ *"... all laws, regulations and other measures of general application pertaining to or affecting trade in goods, and other information concerning relevant procedures, fees, and charges to border-crossing trade"* (China, TN/TF/W/26).

- ◆ *"... all relevant legislation [and other information] on customs procedures relating to the various customs regimes ..."*, including *"the legal basis for administrative decisions"* (Peru, TN/TF/W/30).

It is clear from the listings cited above that there are three main objectives of the proposals.

- ● Their aim is to reaffirm the obligations of GATT Article X and the Agreements on Customs Valuation and Preshipment Inspection.

- ● A few of the proposals aim at creating new obligations. For example, neither GATT nor the Customs Valuation Agreement require countries to determine the standard processing time for the clearance of goods through customs, or require countries to publish the time period, or give reasons for any delay in cases where the procedures take longer than the standard processing time.

- ● Their aim is to broaden the scope and content of some of these obligations by requiring countries to publish information not only about laws and regulations, but also about how some of the measures are applied in practice. In particular, they aim at broadening the scope of the obligations to cover all information regarding:
  - ◆ Internal decision making processes;
  - ◆ The substantive content of each measure affecting foreign trade; and
  - ◆ Border related agency processes and administrative guidelines.

2.1.1 Points for consideration

Any decision regarding the approach towards proposals asking to broaden the scope and content of the present obligations will need to examine whether the additional costs and administrative burdens imposed on the governments of developing countries are commensurate with the advantages accruing to trade through the greater transparency of rules, regulations and practices followed by customs. It is also desirable to examine these proposals in the light of the current trend in which governments of many countries confine themselves to publishing only basic rules and regulations, and leave the explanation of detailed customs clearance procedures and documentation requirements to the manuals and guides published by the Chambers of Commerce or Trade Associations. Thus, it may be more worthwhile to consider rules calling upon governments to encourage business associations to publish manuals on rules and procedures (after obtaining them from customs) or put them on the Internet, rather than impose an obligation on them to publish all such 'information' themselves. Where necessary, governments could also provide financial resources to partly cover the costs of such publications. This would be in keeping with the proposals that have been made for public/private partnership in formulating and overseeing the application of rules.

2.2 Proposals on the publication of standard clearance time

The proposals regarding the obligation to publish also suggest that the rules should be further clarified to require the publication of 'average release and clearance time' (see Box 10).

As a result of the reform programmes and the modernisation of customs procedures, many developing countries have been able to considerably reduce the time needed to clear imported and exported goods. However, some case studies about the experience of reform programmes have expressed apprehension that a number of countries may not be able to sustain the progress made after the technical assistance funds dry up on the completion of the assistance programmes. The main reason for this often lies in the inability of governments to allocate the funds required for the continuation of the reform programme from their own budgets because their priority lies in financing programmes with a more 'developmental orientation.'

The average time taken for the clearance of goods varies from country to country, depending on the prevalence of factors such as customs malpractices (e.g. the tendency on the part of importers to undervalue imported goods), and whether the imports are made in bulk by a few large firms or by numerous smaller companies. Differences in the composition of imports can also influence variations in clearance time. Countries in which a high proportion of imports require approvals before clearance from the Ministries of Industry or Health, the average time taken for the clearance of all imports may be longer than in countries where such imports constitute only a small proportion.

Thus, a number of countries seem to consider it premature to be required to publish the average time it takes to clear goods through customs as also explain periodically the reasons for variations in the standard clearance period.

Box 10: Standard processing time

◆ The publication of *"standard processing period for major trade procedures"* (Japan, Mongolia, Chinese Taipei, Pakistan and Peru, TN/TF/W/8).

◆ *"Establishment of a time limit for customs release…"* (Turkey, TN/TF/W/45).

◆ *"… each Member would establish and agree progressively to reduce its domestic standard processing times for goods release and clearance, based on a common standard such as the WCO Time Release Study. (…) Publication of standard processing times would ensure that such times are in the first place established, and then efforts [are] made to reduce them"* (European Communities, TN/TF/W/46).

◆ See also the reference to EC proposal TN/TF/W/6 in section A.1., first bullet, element (vii).

◆ *Members shall measure and publish their own average time for the release of goods in a consistent manner on a periodic basis, based on the WCO Time Release Study.*

◆ *Members shall endeavour to continuously reduce such average release time.*

◆ *In case of a significant delay in the release of goods, Members shall provide the traders who have made written requests with the reasons for the delay except when such notification would impede the pursuance of legitimate policy objectives.* (Textual proposal, Korea, TN/TF/W/139).

2.3 The publication of reform plans

Another important proposal is that countries should be requested to publish their plans for reforming customs.

The improvement of the effectiveness and efficiency of the services provided by the government is a management function. The concerned government departments are expected to take measures for the modernisation and improvement of services they provide on a continuing basis. However, it is often difficult for the authorities to decide which practices should be treated as 'reform programmes' and, thus, be published for the information of the general public and the governments of other countries. Whether the measures adopted for improving the effectiveness of the services being provided should be published or not and, if published, the amount of publicity to be extended, are decisions that would have to be left to the country concerned. In some cases, customs administrations may be reluctant to publicise measures that are being undertaken until they are sure they can be fully implemented, mainly because of uncertainty regarding the continued availability of financial resources.

2.4 Proposals on Internet publication

The specific proposals regarding the publication of such information on the Internet are listed in the Box 11.

Box 11: Proposals on Internet publication

◆ *"Internet 'publication' of the elements set out in Article X of GATT 1994"* (United States, TN/TF/W/13).

Special and Differential Treatment

◆ *"The unique situation of each individual Member regarding implementation of the proposed commitment could be addressed early in the negotiations through the use of diagnostic tools providing an assessment of specific needs, which can lead to appropriate and workable transition periods combined with assistance targeted at individual situations"* [58] (United States, TN/TF/W/13).

Technical Assistance and Support for Capacity Building

◆ *"It would be useful if (...) Members and, as appropriate, International Organisations would provide information on experiences and available resources specifically related to this particular proposal"* [59] (United States, TN/TF/W/13).

Internet publication is only one of the modes by which laws, rules and regulations can be made available to the public. This method of publication would only be useful in those developing countries in which the use of IT among traders and the business community is widely prevalent.

The clarification of the provisions of Article X encouraging countries to publish rules, regulations, and other customs related information on the Internet could – by providing traders with improved and easy access to information – add to their transparency. However, whether the publication of such information on government websites should complement paper publication or be a substitute for it is a question that needs to be addressed. Another related question is whether Internet publication by itself would meet the

---

58   Applies also to section A:3:b.
59   Applies also to section A:3:b.

requirements of the provisions of GATT Article X (2) which, *inter alia*, lays down that duties and taxes should not be collected unless the rules authorising their collection are published.

2.5 Proposals on the interval between the publication and enforcement of rules

The proposals on the provision of a reasonable interval between the publication and entry into force of rules and regulations are listed below.

Box 12: The interval between publication and entry into force

Members shall ensure that a reasonable interval is provided between the publication of new or amended laws, regulations and administrative rulings of general application, or their drafts or summaries, and their entry into force in such a manner as to allow traders to become acquainted with and well prepared for compliance with them. (*Hong Kong China, Japan, Korea, Mongolia, and Switzerland,* TN/TF/W/115)

◆ Allow for *"an adequate time period between the publication of rules and their implementation"* (European Communities, TN/TF/W/6). See also a related EC-Australia proposal in TN/TF/W/23 as reflected in section G:2, first bullet.

◆ *"... allow a reasonable amount of time between the publication of new or amended measures and their entry into force; if desirable, Members may even go further to specify the time period"* (Korea, TN/TF/W/7).

◆ *"Publication of laws and regulations (or final draft regulations) before their implementation"* (Japan, Mongolia, Chinese Taipei, Pakistan and Peru, TN/TF/W/8).

◆ *"There should be a reasonable interval (e.g., at least 30 days) between the publication of regulations and their implementation or enforcement ..."* (China , TN/TF/W/26).

◆ *"Establishment of minimum time periods before the entry into force of new regulations"* (Peru, TN/TF/W/30).

The proposals also suggest that, in addition to strengthening publication obligations, the new rules should provide that there should be an adequate period of time (at least 30 days) between the publication of the regulations and their entry into force.

The basic objective of these proposals is to provide sufficient time to traders and business firms engaged in imports and exports to get acquainted with the new regulations, as also with any amendments in existing regulations. While these proposals on allowing time between the publication and enforcement of new rules should not pose serious problems, they would have to recognise that there could be cases where authorities consider that the new rules should be complied with immediately after they are made public.

2.6 Proposals on the right of other countries to comment on new regulations or amendments

The proposals also impose an obligation on governments to take into account the views of the business sector, consumer organisations, academics, professionals, and any other interested stakeholders while formulating new regulations or making major amendments in the existing rules. Some proposals also envisage that the regulations should provide the governments of other countries the right to comment on the drafts of new laws and regulations being formulated, and that there should be an obligation requiring the concerned country to take such comments into account when finalizing them. Another proposal even suggests that the country adopting the regulations should be required 'to provide an explanation to the traders and other WTO members as to why their comments have not been taken into account.' Box 13 provides an overview of these proposals.

Box 13: The right of other countries to comment on the proposed new regulations or amendments

"Members shall afford appropriate opportunities to interested parties to comment on proposed introduction or amendment of trade-related laws, regulations and administrative rulings of general application. Members shall provide information of their legitimate policy objectives pursued and allow reasonable period for interested parties to submit comments" (*Hong Kong China, Japan, Korea, Mongolia, and Switzerland*, TN/TF/W/115).

◆ *"A provision requiring consultation between interested parties, notably governments and the private sector, on proposed new rules and procedures applied to import and export administration and goods in transit"* (European Communities, TN/TF/W/6).

◆ Provide interested parties with an opportunity to submit comments in writing on proposed new *"core measures"* or amendments to the same, followed by Members *"giving due consideration to these comments"* before finalizing the proposed measures (Korea, TN/TF/W/7).

◆ Provide *"opportunities for interested parties including the private sector to comment on prospective trade-related laws and regulations"* (Japan, Mongolia, Chinese Taipei, Pakistan and Peru, TN/TF/W/8).

◆ Give *"Members and traders (…) the right to comment on proposed customs rules, procedures, and policy with commercial effects and either amend the proposed rule or procedure, or as the case may be, provide an explanation to traders and other WTO members as to why their comments have not been taken into account"* (New Zealand, TN/TF/W/24).

◆ *"Members should, without discrimination, allow reasonable time for other Members to make comments in writing, and take these written comments into consideration after such laws, regulations and measures are publicised before being implemented or enforced"* (China, TN/TF/W/26).

◆ *"(i) Each Member should establish effective mechanisms for exchanges with traders, whose views should be duly taken into account, concerning the administration of measures referred to in paragraph 1 of Article X of GATT 1994. (ii) When formulating, implementing and reviewing any measures referred to in paragraph 1 of Article X of GATT 1994, opportunities should be provided for consultation with traders if substantial trade interests or major changes to the existing measures are involved"* (Hong Kong, China, TN/TF/W32).

2.6.1   Points for consideration

There is increasing recognition on the part of the governments of most countries (including those of developing countries) of the need to consult all interested stakeholders when formulating new laws and regulations, or when reviewing the existing ones. However, as one of the proposals recognises, it would also be necessary to leave it to the judgement of the country concerned to decide on how such consultations should be arranged, and whether any views expressed by traders or other stakeholders should be accepted. Any requirement imposing an obligation on governments to justify why the views of their traders or of other governments have not been accepted may put the governments in an embarrassing situation, particularly with reference to laws and regulations dealing with customs matters. Many of these regulations aim at striking a balance between the control functions of customs which aim at ensuring that due revenues are fully collected and that there is full compliance with customs rules, and the interest of traders by keeping such controls to the minimum in order to facilitate trade.

The proposals regarding giving the right to the governments of other WTO member countries to comment on the drafts of laws and regulations may also raise difficult policy issues. The idea appears to have been borrowed from similar provisions in the Agreements on Technical Barriers to Trade (TBT) and on Sanitary and Phytosanitary (SPS) measures.

The two Agreements impose an obligation on countries to base their technical regulations and SPS measures on international standards. It is possible for countries to deviate from this obligation in specific circumstances in which they consider that the adoption of the international standard is not appropriate. However, in all such cases, the two Agreements require the country proposing to adopt the technical regulations and SPS measures to notify its intentions to the WTO as well as publish them in draft form so that if any country wishes to comment on the draft, it could request to do so. The two Agreements also impose an obligation on the countries to subsequently take such comments into account when adopting the new regulations.

The rationale for these rules is that where technical regulations and SPS measures are based on international standards, the views of other WTO member countries would already have been taken into account since they would have participated in the preparatory work on the formulation of the international standards. The situation is different in cases where a country does not apply international TBT and SPS standards. In such cases, other countries must have the right to comment on them before the rules are adopted in order to ensure that the characteristics of the products produced by them and the processes used in production by the respective industries are fully taken into account by the country adopting the regulation or measure. This is necessary to ensure that they do not cause non-tariff barriers to trade.

Whether countries should be obliged to take into account the views and comments of other WTO member countries when adopting new customs related regulations or amending existing ones, is an issue that needs to be examined carefully. The basic condition applicable to the adoption of technical regulations and SPS measures is that they should be based on international standards. This condition does not apply to customs related laws and regulations which are adopted by governments after taking into account the views and needs of their customs authorities and, where considered desirable and appropriate, the views of the industry, trade associations, and other stakeholders. In other words, they are tailored to the trade situation prevailing in the country. Their main aim is to strike a balance between the extent of control of import and export transactions needed (taking into account the prevalence of the undervaluation of goods and other malpractices as well as other forms of customs related corruption) and the desire of the business community to keep such controls to the minimum in order to facilitate trade. Thus, the approach adopted, and the detailed provisions included in the laws and regulations, would necessarily vary from country to country. Security considerations are also making those countries facing risks from terrorism impose greater degrees of scrutiny of import documentation as well as increase physical checking.

A number of countries also appear to be apprehensive about the right of other member countries to comment on their domestic laws and regulations. This could lead to unnecessary tension between countries. This is particularly so if a country is put under obligation to explain the non-acceptance of comments made by other countries about the new rules and regulations they want to adopt. Any such requirement could be considered unnecessary interference by a foreign government in the work of the national parliament, especially in the formulation of laws.

This does not mean that WTO member countries should not be permitted to comment on any new
regulations or amendments in existing laws, especially if they consider that they are likely to affect their

trade interests adversely. Today, a number of countries require their commercial attachés to follow the development of new laws and regulations in the countries of their posting. It is normal for these officials to obtain drafts of new legislations and regulations, and send them to their governments for comment. Any comments and suggestions received by them are also made available to the concerned authorities for consideration. The officials also inform their governments about the views expressed by the authorities after they have examined the comments. A greater reliance on such practices is likely to produce more fruitful results rather than those consequent upon the provision of legal rights under the WTO system to comment on draft legislations.

The proposal further envisages that in order to facilitate comments on draft legislations by other countries, the 'core subjects or measures' that are expected to have a significant effect on trade on which new rules would be adopted, should be notified to the WTO. By bringing the attention of the government of other countries to the subject about which new legislation is being adopted, the WTO would help them decide whether they should examine the draft legislation for comments. The practical problem that would be encountered in complying with this notification obligation is how to identify the measures that are likely to have a 'significant effect' on trade.

2.7 Proposals on the establishment of enquiry points or offices

Nearly all of the proposals suggest that there should be an obligation on countries to establish enquiry points or a single national enquiry point (SNEP) which could supply, on request, all the information regarding documentation requirements, duties, and other charges payable on imported and exported products, and on the procedural aspects of customs administration to interested traders, other stakeholders from the country, and to other WTO member countries.

Box 14 lists some of these proposals.

Box 14: The establishment of enquiry points or offices

Members shall ensure that one or more enquiry points exist which are responsible for the provision of relevant information and documents related to trade procedures ...to traders in a non-discriminatory and convenient manner (Japan, Mongolia and Switzerland, TN/TF/W/114).

◆ "*Establish enquiry points or trade desks, providing information on all* (...) *measures and information* [proposed by the EC for publication in section A:2:1 of document TN/TF/W/6] ... ." "*Such provisions could be based on provisions on enquiry points in certain WTO Agreements such as TBT and SPS*" (European Communities, TN/TF/W/6).

◆ Establishment of a Single National Focal Point as a centre for communication with other domestic competent authorities to more efficiently respond to inquiries. "*The SNFP should, within a reasonable period of time, supply not only the information requested but also any other pertinent information, which the SNFP considers the interested parties, should be aware. In addition, the contact information relating to the SNFP should be notified to the WTO Secretariat. The Secretariat should make such information available to the other Members and interested parties*" (Korea, TN/TF/W/7).

◆ "*Establishment of inquiry points responsible for providing relevant information or documents related to trade procedures to the traders (including co-ordination among existing inquiry points of each border authority)*" (Japan, Mongolia, Chinese Taipei, Pakistan and Peru, TN/TF/W/8).

◆ Set up information centres or inquiry points with competent officers to provide responses to inquiries (Chinese Taipei, TN/TF/W/10).

- "Each Member shall, in accordance with their real situations, establish or designate one or more trade policy enquiry points where, upon request of any individual, enterprise or WTO Member, all information relating to the above-mentioned laws[60], regulations and measures may be obtained" (China, TN/TF/W/26).

- "Establishment of enquiry points facilitating access to trade-related information, for example, the creation of a National Enquiry Point operating a free-of-charge 24-hour service or an informative website providing a broad range of customs information with links to other relevant sites" (Peru, TN/TF/W30).

- Establish "national trade enquiry points (...)". A "parallel work may be effected at the WTO through a trade portal. The system suggested (...) is similar to the system provided at the 'International Portal on Food Safety, Animal & Plant Health' (www.ipfsah.org) (...)" (Turkey, TN/TF/W/45).

- "Establish enquiry points at the national level or in the case of SVEs/developing countries involved in a Customs Union/RTA/FTA, the option of the establishment of enquiry points at the regional level, to provide relevant information on trade procedures to trade."

- "Members and the WTO, within its competence, shall provide technical and financial assistance on mutually agreed terms to SVEs/developing countries to support the establishment, modification and maintenance of these national and/or regional enquiry points" (Antigua and Barbuda, Barbados, Dominica, Fiji, Grenada, Papua New Guinea, The Solomon Islands, St. Kitts And Nevis, St. Lucia, and St. Vincent and The Grenadines (TN/TF/W/129/Rev.1).

The Agreements on Technical Barriers to Trade (TBT) and on Sanitary and Phytosanitary measures (SPS) also call on countries to establish enquiry points that are responsible for replying to reasonable questions from WTO member countries, as well as from other parties on, *inter alia*, technical regulations, sanitary and phytosanitary measures, procedures for control and inspection, and of quarantine treatment.

Case studies as well as anecdotal evidence about the experience with these enquiry points shows that while in most developed countries and some developing countries they are playing a useful role, in many developing countries and least developed countries, they have not always been able to provide the requested information. There are two reasons for this:

- They are not able to obtain updated information because of the lack of cooperation from other government departments, and

- Budgetary constraints have curtailed the resources allocated to such information points.

Case studies undertaken by the World Bank and OECD regarding the operational experience of enquiry points established under the technical assistance-supported customs reform programmes in some developing countries show that they have been playing a useful role in providing information to interested traders about customs procedures and duties payable. The effectiveness of the enquiry points in responding to queries is largely due to the importance attached to their role by the higher authorities in the government. This has assured the cooperation of officials from other departments in keeping the information always updated and available. However, there are fears that after the termination of the technical assistance programme, the resources required for the effective operation of the enquiry points may not continue to be available from the governments because of budgetary constraints. These considerations may have to be taken into account while deciding whether the rules should impose a binding obligation to establish enquiry points, or leave it to the country concerned to decide how the required information should be provided.

---

60   '... laws, regulations and other measures of general application pertaining to or affecting trade in goods, and other information concerning relevant procedures, fees, and charges related to border crossing trade.'

Thus, past experience should determine whether the obligation of developing countries should be binding or voluntary. Of relevance here is that the guidelines in the Kyoto Convention on the application of standards relating to information, decisions, and rulings by customs state that the following prerequisites are necessary for the successful functioning of enquiry offices:

- Availability of sufficiently trained staff to deal with the broad range of questions raised, and
- Speedy access to information sources so as to provide comprehensive service.

The increasing availability of information on the Internet may also gradually reduce the need for the establishment of enquiry points. Thus, it would be desirable to leave the structure of such points and their location to be determined by the country concerned.

In this context it is relevant to note that some countries have proposed that small, vulnerable economies, and developing countries which are parties to regional trade arrangements, should be permitted to establish enquiry points at the regional level.

It would also be necessary to ensure that the information provided by such enquiry points does not entail any legal consequences.

Chapter 9: The level of fees connected with importation and exportation

General

Article VIII of GATT 1994 consists of two elements. First, it provides that countries should ensure that the fees and charges levied by them in connection with importation and exportation should be limited to the approximate cost of the services rendered (Para 1 (a). Second, it calls upon countries to minimise the incidence and complexity of import formalities, and to decrease and simplify import and export documentation (Para 1 (c).

This chapter examines the proposals that have been made for the clarification of the rules of Article VIII regarding fees and other charges.

1. The clarification of rules

The GATT rules envisage member countries reducing their customs duties by participating in trade negotiations held periodically under the auspices of the WTO, and that the tariffs reduced in such negotiations should be bound against further increase. Thus, the rules prevent countries from collecting duties on imported products at a rate higher than the bound rate. Countries are also prevented from imposing other taxes on such imported products.

There are, however, two exceptions to this rule.

First, in addition to customs duties, member countries are permitted to collect internal taxes on imported products, such as value added tax or excise duties. However, Article III (which lays down a national treatment rule) requires that such taxes can be levied on imported products only if they are also levied on other 'like' products produced domestically. Moreover, the rate of such taxes should not exceed the level payable on domestically produced products.

Second, in addition to customs duties and internal taxes, member countries are permitted to collect fees and charges to cover the costs of the services provided by customs in connection with importation and exportation.

Article VIII, para 1 (a) allows member countries to impose fees and charges in connection with importation and exportation only if the following conditions are met:

- They are 'limited in amount to the approximate cost of services rendered,' and
- They shall not represent 'an indirect protection to domestic products or a taxation of imports or exports for fiscal purposes.'

Thus, all fees and charges in excess of the cost of services provided by customs to importers and exporters would constitute taxation for fiscal purposes and would, therefore, not be consistent with the rules of Article VIII.

2. Interpretation of the provisions by Panels

The provisions of the Article VIII have been subject to interpretation by various Panels of the WTO. In the **US–Customs Users Fee**[61] case, the Panel examined what the term 'services rendered in a more artful political sense' meant in actual practice. It took the view that the term was not used in its usual 'economic sense' since the regulation of imports and exports by customs is 'not necessarily desired' by importers, and does 'not necessarily add value' to imported goods. The Panel went on to explain that the drafters must have used the term 'services rendered' to imply 'government activities closely connected to the process of importation and exportation.' Although not all analysts may share the view of the Panel – that business considers customs activities as not being a service but a barrier to trade – the subsequent explanation (suggesting that the term should be treated as covering the 'activities performed by customs') may, in practice, be helpful in appreciating the scope of the provisions.

The Panel further observed that:

- The assessment of whether fees and charges are limited to the cost of services should be measured on the basis of the 'costs of the period for which revenue is collected,' and

- The level of fees and charges should be further determined by taking into account the approximate costs for individual importers.

The Panel has also ruled that since ad valorem fees (with no fixed maximum level) results in a greater incidence on high-value goods and a lower incidence on low-value goods, it is, in its very nature, inconsistent with the rule stipulating that such fees and charges should be limited to the costs of services rendered.

3. Overview of the fees and charges levied by selected countries

The **Annex** to this chapter provides an overview of the fees and charges being collected in selected countries, and their approximate rates. It is to be noted that, in addition to customs duties, certain fees and charges are payable on imported or exported goods. A large number of developing countries levy such fees and charges. The fees take the following forms:

- Customs surcharge;
- Tax on foreign exchange transactions procedures;
- Stamp tax;
- Import license fee;
- Statistical tax;
- Tax on transport facilities;
- Taxes or charges on sensitive products;
- Surcharge for the development of port facilities and housing for fishermen; and
- Fees charged to finance the activities of the Regional Trade Area Secretariat.

---

61   See the WTO Guide to GATT Law and Practice, Vol. 1, pp. 269-276 (WTO, 1995).

It is doubtful that all of the fees and charges listed in the **Annex** actually meet the criteria in Article VIII which stipulates that:

- Such fees must relate to the services rendered by customs in relation to imports and exports, and

- Such fees should not exceed the approximate cost of such services.

4. Proposals tabled by delegations

4.1 Proposals on the clarification of the concept of the approximate cost of services rendered

The proposals aim primarily at clarifying Article VIII which stipulates that the fees charged should not exceed the approximate cost of the service provided. The proposals made are described in Box 15.

Box 15: The concept of approximate cost of services rendered

- *"Establish specific parameters for fees charged by Members under Article VIII of GATT 1994"* (United States, TN/TF/W/14).

- Establish disciplines for GATT Article VIII-related fees and charges applying to *"all fees and charges imposed by customs authorities or by any other government body (including tasks undertaken on their behalf), or in connection with importation or exportation, or as a condition for importation or exportation, to the extent not already covered by other WTO Articles and Agreements"* (European Communities and Australia, TN/TF/W/23).

- Ensure that (i) *"the service provided is related to the goods in question* (ii) *fees and charges refer to the approximate cost of the service provided* (iii) *fees and charges (...) [are] not (...) calculated on an ad valorem basis* (iv) *administrative or operational costs not constituting a service associated with the treatment of imports or exports (...) [are] not (...) imposed on such imports or exports* (v) *[there is] non-discrimination in the design and application of fees and charges"* (European Communities and Australia, TN/TF/W/23).

- Calculate the approximate cost of services rendered by breaking down costs into (i) direct costs (in the sense of costs directly related to the specific services rendered, including labour, materials, equipment, and utilities) and (ii) indirect costs (consisting of costs incurred that are not directly related but are, nonetheless, attributable to the specific services rendered e.g., costs of supporting labour, equipment, and office rent). (Chinese Taipei, TN/TF/W/25).

- *"Establishment of objective criteria for the application of fees and charges by Members to import and export operations"* (Peru, TN/TF/W/30).

4.1.1. *Kyoto Convention Provisions*

The issue of fees and charges being limited to the approximate cost of services rendered by customs was discussed and debated during the revision of the WCO Kyoto Convention. However, no standard could be agreed upon due to the divergence of views among countries regarding, *inter alia*, how the cost for determining fees should be calculated.

4.1.2   Points for consideration

One of the major constraints developing countries encounter in adopting new and innovative methods in customs clearance – such as the application of the techniques of risk management, post-audits, and the recognition of authorised importers – arises from a lack of financial resources. Where only the initial outlay required for the development of physical infrastructure, equipment (e.g. computers and scanners), and the training of officials is made available to developing countries under technical assistance programmes, experience has shown that the majority of these countries – particularly the least developed ones or those at a lower stage of development – are not able to meet the recurring expenditure needed for maintaining and strengthening the reform programme due to budgetary constraints.

Thus, while clarifying the rules, it may be desirable to ensure that countries – particularly developing countries – are able to recover the costs incurred by them in adopting the reform programmes as well as be able to afford the recurring expenditure needed for their continued application.

The proposal made by Chinese Taipei suggesting that both direct costs (costs for equipment, material, and utilities) and indirect costs (recurring expenditure on maintenance of equipment, office rent, etc.) should be included in the calculation of costs, could provide a useful basis for the further examination of these issues. It may also be necessary to consider whether the costs should include other elements, such as the costs of training and the salaries of additional staff needed while adopting the reform programme. In order to ensure that the fees or charges calculated on such a basis do not impose a heavy additional burden on importers and exporters, the recovery of direct costs should be spread over a reasonably long period of time. However, the period over which such costs should be recovered should be determined by the country concerned.

If, for these reasons, a country decides on levying a 'customs reform fee,' it would be necessary to ensure that the additional financial burden on importers and exporters does not result in offsetting the benefits obtained by adopting the reform programme regarding the reduction of clearance time, and the consequent lowering of the total costs of the imported goods. The fee should also be kept under continuous review, and reduced after the 'direct costs' segment of the reform programme is recovered. The rules should recognise that any such fee aimed at recovering direct costs of the reform programme and meeting the recurring expenditure of its implementation would not be considered as constituting the 'direct protection of the domestic industry' or 'taxation of imports for fiscal purposes,' provided that:

- The fees levied do not exceed the actual expenditure incurred on meeting direct costs, and
- The recovery of such costs is spread over a reasonable period of time.

The imposition of such taxes would be consistent with the practice followed by governments to recover the costs of services provided by levying taxes on the user. The fees thus collected do not form a part of general revenue but are used for providing a specific service or for improving existing services. A good example of such a tax is airport tax which is made available to airport authorities for the improvement of services and for taking security measures against terrorism. Other examples include tolls collected from users of auto routes, the proceeds of which are used for the maintenance of roads.

4.2 Proposals on publication, notification and review obligations

In addition to the proposal on the clarification of the rules of Article VIII relating to the concept of the cost of services rendered, it is suggested that countries should be under an obligation:

● To notify WTO of the fees, and

● To periodically review them in order to, *inter alia*, reduce or minimise their number and diversity.

4.2.1 Points for consideration

Whether the rules should impose an obligation on countries to notify fees to the WTO is an issue that needs careful consideration. If the main purpose of the notification is to ensure transparency, then, as countries begin to publish such information on the Internet, interested traders in other countries (and their governments) will have easy access to it. In such circumstances, the obligation to notify fees to the WTO would impose an unnecessary and avoidable administrative burden on the governments of member countries.

In order to ensure that they do not exceed the costs of services provided, the proposal about keeping fees and charges under review could, as noted earlier, form an integral part of the clarification of the rules of Article VIII, especially how such costs should be calculated for the purpose of determining the level of fees.

ANNEX

Examples of customs fees and charges levied by selected countries[62]

A. CUSTOMS SURCHARGES

Country	Purpose	Rate (%)	Date of introduction
Bangladesh	Temporary infrastructure development surcharge.	2.5	1997
Benin	Specific fee for National Dockers' Council.		
Brazil	Merchant Marine Renewal tax to modernise and improve its merchant fleet; and a Dock Worker Severance pay to indemnify workers whose registration had been cancelled.		
Costa Rica	Welfare, medical, and child care centres.	1	
Haiti	Fund for the 'Management and Development of Local Communities.'	2	
Ghana	Import levy on all non-petroleum products imported in 'commercial quantities.'	0.5	
Nigeria	(a) Port Development Tax. (b) Raw materials and Development Council surcharge. (c) Shippers' Council surcharge.	5 1 1	
Peru	Surcharge to pay for the Agricultural Development Fund (tariff surcharge on 331 agricultural products).	5	1997
Senegal	Senegalese Loaders' Council; Livestock Fund levy.	0.2	
Turkey	Mass Housing Fund – imports on fish and fishery products to finance its Government low-cost housing schemes for poor and middle-income families.	3	
Uruguay	On imports transported by sea, to finance the severance packages of the national Ports Administration personnel.	0.25	

B. TAX ON FOREIGN EXCHANGE TRANSACTIONS

Country	Purpose	Rate (%)	Date of introduction
Antigua and Barbuda	Foreign exchange transaction tax on all transactions.	1	

---

62   The information in the table draws on data from the OECD Trade Policy Working Paper No. 14: 'Analysis of non-tariff measures: Customs fees and charges on imports' (TD/TC/WP(2004)46/FINAL), 8 March 2005.

C. STAMP TAX

Country	Purpose	Rate (%)
Jamaica	Additional stamp duty on customs warrants. Aim: protection of local production of certain product categories, e.g.: (a) Primary aluminium products; (b) Vegetables and beans; (c) Alcoholic beverages; and (d) Tobacco products.	 20-25 35 34 56
Madagascar	Customs stamp duty.	1
Morocco	Verification and stamp tax on carpets.	5
Niger	Stamp tax discriminating between WAEMU and non-WAEMU countries.	(small fee)

D. IMPORT LICENSE FEE

Country	Purpose	Rate (%)
Bangladesh	*Ad valorem* import license fees on imports valued above Tk 100,000.	2.5
Sri Lanka	*Ad valorem* import license fees on 474 items.	0.1
Swaziland	*Ad valorem* import license fees.	0.05
Uganda	*Ad valorem* import license fees on all imports.	2%

E. CONSULAR INVOICE FEE

Country	Purpose	Rate (%)	Date of introduction
Dominican Republic	For approval of transactions.		
Nicaragua	Ad Valorem fee.	0.05	
Paraguay	Consular tax on total merchandise value.	7.5	1972

F. STATISTICAL TAX

Country	Purpose	Rate (%)	Date of introduction
Benin	Fees on imports from non-ECOWAS and non-WAEMU countries.	1	
Burkina Faso	"	1	
Mali	"	1	
Niger	"	1	
Senegal	"	1	
Madagascar	Statistical taxes between 2-3%.	2-3	
Côte d'Ivoire	"	2-3	
Mauritania	"	2-3	
Togo	"	2-3	
Suriname	On the c.i.f. value of all imports, except those of bauxite companies for which statistical tax quadrupled.	0.5	
Argentina	Statistical tax applied on non-MERCOSUR countries.	0.5	1998

G. TAX ON TRANSPORT FACILITIES

Country	Purpose	Rate (%)	Date of introduction
Israel	Wharfage fee/port use fee: (a) Importers, and (b) Exporters.	1.1 0.2	

H. TAXES AND CHARGES ON SENSITIVE PRODUCT CATEGORIES

Country	Purpose	Rate (%)
Korea	Environmental waste charges on certain plastics. Domestic producers: specific fee. Foreign imports: *Ad valorem* fee, 0.7%	0.7
Belize	Environmental tax on most imported products.	1
Grenada	Environmental levy on a range of goods.	1

I. ADDITIONAL CHARGES (n.e.s)

Country	Purpose	Rate (%)	Date of introduction
Belize	Administrative charge.	1.5	
Mauritius	Tea.	20	
El Salvador	Empty sacks and bags of synthetic fibre.	80	
Chile	Dispatch tax on merchandise exempt from import duties.	5	
Morocco	Para-fiscal tax.	0.25	
Suriname	Consent fee.	1.5	
Nicaragua	Municipal tax.	1	

J. FEES RELATED TO CUSTOMS PROCEDURES

Country	Purpose	Rate (%)
Bangladesh	*Ad valorem* customs 'service fee'.	1
Venezuela	"	1
Uruguay	"	0.35-1.1
Dominica	"	2
St. Lucia	"	4
St. Vincent and the Grenadines	"	4
Antigua and Barbuda	"	5
Grenada	"	5
St. Kitts and Nevis	"	5
Cambodia	Pre-shipment inspection fee.	0.8

Country	Purpose	Rate (%)
Laos	Pre-shipment inspection fees with minimum fees and 1% of goods valued above USD 30.000.	1
Myanmar	Landing charge.	0.5
Argentina	*Ad valorem* fees for inspection or pre-shipment inspection of imports.	
Bolivia	"	1.92
Burkina Faso	"	1
Ghana	"	1
Guinea	"	1.05
Haiti	"	4
Malawi	"	0.85
Mauritius	"	Specific fee.
Niger	"	1
Nigeria	"	1
Peru	"	Up to 1
The Gambia	Processing fees.	1.05
Mexico	"	0.8
Norway	Inspection or foodstuff taxes.	0.58-0.82
Egypt	(a) Service and inspection fee 1%;. (b) Additional service charge of 2% on goods subject to import duties of 5.29%; and. (c) 3% on goods subject to duties of 30% or higher.	1 2 3
Burundi	Service tax on all imports – in addition to the pre-shipment inspection fee (for imports of a value of more than USD 5.000) that amounted to 1.5% of the customs value.	6
Côte d'Ivoire	Service fee on imports carried by sea. Inspections firms charge an additional 0.75%.	0.6 0.75
Romania	Customs commission.	0.5
Hong Kong, China	Mandatory electronic system (EDI) for trade declarations – charge: 11HK$ in 1999.	11HK$.
Kenya	Import declaration fee, 2.75% on the customs value of all imports.	2.75

K. COMMUNITY LEVIES

Country	Purpose	Rate (%)	Date of introduction
Benin (ECOWAS)	ECOWAS customs community levy on imports from non-ECOWAS members.	0.5	
Burkina Faso (ECOWAS)	"		
The Gambia (ECOWAS)	"		
Ghana (ECOWAS)	"		
Guinea (ECOWAS)	"		
Mali (ECOWAS)	"		
Niger (ECOWAS)	"		
Senegal (ECOWAS)	"		
Togo (ECOWAS)	"		
Benin (WAEMU)	WAEMU community solidarity levy from non-WAEMU members.	1	
Burkina Faso (WAEMU)	"	1	
Mali (WAEMU)	"	1	
Niger (WAEMU)	"	1	
Senegal (WAEMU)	"	1	
Togo	WAEMU community solidarity levy in the beginning of 1998.	0.5	
Niger	Special import tax (TCI) on rice during 2000-2002.	10	

Chapter 10: The establishment of appeals procedures at the national level

General

Where an importer or exporter is dissatisfied with a decision taken by customs officials, he/she should have the right to request a reconsideration of the decision. The practice in most countries is to permit the concerned party to appeal against the decision to higher authorities in the customs administration, or to a tribunal within the department. The right to appeal to a court or a judicial body is generally available if the ruling by the higher authority or tribunal is not found satisfactory by the aggrieved party.

1. Proposals tabled by delegations

The proposals tabled by delegations suggest that any new rules that may be adopted should specifically provide for, *inter alia*:

* The right to appeal.
* Transparency.
* Standard time for the resolution of minor appeals
* The costs of such appeals are kept to the minimum

These proposals are listed in Box 16.

Box 16: The right to appeal and the release of goods

* *The legislation of each Member shall ensure that traders have the right of appeal, without penalty, against rulings and decisions by customs and other relevant border agencies concerning the specific importation, exportation, and transit of goods conduced by them. The appeal may be initially heard by the same agency or its supervisory authority prior to a review by separate and independent judicial, arbitral, or administrative tribunal (Japan and Mongolia, TN/TF/W/116).*

* *Members shall ensure that appeal procedures are carried out in a non-discriminatory manner, and that information concerning such procedures is made available to traders. Traders shall be allowed to be represented at all stages of appeal procedures by independent legal counsel (Japan and Mongolia, TN/TF/W/116).*

* *Members shall ensure that customs and other relevant border agencies set out a standard period for their review and correction of decisions and rulings under the appeal procedures (Japan and Mongolia, TN/TF/W/116).*

* *Members shall ensure that customs and other relevant border agencies afford opportunities for traders to raise complaints concerning rulings and decisions in an informal and convenient manner prior to the commencement of the appeal procedures. The relevant agencies shall, upon request, inform the traders of reasoning of the rulings and decisions including applied laws and regulations (Japan and Mongolia, TN/TF/W/116).*

* *"For imports, exports and goods in transit, there should be an obligation to provide a non discriminatory, legal right of appeal against customs and other agency rulings and decisions, initially within the same agency or other body, and subsequently to a separate judicial or administrative body. A standard time should be set for resolution of minor appeals at the administrative level (....) Companics should have the right to be represented at all stages of appeal procedures by an agent or legal representative..." (European Communities, TN/TF/W/6).*

◆ *"Development of legal and administrative appeal systems for lodging objections" (...) "against unfair administration of trade-related procedures"; "Publication of major judicial and administrative decisions against lodged appeals"; "Establishment of a complaints desk"* (Japan, Mongolia, Chinese Taipei, Pakistan and Peru, TN/TF/W/8).

Suggested Approach/Means

◆ *"[N]on discriminatory" "[p]rocedures for appeal should be easily accessible, including to SME's, and costs should be reasonable and commensurate with costs in providing for appeals"* (European Communities, TN/TF/W/6).

◆ *"Where a disputed decision is the subject of an appeal, goods should normally be released and the possibility be available in given circumstances for duty payment to be left in abeyance. This should be subject, where required by national legislation, to the provision of a guarantee, such as a surety or deposit"* (European Communities, TN/TF/W/6).

2. Applicable GATT rules

Since the provisions requiring countries to provide a right to appeal in their legislations already exist in Article X of GATT 1994 as well as in the Agreement on Customs Valuation, the intention of the delegations making the proposals appears to have been to secure a further clarification of these rules.

Para 3(b) of Article X requires all members to maintain 'judicial, arbitral or administrative tribunals or procedures for the purpose, *inter alia*, of the prompt review and correction of administrative action relating to customs matters.' It further provides that administrative tribunals or procedures established for reviewing customs decisions 'shall be independent of the agencies entrusted with administrative enforcement.'

The Agreement on Customs Valuation elaborates these provisions by requiring countries to provide a right to appeal against the determination of the customs value of the imported goods by customs. An initial right should be provided to appeal to an 'authority within customs' or to an 'independent body.' In case the importer is not satisfied with the decision, they should have a right to appeal without penalty to a judicial body (Article 11).

3. Provisions of the Kyoto Convention

The Kyoto Convention also contains provisions on Appeals on Customs matters. Box 17 contains the relevant standards.

Box 17: Appeals in customs matters

CHAPTER 10, WCO Kyoto Convention (General Annex)

A. RIGHT OF APPEAL

10.1. Standard
National legislation shall provide for a right of appeal in Customs matters.

10.2. Standard
Any person who is directly affected by a decision or omission of the Customs shall have the right of appeal.

10.3. Standard
The person directly affected by a decision or omission of the Customs shall be given, after having made a request to the Customs, the reasons for such decision or omission within a period specified in national legislation. This may or may not result in an appeal.

10.4. Standard
National legislation shall provide for the right of an initial appeal to the Customs.

10.5. Standard
Where an appeal to the Customs is dismissed, the appellant shall have the right of a further appeal to an authority independent of the Customs administration.
General Annex/Chapter 10 32.

10.6. Standard
In the final instance, the appellant shall have the right of appeal to a judicial authority.

B. FORM AND GROUNDS OF APPEAL

10.7. Standard
An appeal shall be lodged in writing and shall state the grounds on which it is being made.

10.8. Standard
A time limit shall be fixed for the lodgement of an appeal against a decision of the Customs and it shall be such as to allow the appellant sufficient time to study the contested decision and to prepare an appeal.

10.9. Standard
Where an appeal is to the Customs they shall not, as a matter of course, require that any supporting evidence be lodged together with the appeal but shall, in appropriate circumstances, allow a reasonable time for the lodgement of such evidence.
General Annex/Chapter 10 33.

C. CONSIDERATION OF APPEAL

10.10. Standard
The Customs shall give its ruling upon an appeal and written notice thereof to the appellant as soon as possible.

10.11. Standard
Where an appeal to the Customs is dismissed, the Customs shall set out the reasons therefore in writing and shall advise the appellant of his right to lodge any further appeal with an administrative or independent authority and of any time limit for the lodgement of such appeal.

10.12. Standard
Where an appeal is allowed, the Customs shall put their decision or the ruling of the independent or judicial authority into effect as soon as possible, except in cases where the Customs appeal against the ruling.

4. Points for consideration

The need to adopt new rules in this area would have to be considered, and would have to take into account that the provision of the rights of traders to appeal first to a higher authority within the customs administration or a tribunal and, if necessary, to a judicial body, already exist in GATT as well as in the Agreement on Customs Valuation. The Kyoto Convention also contains detailed provisions on all aspects of appeals procedures.

The proposals requiring countries to fix a 'standard time for the resolution of minor appeals' and to ensure that the costs of appeal are kept low may, however, pose problems for many developing countries in which there are backlogs of undecided cases due to many reasons, including a shortage of staff. Likewise, the costs of appeal depend largely on the level of fees charged by lawyers specialising in the field of customs law. Thus, there are limits to government intervention in keeping the costs of appeal as low as possible.

Another question relating to the above is how to identify 'a minor appeal.' According to some proposals, the obligation to fix a standard time is expected to apply only to this category of appeals. The proponents of the proposals have clarified that minor appeals may be defined as covering those cases involving low-value consignments, imports by individuals, payment of duties of less than EUR 1000, and others raising minor legal issues.

Chapter 11: The simplification of formalities and procedures

General

In addition to the rules governing the use of fees and other charges on imported and exported goods, Article VIII contains rules which, *inter alia*, call upon governments to:

- Minimise the incidence and complexity of import and export formalities;
- Simplify import and export documentation; and
- Review disciplines and formalities, if requested by another member country.

Specific proposals have been made regarding the improvement and clarification of these rules to ensure that:

- Import and export formalities are applied on a non-discriminatory basis;
- Periodic reviews of the procedures and formalities are undertaken;
- Consular formalities should be abolished;
- Documentation and other requirements are simplified and kept to the minimum; and
- Procedures and formalities are kept at the least trade restrictive level, or at levels that are not more burdensome and trade restrictive than necessary for meeting legitimate objectives.

1. Application of the non-discrimination principle

1.1 Proposals on the application of export and import formalities on a non-discriminatory basis

It is proposed that the commitment to apply non-discriminatory treatment should be built into the design and application of import and export customs procedures. However, the proposals recognise that in the exercise of their control functions, customs may have to be rigorous in their examination of goods originating in certain countries.

1.1.1 Points for consideration

Rigorous controls involving documentation scrutiny and physical checking are generally applied to imports from countries where past experience has shown that exporters from these countries are routinely engaging in the undervaluation of goods or other customs frauds. Customs may decide to apply such controls on the basis of risk assessment criteria or, where it has not been possible for them to adopt such a technique, on the basis of the confidential information collected. Thus, in actual practice, difficulties would arise while applying the principle of non-discrimination to procedures followed by customs in the clearance of goods.

Of relevance here is that para 3(a) of Article X imposes an obligation on countries to administer all their laws, regulations and decisions relating to customs matters in a 'uniform, impartial and reasonable way.' The difficulties encountered by customs in abiding by the principle of non-discrimination in the clearance of goods seem to be the reason why its application has not been included in the rules which only state that they should be applied in an impartial and reasonable manner.

1.2   Proposals on the periodic review of import and export procedures

Article VIII stipulates that countries should review import and export formalities when requested by another member.[63] The aim of the proposals is to clarify the rules asking members countries to voluntarily review their fees, charges, formalities and other requirements at reasonable intervals, irrespective of whether or not a request for such a review has been made by another member country.

1.2.1   Points for consideration

The proposal made by Hong Kong China recognises the difficulties that would arise in imposing a binding obligation on countries under the WTO system to undertake periodic reviews. In particular, it states that while countries could be urged to undertake such reviews, it may not be possible to define a rigid period of interval time, keeping in mind the differing circumstances in, and the measures adopted by different countries.

Constantly reviewing procedures involved in the implementation of customs and other rules is a management function, and is an important element of good governance. Thus, it should be left to each country to decide whether there is need for a review and if so, when it should be undertaken. International rules requiring countries to undertake reviews on a periodic basis could be counterproductive, and add unnecessary administrative burdens and costs.

2.   Proposals on the abolition of consular formalities

2.1   Proposals regarding the abolition of consular formalities

There is broad agreement among WTO member countries on the need to abolish consular formalities.

The term 'consular formalities' refers to the obligations of exporters to have invoices and other documents authenticated by its consular office or embassy (in the exporting country), before exports can take place.

Consular formalities create export delays, and increase transaction costs for exporters, particularly as consular offices charge special consular fees for copies of documents and airmail postage to the customs offices in the country.

As a result of the recommendations adopted in the years following the establishment of GATT, and subsequently after the Tokyo Round of Negotiations (1971 1979) calling on countries to abolish consular formalities,[64] very few countries are applying such formalities today. The proposals aim at ensuring the full implementation of the recommendations adopted in the past on the abolition of fees and formalities. Box 18 lists these proposals.

---

63   Para 2 of Article VIII reads as follows: 'A contracting party shall, upon request by another contracting party or by the CONTRACTING
      PARTIES, review the operation of its laws and regulations in the light of the provisions of this Article.'

64   See the WTO Guide to GATT Law and Practice, Vol. 1, p. 280 (WTO, 1995).

Box 18: The abolition of consular formalities

- ◆ *"Prohibition of requiring consular transactions, including consularization-related fees and charges, in connection with the importation of goods"* (Uganda and the United States, TN/TF/W/22).

- ◆ *"Practices such as the levying of "consular fees" or "consular invoices" and the like should be discontinued"* (European Communities and Australia, TN/TF/W/23).

- ◆ *" .... we often hear complaints from traders about high fees for consular invoices and certificates charged by importing Members"* (Chinese Taipei, TN/TF/W/25).

- ◆ *"Members could also agree to abolish documentation requirements such as demands for consular invoices (...)"* (New Zealand, Norway and Switzerland, TN/TF/W/36).

2.1.1 Points for consideration

Consular formalities have become outdated in situations where embassy officials seek to verify whether the value displayed on the invoice reflects the correct value of the goods being exported. This is because it is becoming increasingly possible for customs officials in importing countries to carry out such checks using data available on prices charged in the past, and other price data.

Such formalities are also inconsistent with the rules of the Agreement on Customs Valuation which, *inter alia*, require that except in cases where customs have doubts about the truth or accuracy of the value declared by the importer, they shall use it as a basis for determining the customs duty payable by the importer. Moreover, as such formalities are required only in a few countries, it may be possible to adopt a rule prohibiting their use.

3. Keeping documents simplified

3.1. Lodgement of the customs declaration by the importer

Goods may be imported not only for home use but also for exports after processing, within a certain time limit. They may be imported for transit to other countries. To facilitate the initiation of appropriate procedures, the importer (or another person acting on his behalf), lodges a Declaration informing customs about the purpose for which the goods have been imported.

Such a Declaration can be lodged in paper form or electronically. In certain cases where the value of the goods is low or below a certain threshold — particularly when such goods are brought into a customs territory by travellers — an oral declaration is considered sufficient by customs.

The declarants are expected to provide all the information in their goods Declaration that is deemed necessary by customs for:

- The assessment of duties and taxes;
- The collection of statistics; and
- The application of customs law.

In addition, the declarant may be required to furnish information needed by other agencies for ensuring that the imported products meet the requirements relating to technical regulations as well as safety and health standards.

3.2   Minimising documentation by using the UN Layout Key

In order to reduce the number of documents needed for submission, the United Nations Centre for Trade Facilitation and Electronic Business (UN/CEFACT) has developed the UN Layout Key for trade documents that could be used to facilitate the declaration. Taking into account the experience of the application of the Key, the WCO developed the Single Goods Declaration (SGD) in 1990. The form has been adapted, with minor modifications, by the European Union to meet the requirements of the customs administrations of its member countries. This single form has come to be known as the Single Administrative Document (SAD). The SAD form is widely used not only by the member countries of the European Union but also by other European countries. A modified form of SAD is also used by countries which have implemented the UNCTAD's Asycuda System.

The UN Layout Key (or its adaptations SGD and SAD) prescribes the size of the form and the 'minimum data' to be provided in a goods Declaration. It aims at ensuring that all the information needed for the clearance of goods by customs, and for approval by other agencies, is available in one place.

3.3   Supporting documents

Customs procedures generally require that the Declaration should be accompanied by other supporting documents at the time of submission to ascertain the correctness of the information provided. Examples of such documents are:

- The Commercial invoice;
- The Import and export licence;
- Documentary evidence of origin;
- The Document for preferential tariff treatment;
- The Health and Transport certificate; and
- Transfer documents.

The requirements relating to the presentation of such documents varies from country to country. Some countries require such documents to accompany the Declaration; others permit their presentation at a later stage; still others do not require them at all, provided they are available with the declarant.

3.4 The provisions of the Kyoto Convention

The Kyoto Convention prescribes guidelines and standards that countries should apply in the documents submitted to customs. These are listed in Boxes 19 and 20.

Box 19: Clearance and other customs formalities

Chapter 3, General Annex Guidelines, WCO Kyoto Convention:
Extract from Guideline No. 3.2 on 'Minimum data requirements'
'Standard 3.12'

Customs usually requires the following particulars in full detail or by code sets, as applicable:

(a) The Customs procedure requested.

(b) Particulars relating to persons:
- name and address of the declarant,
- name and address of the importer, and
- name and address of the consignor.

(c) Particulars relating to transport:
- mode of transport, and
- identification of the means of transport.

(d) Particulars relating to the goods:
- description of the goods,
- tariff classification of the goods,
- country of origin,
- country of dispatch or export,
- country of destination,
- description of the packages (number, nature, marks and numbers), and
- quantity, gross weight and net weight of the goods.

(e) Particulars for the assessment of import or export duties and taxes:
- rates of import or export duties and taxes,
- dutiable value or invoice price,
- exchange rate,
- information concerning tax bases other than value, such as weight, litres for alcohol products, carats for gold or gems, etc., and
- terms of delivery.

(f) Other particulars:
- information concerning preferential or other special treatment;
- reference to documents submitted in support of the Goods declaration; and
- place, date and signature of the declarant.

Where automated systems are used for Customs clearance, fewer data elements may be required since some of these can be generated automatically from other sources. For instance, the dutiable or Customs value can be obtained from the invoice price with some deductions and/or additions as necessary from the terms of delivery (f.o.b, c.i.f, c&f, etc.), or from information already available in the automated system such as the rate of exchange.

Box 20: The goods declaration (General Annex)

Chapter 3, WCO Kyoto Convention

(a) Goods declaration format and contents

3.11. Standard
The contents of the Goods declaration shall be prescribed by the Customs. The paper format of the Goods declaration shall conform to the UN-layout key.
For automated Customs clearance processes, the format of the electronically lodged Goods declaration shall be based on international standards for electronic information exchange as prescribed in the Customs Co-operation Council Recommendations on information technology.
General Annex/Chapter 3 8.

3.12. Standard
The Customs shall limit the data required in the Goods declaration to only such particulars as are deemed necessary for the assessment and collection of duties and taxes, the compilation of statistics and the application of Customs law.

3.13. Standard
Where, for reasons deemed valid by the Customs, the declarant does not have all the information required to make the Goods declaration, a provisional or incomplete Goods declaration shall be allowed to be lodged, provided that it contains the particulars deemed necessary by the Customs and that the declarant undertakes to complete it within a specified period.

3.14. Standard
If the Customs register a provisional or incomplete Goods declaration, the tariff treatment to be accorded to the goods shall not be different from that which would have been accorded had a complete and correct Goods declaration been lodged in the first instance.
The release of the goods shall not be delayed provided that any security required has been furnished to ensure collection of any applicable duties and taxes.

3.15. Standard
The Customs shall require the lodgement of the original Goods declaration and only the minimum number of copies necessary.
General Annex/Chapter 3 9.

(b) Documents supporting the Goods declaration

3.16. Standard
In support of the Goods declaration the Customs shall require only those documents necessary to permit control of the operation and to ensure that all requirements relating to the application of Customs law have been complied with.

3.17. Standard
Where certain supporting documents cannot be lodged with the Goods declaration for reasons deemed valid by the Customs, they shall allow production of those documents within a specified period.

3.18. Transitional Standard
The Customs shall permit the lodgement of supporting documents by electronic means.

3.19. Standard
The Customs shall not require a translation of the particulars of supporting documents except when necessary to permit processing of the Goods declaration.

4. Proposals on the simplification of documentation

4.1 Proposals on the reduction of import documentation tabled by delegations

The proposals call on countries to reduce import documentation required to be submitted by importers by adopting the UN Layout Key for customs declaration.

4.1.1 Points for consideration

Some developing countries have adopted the UN Layout Key as the format to be used by importers. However, a number of other developing countries appear reluctant to adopt it. Past experience of its use by EU members and other countries has shown that its format may have to be modified to suit the trading realities and conditions prevailing in a specific country.

A number of developing countries also require other supporting documents to be submitted alongside the main Declaration. While some of these may otherwise be considered redundant, in countries where the undervaluation of goods and other customs frauds are widely prevalent, the customs authorities consider them essential for ascertaining the authenticity of the information provided by the importer in his Declaration.

4.2 Proposals on the reduction of formalities, procedures and documentation requirements to the least trade restrictive levels

The proposals tabled on the simplification and reduction of formalities also suggest that there should be an obligation on countries to ensure that import and export formalities and procedures are not more trade restrictive than necessary to fulfil legitimate objectives (Hong Kong, China and Switzerland TN/TF/W/124/Rev.1 and the European Communities, TN/TF/W/46).

5. The relevance of the provisions of GATT and of the Agreement on TBT and SPS

The proposals are based on similar provisions in GATT Article XX and in the Agreements on TBT and SPS.

5.1 GATT Article XX

Art XX provides exceptions and allows countries to take measures that are not permitted under GATT rules in specific situations referred to in the Article, provided that they do not constitute 'arbitrary or unjustifiable discrimination' between countries where the same conditions prevail or 'disguised restrictions on international trade'. In taking such measures, countries are expected to rely on those that are least trade restrictive.

5.2 The TBT and SPS Agreements

The two Agreements lay down an obligation on all member countries to use international standards developed by international standard setting bodies as a basis for national technical regulations and SPS measures. Both Agreements provide that, where such regulations or measures are based on international *151* standards, it shall be presumed that they do not create unnecessary obstacles to international trade, although members may challenge this presumption (Article 2.5 TBT Agreement and Art 2.4 of the SPS Agreement).

These Agreements permit countries to deviate from the above rule to use international standards if certain conditions are met. The TBT Agreement permits such a deviation where the country adopting the standard considers that the international standard is inappropriate for inclusion in its national technical regulations. In the case of SPS measures, such a deviation is permitted where the country adopting the standard considers that the international standard would not result in providing the level of protection that is considered appropriate.

The two Agreements also lay down factors that should be taken into account in adopting technical regulations and SPS measures that are not based on international standards. The factors to be taken into account in the case of technical regulations include: available scientific evidence, technical information, related processing technology, and the intended use of the product. The SPS measures that are not based on international standards are permitted to be applied only after the country has carried out risk management based on available scientific evidence to determine the appropriate level of sanitary protection.

The adoption of technical regulations and SPS measures generally result in the prohibition or restrictions on the import of products that do not conform to the standards. In order to ensure that such standards do not cause unnecessary barriers to trade, the TBT Agreement calls on countries to ensure that technical regulations are not more trade restrictive than required for the attainment of legitimate objectives, taking into account the risks following non-fulfilment (Article 2.2 TBT Agreement). Likewise, the SPS Agreement requires countries to ensure that SPS measures are not more trade restrictive than necessary to achieve the appropriate level of sanitary and phytosanitary protection.

5.3 The feasibility of applying the concept of 'least trade restrictive' to trade facilitation

How far is it possible to incorporate the above concept in the new rules that may be developed and adopted in the area of trade facilitation? The answer to this question lies in the difference between the character of the measures taken under GATT Article XX as well as the TBT and SPS Agreements, and the procedures adopted for the clearance of goods through customs.

The measures taken under the 'exception' provisions of Art XX result in a violation of the GATT rules. Thus, they are permitted only if the conditions laid down by the Article are met. Also in reviewing such measures, the GATT panels generally examine whether the alternative measure which was less trade restrictive and could have been employed was available to the country taking the measure.

Technical regulations and SPS measures result in the prohibition of imports if the imported products do not conform to the standards prescribed by them. For instance, in determining the level of protection in the case of SPS measures, the concerned authorities, in most cases, have to consider some specific trade restrictive measures in order to maintain the level of sanitary protection they wish to extend for public health reasons. For instance, they may decide to only allow the imports of those products that meet the standards prescribed by the SPS measures, and prohibit others that do not meet such standards. Alternatively, they may – in the case of SPS measures – permit imports by requiring countries to adopt certain processing methods. A good example is fumigation which reduces the risk of imported products bringing in diseases prevailing in the exporting country.

The procedures and formalities adopted by countries for the clearance of goods through customs do not in themselves provide for the prohibition or restriction of imports and exports.

It could be argued that even though customs procedures do not in themselves impose trade restrictions, the way they are applied could have a restrictive or negative impact on trade. Thus, countries should be under obligation to apply them in such a way that they do not create more 'trade restrictive effects, than are necessary 'for the attainment of the legitimate objectives' for which such procedures are adopted.

This view raises two difficult issues:

● The nature of the criteria to be applied while determining whether a given customs procedure has more trade restrictive effects than necessary for the attainment of legitimate objectives, and

● The determination of the 'standard for review' to be adopted by Panels in examining the disputes that are brought to the WTO.

5.4   Difficulties in applying the necessity test

Under WTO jurisprudence, countries are expected to apply the 'necessity' test at the national level for this purpose. The TBT and SPS Agreements prescribe rules clarifying how the necessity test should be applied while adopting technical regulations and SPS measures. They state that the standards used in such regulations and measures must be based on 'scientific evidence.' The obligation to use scientific standards is stated more explicitly in the SPS measures than in the technical regulations. Because the criteria used for adopting the standard are based on 'science,' it is possible to make a relatively objective judgement about whether the SPS measures are justified and 'necessary'. It is assumed that the physical and chemical sciences, with their more theoretical foundations and well-defined methods for analysis, provide the most objective criteria to judge the need to apply the 'necessity' test.

However, despite the greater certainty and predictability of science-based criteria, the practical experience of the application of such provisions in the SPS Agreement has shown that many difficulties still remain. They arise because of serious differences in the opinions of scientists in a number of areas. Thus, national policy makers often have to choose between two or three conflicting opinions.

Even with such limitations, any criteria 'based on science' provides the most sound and objective basis for the investigating authorities to examine whether the measures adopted are not more trade restrictive than necessary for the attainment of legitimate objectives. In the area of trade facilitation, the investigating authorities do not generally use such predictable and definitive 'science based' criteria. Customs determine the extent of the control they wish to exercise over import or exports through document scrutiny, physical checking, or on the basis of information derived from past records of an importer's compliance with customs rules. Even though such information may have been collected by applying methods that are 'scientific,' the final judgment on the nature, type, and extent of control needed involves the exercise of a large degree of discretion by the checking authority. Morcover, some of the information which customs rely upon may be of a confidential nature, not to be disclosed to any outside investigating authorities.

5.5   The application of standards for the review of decisions of the regulatory authorities by judicial bodies

There is considerable debate among legal analysts about how trade restrictive rules and measures adopted on public health grounds causing unreasonable barriers to trade are being interpreted by judicial bodies in settling disputes. This is so even though the criteria used to decide the justification of such measures are based on science and, thus, provides a more predictable basis to the courts or judicial bodies on which to examine disputes in the area of trade facilitation.

While reviewing actions at the national level, regional and international investigating authorities rely on two standards which differ considerably from one another. The first is the 'deference standard.' Except in cases of 'manifest error,' under this standard the investigating authorities show deference to the 'inference of scientific justification' drawn by the authority taking the measure. The second standard is the *de novo* standard.' Under this standard, the investigating authorities have complete freedom to review the facts and make their own judgment about whether the inference drawn from the data or facts is really justifiable.

Generally speaking, national and regional courts appear to apply the deference standard in public health cases. For instance, while reviewing cases involving the prohibition of the import of meat from countries where the mad cow disease was widely prevalent to other member states of the EU, the European Court of Justice (ECJ) observed that the '[c]ommunity judicature must, when reviewing such measures, restrict itself to examining whether the exercise of such discretion is vitiated by a manifest error or omission or misuse of power, or whether the Commission did not clearly exceed the bounds of its discretion.'[65] Some legal scholars consider that the ECJ relies on the 'deference standard' in examining complaints against the Commission because it is a member of the 'family of Community institutions' and, thus, it proceeds on the basis that if restrictive measures are applied, the Commission has 'probably good reasons for doings so.'

The WTO's Dispute Settlement Understanding, as well as WTO Agreements are silent about which standard the Panels or Appellate Body should apply for review. The only exception to this is the Agreement on Anti-dumping Practices (AD Agreement). Art 17 of the AD Agreement incorporates a standard which comes quite close to the 'deference standard.' The Article provides that the Panels and Appellate Body shall:

*   In assessing whether the establishment of facts by the investigating authorities was 'proper' and whether the evaluation was objective and unbiased, not overturn the conclusion even though it might itself have reached a different conclusion, where the objectivity of the investigating authorities is not in doubt, and

*   In examining issues of law, where the relevant provision of the Agreement admits more than one possible interpretation, find the measure complained about to be in conformity with the Agreement if it rests on one of the permissible interpretations.

In the US Hormone-Treated Meat case, the EC argued that the Panel should apply the 'deferential reasonableness standard' while reviewing a member's determination that a 'particular inference from the available data is scientifically plausible.' It considered that this standard should normally be applied in all cases where the panels are examining cases involving 'highly complex factual situations,' as the *de novo* standard could lead to a substitution of the judgment' made by the authority taking the measure by the judgment of facts by the Panel.

---

65   Natalie McNeils, 'The Role of the Judge in the EU and WTO: Lessons from the BSE and Hormones Cases' in T. Cottier and P.C. Mavroidis (Eds.), P. Blatter (Associate ed.), The Role of the Judge in International Trade Regulation – Experience and Lessons for the WTO, pp. 230-234.

The Appellate Body rejected the plea. Taking into account the guidance provided by the SPS Agreement, it stated that the standards they proposed to apply could neither be 'total deference' nor '*de novo*' – it had to be somewhere in between.[66]

In the Mad Cow case, the ECJ held that the Commission's ban was justifiable; in the Hormone-Treated Meat case, the WTO Appellate Body ruled that the ban was not justified. It would by unrealistic to hold that the opposing decisions were entirely influenced by the different standards used; both the decisions may have been appropriate on the basis of merit. At the same time, it has to be recognised that the final outcome may be influenced by the standard that is used – either total 'deference' or '*de novo.*'

In this context, it appears that there may be insurmountable difficulties in applying the concept that the measures adopted should 'not be more trade restrictive than necessary for the attainment of [the] legitimate objectives' embodied in the TBT and SPS Agreements in any disciplines that may be adopted in the area of trade facilitation. This is so for the following reasons:

- The criteria for determining whether the customs procedures are creating 'more than necessary' barrier effects, would not be based on science (as is the case with technical regulations and SPS measures) but on standards involving judgments made by customs authorities on the basis of the information available to them, and

- Unless it is clearly recognised that the bodies reviewing national decisions must apply the standard which requires them to show 'deference' to the judgment by the customs authorities (except in the case of manifest error), the possibility of the reviewing bodies substituting their own judgment for that of the customs authorities is likely to exist.

Also, these issues would have to be kept in mind while considering how far, and to what extent, the WTO dispute settlement procedures can be applied at this stage for sorting out the differences that may arise in the application of rules in this area.

---

66   *Ibid*, p. 232

Chapter 12: The establishment of a mechanism for the exchange of customs related information among WTO member countries

General

It is reasonably clear that, for the effective and efficient administration of customs clearance procedures, customs authorities must have ready access to data regarding prices and other information. In order to overcome the relative absence of such data, proposals have been tabled for the establishment of a multilateral mechanism for cooperation among countries about the exchange of information needed by the customs authorities.

These proposals divide the information required by customs into two categories:

- Information required by customs *generally* to ensure compliance of domestic laws and regulations, and

- Information required by them for the specific investigations of cases of non-compliance.

A proposal on the establishment of a multilateral mechanism for the exchange of information under the first category has been tabled by India and the USA (TN/TF/W/57). Another proposal on the establishment of a similar mechanism for the exchange of information under the second category has been tabled by India (TN/TF/W/68).

1. The information required by customs to ensure compliance of domestic laws and regulations

It has been proposed that a multilateral mechanism should be established for the exchange of a 'defined universe of trade transaction information.' Such information could include 'documentation' or 'data elements' that relate to the movement of goods across borders (e.g. the name of the importing or exporting party, the origin of goods, the description of goods, their classification, their declared value, the shipper etc). The establishment of such a mechanism would serve a dual purpose.

- It would enhance the ability of customs administrations to ensure compliance with domestic laws and regulations, and

- It would improve their ability to adopt new methods for performing functions 'away from the border' with a view to facilitating trade. Such methods include the 'pre-arrival clearance of goods' and allowing the clearance of goods by authorised importers subject to post-import audit.

The proposal suggests that the establishment of such an information exchange mechanism would have to be 'linked to the implementation of the WCO Data Model.' Advancements in Information Technology and logistics have now made it possible to establish such a mechanism at the multilateral level. The establishment of such a mechanism would benefit 'not only individual members but also the whole trading system.'

Thus, negotiations in this area should aim at, *inter alia*:

- Defining the 'universe of trade transactions' that should be covered;

- Exploring the potential of the use of the WTO Customs Data Model for this purpose;

- Addressing confidentiality matters;

- Assessing the technical assistance needs, implementation, transitions, and other requirements of developing countries; and

- Identifying the possibility of cooperating with other international organisations and resource providers in meeting the technical assistance needs of developing countries.

The genesis of the proposal can be traced to the initiatives taken by the Group of 7 – the seven largest economically developed countries. At a meeting of their Heads of States in 1996, it was decided that action must be taken to deal with the 'redundant and non-standardised systems' used by customs in different countries which were posing barriers to international trade.

To pursue this Decision, a Group of customs experts was established 'to standardise and reduce the amount of data necessary to meet customs requirements.' The Customs Data Model developed by the Group was transmitted to the WCO to encourage its application by other countries as well as by international trade and development organisations.

Box 21 provides further information on the Customs Data Model.

Box 21: The WCO Customs Data Model

'What is the WCO Customs Data Model?

The WCO Customs Data Model provides a maximum framework of standard and harmonised
sets of data and standard electronic messages to be submitted by trade for Customs and other regulatory purposes to accomplish formalities for the arrival, departure, transit and clearance of goods in international cross-border trade.

What are the benefits of the Customs Data Model?

The Customs Data Model enables the various information systems of a Customs service, its trading partners as well as co-operating Customs and other regulatory authorities to work together in the most effective way possible.

The many benefits of the Customs Data Model include:

- Promoting safe and secure borders by establishing a common platform for regulatory data exchange enabling early sharing of information;

- Helping co-operating export and import Customs to offer authorised traders end-to-end premium procedures and simple integrated treatment of the total transaction;

- Contributing to rapid release;

- Eliminating redundant and repetitive data submitted by the carrier and the importer;

- Reducing the amount of data required to be presented at time of release;

- Reducing compliance costs;

- Promoting greater Customs cooperation.

How and when will the Customs Data Model be implemented?

The implementation of the WCO Customs Data Model will take place at the national level. However, the full benefits of the Customs Data Model will be materialised by implementation on a bilateral or multilateral basis. G7 countries and Russia have so far agreed to implement the WCO Customs Data Model where possible by 2005. The implementation should take place only after close consultation with trade. It is recognised that the implementation will happen over a period of time thus requiring flexibility from all parties.'

Source: All quotes are from the WCO Fact Sheet on the 'The WCO Customs Data Model', see the WCO website (visited on 21 November 2005): http://www.wcoomd.org/ie/En/Topics_Issues/FacilitationCustomsProcedures/facil_wco_data_model.htm

1.1   Points for consideration

The main objective of the model is to standardise the information needed by customs, both for the clearance of goods and for the security of borders, by developing 'data sets' for cargo reports, and for import and export data (see Box 21 for details), and align the standards adopted to electronic transmission systems. This would enable traders to submit import and export declarations electronically, and facilitate the speedy clearance of goods by adopting such systems as 'single window clearance' and 'authorised importers.'

The ability of countries to participate in the system for the exchange of information on the basis of the WCO Customs Data Model would depend greatly on how far the use of Information Technology is developed and spread among the trading community. Thus, participation in the system would have to remain optional for a number of countries that have not been able to adopt Information Technology for the submission of the data required for the clearance of goods through customs by traders and nor has its use penetrated the business community.

2. The establishment of a separate mechanism for the exchange of information when there is reason to doubt the declarations made by importers/exporters

In addition to the establishment of the general mechanism for the exchange of data and information as described above, another proposal, tabled by India, envisages a separate mechanism for:

● Exchanging specific information upon request, about matters such as customs valuation, HS classification, the full and accurate description of goods, quantity, the origin of goods etc. in identified cases where there is reason to doubt the truth or accuracy of the declaration filed by the importer or exporter. The request for information would be limited to the data elements contained in the import or export declaration.

● Providing the document(s) filed in support of goods declarations to the requesting country for investigative and/or judicial processes in appropriate cases.

This proposal emphasises that, in order to ensure that such requirements do not put an additional burden on customs administrations in terms of resources, requests should be confined to a 'limited number of cases' in which investigating authorities, after carrying out necessary internal verification, have reasons to doubt the truth or accuracy 'of any element of the import and export declaration or supporting document.' Moreover, the proposal also indicates guidelines regarding, *inter alia*, the nature of the information and the supporting documents that could be required; procedures that could be established at the national level for the exchange of information, and for ensuring the confidentiality of the information. Box 22 provides further details on the proposal.

Box 22: Proposal on the information required in cases of doubt about the declaration made by an importer/exporter (TN/TF/W/68)

The information to be requested would contain specific details (e.g. description of goods, grade or specification, HS classification, value, quantity, country of origin, etc.) concerning the transaction. Supporting documents, wherever required, would include the commercial invoice, packing list, certificate of origin etc. These documents would be certified or authenticated copies. The information sought could also be used for confirming the authenticity of supporting document(s).

The procedure to be followed for the exchange of information could be through a nodal agency, to be designated by each customs administration and notified to the WTO. The designated nodal agency would be required to confirm that all necessary internal checks have been carried out within the country of import or export, and that the information sought is necessary to secure compliance with the customs requirements of the requesting country. The request for assistance should be made in one of the three official languages of the WTO. Such requests could be made in writing (also submitted electronically). Any request for information should include brief details of the case, nature of doubt, and reasons for doubting the truth or accuracy of the declaration, results of the internal verification already carried out, and the details of the information required from the requested administration. It would be desirable to lay down a reasonable time limit for furnishing the information so that the requesting country is assured of a response.

This proposal envisages that the information exchanged should be subject to a confidentiality clause; viz. that the information supplied should not be disclosed, except to the extent required in judicial proceedings. A similar provision exists in Article 10 of the WTO Agreement on Customs Valuation. Any information exchanged through this cooperation mechanism can hardly be effective unless it can be used as evidence in judicial proceedings to secure customs compliance. Under various GATT and WTO provisions (Article X of GATT, Article 11 of the Agreement on Customs Valuation), Members are obliged to have strong judicial systems for the review of decisions taken by customs authorities. Also, during the present negotiations, proposals have been made to improve the system of judicial review. This puts a strict burden of proof on the customs administration to 'establish a violation.' Evidence gathered from other administrations can, many a time, be crucial in discharging this burden of proof. Thus, it is essential that the information obtained through the proposed cooperation mechanism is allowed to be used as evidence in judicial proceedings without citing the cover of confidentiality.

A related concern of some Members is with regard to the sharing of information on account of domestic confidentiality laws. There is need for greater clarity on this issue. The declarations presented before the two customs administrations (importing and exporting) ought to be based on identical information relating to the transaction. In any case, all relevant particulars in respect of goods are to be presented to the customs administrations in both countries. In the case of a true and accurate declaration, the same information would be available with the requesting customs administration as well. Hence, confidentiality concerns should not include the sharing of such information with the customs administration of another Member, but only in terms of making it public. In this regard, a general principle can be adopted stipulating that the information obtained under this mechanism shall be afforded the same degree of confidentiality by the receiving Member that it applies to similar information in its custody.

3. History of the negotiations on a similar proposal

The above proposal is not new. A similar one, tabled by India at the Doha Ministerial Conference, was discussed both in the WTO Committee on Customs Valuation and in the WCO Policy Commission. In the discussions, both the thrust and the approach in the proposal received strong support from many delegations of developing countries. However, it was strongly opposed by the delegations of developed countries.

The reasons for the opposition of the delegations of developed countries are summarised below:

- Their domestic legislations (confidentiality laws, secrecy laws) prevent their customs authorities from 'routinely' providing such information. Except in cases of allegations of fraud or criminal cases, the legislations of some of these countries even contain the outright prohibition on providing such information.

- They felt that the value data at the disposal of the exporting countries is not always reliable, and not subject to the same level of scrutiny as in the importing country. Moreover, they felt that some countries keep export value information only for statistical purposes; others keep data only on a transaction-by-transaction basis.

- They argued that the fact that the declared import value often matches the declared export value does not necessarily mean that the goods are not under- or over-valued, as there could be collusive deals between exporters and importers to declare the same value. Likewise, it may not always be correct to assume that there is fraud simply on the grounds of a discrepancy between the two prices. They felt that, in all such cases, verification by the customs administrations of the exporting countries is needed. Thus, in the view of the developed countries, this could lead to the shifting of the burden of investigation from importing to exporting countries – a situation they were not willing to accept.

- They argued that the establishment of a mechanism could lead to an avalanche of requests that would place an unnecessary burden on customs administrations of the exporting country to provide information to the importing country. Some customs administrations may not have the resources required for this purpose.

In response to the concern of developed countries that the establishment of the mechanism could lead to a large number of requests, the WCO Technical Committee on Valuation adopted a Guide for the Exchange of Customs Valuation Information in early 2003. The Guide was also submitted to the WTO Committee on Customs Valuation. This Guide lists practical measures to ensure that the requests for information made to an exporting country are kept to the minimum. It provides a 'checklist for valuation actions' to be taken by an importing customs administration before requesting information from the exporting country. The steps are quite demanding and, according to some analysts, 'would ensure that such requests would neither be frivolous nor substitute for diligent customs work in the country', requesting for such information.[67]

Developing countries have argued that the difficulties encountered by the customs administrations of exporting countries in verifying the values declared by the exporter should not be exaggerated. The fiscal authorities in these countries, responsible for work on the collection of value added tax (VAT), verify most export values when examining the requests of exporters for VAT credits or refunds. Coordination between customs administrations and VAT refund authorities could easily facilitate compliance with the obligations that would be imposed on exporting countries by an information exchange system.

---

67 Adrien Goorman and Luc de Wulf, 'Customs Valuation in Developing Countries and the World Trade Organization Valuation Rules', in Luc De Wulf and José B. Sokol, *Customs Modernization Handbook*, World Bank (Washington D.C. 2005), pp.166-167.

3.1   Points for consideration

The proposal tabled by India adds more precision and specificity to the proposal it tabled earlier. It also attempts to respond to some of the points made by developed countries in past discussions. However, it remains to be seen whether the developed countries would show a readiness to change the positions they have taken so far.

The establishment of the mechanism would also require exporting developing countries to furnish information on export prices when requested by importing countries. As south-south trade increases in the coming years, such requests from importing developing countries to exporting developing countries are expected to increase. The Indian proposal recognises that developing countries may need technical assistance to meet such requests. However, it points out that the 'technical assistance needs are not likely to be significant as such cooperation can be effected through the existing administrative set up of the customs administrations.'

Chapter 13: Preshipment inspection

General

Delays in the clearance of goods often occur in many developing countries because, in doubtful cases, customs do not have reliable and updated price information to ascertain whether the value declared by importers reflects the correct value of the goods imported. Such delays may also occur as the information required for determining the tariff classification of the imported goods, or the rules of origin, are not readily available with the customs authority. To overcome these difficulties, a number of developing countries are currently using the services of preshipment inspection (PSI) companies for:

- The physical checking of the goods to be imported in the countries of export;
- Advice on the prices of the products to be imported; and
- Advice on tariff classification.

The European Union has proposed that 'members set a deadline for the elimination of PSI where it substitutes for functioning customs services and use the time available to make domestic customs administration become more fully functional'. During the transition period, WTO members should also 'not ... introduce new PSI arrangements' (European Commission (TN/TF/W/46).

This chapter provides the background information useful to delegations in examining how far it is possible for countries using the services of PSI companies (or for those that may need PSI services) to make binding commitments in this area.

1. The use of PSI Services

Preshipment inspection companies have been providing services to the governments of developing countries in the area of customs since the mid-1980s. Prior to this period, their services were used by central banks to help them address the issue of capital flight resulting from the overvaluation of imports. With the gradual removal of control over capital flows, the focus of PSI services shifted to assisting governments in ensuring that the revenues from customs duties were fully collected (by controlling the 'under-invoicing' of imported goods by traders), and to advising them about the correct tariff classification of goods.

The early programmes aimed at preventing the flight of capital through the 'over invoicing' of imported goods, reviewing contract prices, and requesting price reductions if they were considered to be in excess of prevailing export prices. All these issues, along with claims about delays in conducting the inspection of goods to be imported, caused friction and complaints by exporters. Since the 1980s, the emphasis of PSI programmes has gradually changed from controlling the flight of capital to assisting countries in collecting the customs duty that is due, and to identifying transactions in which goods are being undervalued by importers. The practices followed by these companies for assessing the correct value, and for the physical checking of goods made some developed countries exporting to the countries using PSI services complain that the size of such services were constituting non tariff barriers to trade.

2. The provisions of the Agreement on Preshipment Inspection

The concerns of some exporting countries with the use of PSI services resulted in the adoption of a WTO Agreement on Preshipment Inspection in the Uruguay Round. The Preamble to the Agreement notes that developing countries were relying too much on the services of preshipment inspection companies, and states that they should be permitted to use them only as long as they felt there was 'need' to rely on their services for the verification of the 'quality, quantity or price of imported goods.'

The substantive provisions of the Agreement establish a framework of rights and obligations for both 'PSI-using countries' and 'exporter countries.'

3. The obligations of countries using PSI services

Under the Agreement, the obligations on countries using the services of PSI companies aim at ensuring the reduction or elimination of the practical problems encountered by exporters. These include lengthy procedures for price verification and for carrying out physical inspections causing unnecessary delays, the lack of transparency in the procedures followed, and the treatment of confidential information. Towards this end, the Agreement contains provisions covering, *inter alia*:

- The extension of MFN and national treatment;
- The protection of confidential business information;
- The avoidance of unreasonable delays; and
- The use of specific guidelines for conducting price verification.

In order to control foreign exchange and minimize the flight of capital, the Agreement provides price verification guidelines for checking whether a declared contract price is in line with the export market price. PSI companies may compare the contract price with the price of identical or similar goods offered for export from the same country of exportation:

- To the country of importation, and
- To other markets.

However, where for price comparison purposes, the prices charged for export to countries other than the country of importation are used, economic and other factors influencing the prices charged to different countries should be taken into account. In other words, the rules recognise that firms often charge varying prices for different markets, taking into account demand and growth potential as well as factors such as per capita income and standards of living. For example, an exporting firm may charge higher prices for its export of shirts to Europe than it does for its export of shirts to Africa. The Agreement stipulates that when third-country prices are used for price-comparison purposes, the factors responsible for variations in the prices charged to importers in different countries should be taken into account. PSI companies should not 'arbitrarily impose the lowest price upon the shipment.' In addition, it states that PSI companies should make appropriate allowances for certain 'applicable adjusting factors' regarding the export price of the goods being inspected and the prices of identical or similar goods used for price comparison.

The Agreement stipulates, as per Footnote 4, that the obligations of user members with respect to the services of PSI entities in connection with customs valuation shall be the same as the obligations they have accepted under GATT 1994 and other Multilateral Trade Agreements. In essence, PSI entities are required to follow the provisions of the Agreement on Customs Valuation when providing technical advice to Customs Administrations for customs valuation purposes.

The Agreement also imposes certain obligations on countries which export to PSI-using countries. These are designated in the Agreement as 'exporting countries.' The main obligations imposed by the Agreement are two.

- Non-discrimination: laws and regulations that may have been adopted to govern the operation of PSI services should be applied on a non-discriminatory basis; and

- Transparency: all such laws and regulations should be published.

As noted above, the Agreement envisaged the use of preshipment inspection by developing countries only in the short term. In the long term, the objective of these countries should be to reduce the reliance on PSI services in the detection of customs malpractices and fraud by gradually developing the technical capacities of their customs administrations to deal with such practices. To assist PSI-using countries in building such capacities, the Agreement calls on exporting countries to provide them with technical assistance to reduce their reliance on PSI services for verifying prices.

4. The present situation regarding the use of PSI Services

About 30 developing or transition economies are currently using PSI services (see Table 2 at the end of this chapter). The majority of them are least developed countries. Some of these countries use the services of more than one company. In such cases, contracts are allocated to the companies either on a geographical basis or on an importer choice basis. A few countries use the services of these companies in relation to the imports of a limited number of products.

PSI programmers frequently require PSI companies to physically inspect all imports except:

- Low value shipments (the threshold may vary between US$ 5,000 to US$ 2,000);
- Duty free imports;
- Imports of defence related supplies;
- Diplomatic supplies;
- Works of art and precious stones; and
- Personal effects.

However, in recent years some PSI programmes have adopted selective inspection techniques based on risk assessment. As a result, it is no longer necessary to systematically inspect every shipment.

Goods handled by PSI companies are cleared by customs only if they are accompanied by a 'clean report on the findings'. Such reports indicate that the goods have been subject to inspections before shipment which check whether they conform to the declared contractual specifications (quality/quantity), and to the eligibility requirements (e.g. import prohibitions, product labelling) of the importing country. They also provide technical advice to customs on prices and other related aspects for customs valuation and classification purposes.

Under the rules of the Agreement on Customs Valuation, the primary responsibility for determining the value of imported goods for customs purposes rests with the customs authority itself. Except where there are doubts about the truth or accuracy of the importer's declaration, these rules require customs to determine the duty payable on the basis of the value declared by importers. In these cases, customs may rely on the advisory opinion provided by the PSI companies regarding the value of the goods. Their 'clear report of findings' can help in deciding whether the value declared by the importer should be used for the calculation of the customs duty payable. However, in cases where, on the basis of such advisory opinion, customs decide to reject the importer's declared value, under the rules of the Agreement on Customs Valuation, they cannot determine the value as being based on the one recommended by the PSI company. When the value declared by the importer is not acceptable, they are obliged to determine it on the basis of the methods that have been specified in the Agreement for the determination of the value of imported goods for customs purposes.

5. The cost of PSI services

The use of PSI services costs the government or the importers between 0.6 to 1% of the value of the inspected shipments.

6. Opinions on the benefits of the use of PSI services

The provisions of the Agreement on Preshipment Inspection have generally been regarded as successful in ensuring uniformity and transparency in the conduct of PSI companies by the different PSI entities. The International Federation of Inspection Agencies (IFIA), of which most PSI entities are members, has integrated the provisions of the Agreement on PSI into their PSI Code of Practice, compliance with which is periodically audited by independent certification bodies as a condition of IFIA Membership.

However, opinions regarding the benefits accruing from the use of PSI services vary. Some analysts consider the use of such services as facilitating the clearance of goods in countries where, because of the lack of data required for price comparison purposes, the customs administration face serious difficulties in verifying invoice prices; others consider the use of such services as being a disincentive to customs administrations in building their own a databases, thus leading to the postponement of customs reform.

The success of PSI programmes for customs purposes has, to a large extent, been dependent on the commitment and support of the customs administrations. Where there has been good cooperation between customs and the PSI entities, and where the information and training provided by the PSI entities has been properly utilised, positive results have been achieved. On the other hand, where the Government has imposed the support of the Customs, there has been a tendency for the PSI information not to be properly utilised.

In the past, many of the difficulties relating to the use of PSI services have arisen due to the opposition of customs administrations, some of which have regarded PSI as putting unnecessary restraints on their authority. Typically, such resistance has occurred in countries where the decision to use PSI has been taken by governments, no doubt in order to bring customs related corruption under control, but without proper consultation with customs.

In the late 1990s, the image of PSI companies was greatly tarnished by reports about such companies making payments to political leaders and responsible officials in order to secure contracts. Some major PSI companies promptly addressed the situation by adopting codes of professional conduct and, subsequently, IFIA adopted an IFIA Code of Conduct for the entire inspection industry. It should be noted that verification by independent auditing firms of the implementation and compliance with the Code by each PSI company is now a prerequisite for its IFIA Membership.

6.1   Points for consideration

The evidence regarding the usefulness of PSI companies is, at best, anecdotal. There is a wide gap between the views of analysts considering such services useful, and others who maintain that they should be prohibited. Broadly speaking, however, it would appear that in countries where the practice of the undervaluation of goods is widely prevalent and where it is not possible for customs to ascertain the true value of imported goods, the use of such services has probably resulted in the facilitation of trade and a fuller collection of the revenues due.

Also, technological developments, particularly in the IT field, have made a number of PSI companies change their verification practices: instead of undertaking physical inspections and price verification in the exporting countries prior to the shipment of goods, these are now being performed in the importing countries after the goods have entered their customs territory. This is being done by:

- The use of cargo scanning equipment;
- The establishment of risk management databases; and
- The adoption of IT systems (such as the community network system) to facilitate the implementation of the single window concept.

The fundamental change in the nature of the services provided by PSI companies – i.e. providing services not prior to shipment but after the arrival of goods in the importing country (or country to which the goods are 'destined') – has resulted in a significant reduction in objections by exporting countries to the use of their services by developing countries, as compared to earlier years.

Examples of countries where such services are being provided by PSI companies at the country of destination include the following:

Ghana: in which PSI has been replaced by Destination Inspection requiring the use of cargo scanners on arrival, coupled with customs valuation and classification support. These have been additionally enhanced with the implementation of a trade community network. All these have resulted in the significant reduction of clearance time and an improvement in revenue collection.

Tanzania: in which PSI has been replaced by Destination Inspection with cargo scanning.

Nigeria: in which PSI is in the process of being phased out and replaced by a Destination Inspection programme with cargo scanning, as well as risk management support to Customs.

Madagascar: in which the PSI programme is being progressively phased out in favour of cargo scanning on arrival, and the implementation of a trade community network.

Mexico: in which a post-entry valuation support programme to validate documentation and verify the existence of manufacturers and exporters in an effort to combat fraud is already being implemented.

It should be noted that, along with providing services in the country of destination, PSI companies are also working closely and in cooperation with customs. In most countries, their services form an integral part of capacity building programmes. Typically, these programmes include the establishment of valuation and risk databases as risk management tools.

From the strictly legal point of view, it may not be appropriate to treat the advisory services or technical assistance provided at the country of destination as PSI services, and this even though they may be provided by the same companies which, in the past, provided them in the country of exportation. The Agreement on Preshipment Inspection provides that the term 'preshipment inspection' by definition means 'inspection carried out in the territory of exporter members' (Preamble to the Agreement). The physical inspection of imported goods, and their price verification carried out by private companies in the country of destination, fall outside this definition of preshipment inspection. Consequently, the provisions of the PSI Agreements are, prima facie, not applicable to the services provided by private companies in the country of destination. This situation would suggest that the proposal for the prohibition of PSI services that has been tabled by some delegations would apply only to the inspection and other related services provided by private companies to the governments of importing countries in the country of exportation, and not when they are provided in the country of importation.

In this context, it is important to note that, apart from PSI companies, IT companies are also developing 'data warehouses' on world prices and systems to label and track internationally traded goods. Their programmes could provide information to buyers and sellers worldwide via 'outline access databases' in which prices are updated through an international network of representatives and agents. These representatives are required to keep the specifications and prices of their products updated at all times.

These IT companies could assist customs in building up the national data bases required by customs for price comparison purposes, and keep them updated – especially for products that figure generally in their imports – at all times.

Information on products not included in a country's database could be obtained from the central international database of the company providing the services via the Internet. These companies consider that the price data provided by them could be used by customs for price comparison purposes in accordance with the WTO rules on valuation. This data could also be relied upon by customs in court cases where there is a decision to reject the value declared by customs and fix it on the basis of the information on the price provided by the company.

Table 2: Countries using PSI Services[68]

Programmes for Customs (C) and/or Forex (F) Purposes

Country	Type	Mandated Member(s) of IFIA PSI Committee	IFIA Member Choice
Angola	C	BIVAC	-
Bangladesh	C	BIVAC, Cotecna, Intertek, SGS	Geographical
Benin	C	BIVAC	-
Burkina Faso	C	Cotecna	-
Burundi	F & C (Selective) ❶∞	SGS	-
Cambodia	C	SGS	-
Cameroon	C	SGS	-
Central African Rep.	C	BIVAC	-
Chad	C	BIVAC	-
Comoros	C	Cotecna	-
Congo	C	BIVAC	-
Cote d'Ivoire	C	BIVAC	-
Dem. Rep. Congo	F & C	BIVAC	-
Ecuador	C	Baltic Control, BIVAC, Cotecna, Intertek, SGS	Importer
Ghana	C (Destination Inspection) ❹	BIVAC, Cotecna	Air & land-/sea-freight
Haiti	C (Selective) ❶	SGS	-
Iran	C (Importer's discretion)	BIVAC, Inspectorate, Intertek, OMIC, SGS	Importer
Iran	F	BIVAC, Cotecna, Inspectorate, Intertek, OMIC, SGS	Importer
Liberia	C	BIVAC	-
Madagascar	C (Selective) ❶∞	SGS	-
Malawi	F & C (Selective) ❶∞	Intertek	-
Mali	F & C	Cotecna	-
Mauritania	C	SGS	-
Mexico	C ❷ ,	BIVAC, Intertek, SGS	Importer
Mozambique	C	Intertek	-
Niger	C	Cotecna	-
Nigeria	F & C ❸	Cotecna, Intertek, SGS	Geographical
Nigeria	C (Destination Inspection) ❹	Cotecna, SGS	Port of Arrival
Senegal	C	Cotecna	-
Sierra Leone	C	Intertek	-
Tanzania	C (Destination Inspection) ❹	Cotecna	-
Togo	C	Cotecna	-
Uzbekistan	F & C	CU International, Intertek, OMIC, SGS	Importer / Exporter
Zanzibar	F (Govt. discretion)	SGS	-

❶ "Selective": only certain shipments subject to physical PSI based on risk assessment.

❷ Only certain categories & origins of goods, if their unit value is inferior to estimated prices published by the Government.

❸ Forms M (Inspection Orders) approved by 31 December 2005 subject to PSI, where applicable, until 31 March 2006. (All other imports are no longer subject to PSI but subject to Destination Inspection upon arrival in Nigeria).

❹ Destination Inspection may include price verification and classification on a pre-shipment or post-shipment basis.

68 Programmes subject to the WTO Agreement on PSI, operated by members of the International Federation of Inspection Agencies (IFIA), status as of January 2006.

PART FOUR

Techniques and Methods used by Customs in the Clearance of Goods

Chapter 14: Risk management and other techniques in the clearance of goods: authorised importers and exporters

General

The proposals aimed at clarifying the rules and measures regarding trade policy issues (as discussed in Part Three of the Handbook) need to be distinguished from other techniques and methods which countries are encouraged to adopt in the day-to-day application of customs procedures in order to expedite the clearance of goods. This Part of the Handbook provides background information, and analyses the advantages that could accrue to developing countries by applying risk assessment, risk management and other techniques in the long term, and the difficulties they may encounter in applying such techniques in the short and medium term.

This chapter describes the proposals that have been tabled on:

* The application of risk management techniques;
* Authorised importers; and
* Post-clearance audits.

1. Proposals on the use of risk assessment

The proposals that urge countries to adopt risk assessment and management techniques are listed in Box 23.

Box 23: Risk management

◆ Apply risk management techniques, minimizing customs interventions in the flow of legitimate goods (Chinese Taipei, TN/TF/W/10).

◆ *"Conduct examination and inspection based on risk management." "... introduce simplified import and export formalities for authorised traders which have a high level of compliance with trade related laws and regulations"* (Japan, Mongolia, Peru and Chinese Taipei, TN/TF/W/17).

◆ Introduce and use risk assessment and management procedures (Korea, TN/TF/W/18).

◆ *"Establishment of disciplines on the application of risk assessment criteria ... "* (Peru, TN/TF/W/30).

◆ *"... use of risk management techniques in customs clearance..."* (Turkey, TN/TF/W45).

◆ *"Use of risk analysis methods based, as appropriate, on relevant international standards and practices. (...) In addition, it would be useful if Members were to make a commitment to introduce systems of authorised traders (...)"* (European Communities, TN/TF/W/46).

◆ Use risk management and risk analysis as defined in the WCO Revised Kyoto Convention Guidelines. *"Establishment of a risk management platform by adopting advanced information technology."* Classify enterprises *"into different risk levels upon their compliance records with customs"* and treat them *"differently in terms of providing customs facilitation"* (China and Korea, TN/TF/W/49)

◆ See also input on risk management contained in TN/TF/W/42 (Japan).

- *Members shall conduct documentary and physical examination based on risk management for the purpose of concentrating on the examination of higher risk goods and facilitating the movement of lower risk goods.*

- *In applying risk management techniques, Members shall examine imported goods based on appropriate selectivity criteria in order to provide compliant traders with greater facilitation and expedited customs procedures.*

- *The selectivity criteria may include specific commodity code, country of origin, country whence consigned, licensing indicator, value of goods, compliance level of traders, type of means of transport, and the traders' purpose of the stay in the Customs territory.*

- *Members shall, where practicable, refer to relevant international standards and practices including the revised Kyoto Convention and the WCO Risk Management Guidelines as the basis for its risk management procedures.*

- *Risk management procedures shall not be used if they have the effect of creating disguised discrimination and obstacles to trade.*

- *Risk management procedures shall be applied, to the extent possible, to the relevant trade facilitation measures including pre-arrival processing, post-clearance audit, and authorised traders.*

(Definition)

- **Risk** *means the potential for non-compliance with customs and/or other relevant laws.*

- **Risk Management** *means the systematic application of management procedures and practices providing customs and other relevant border agencies with the necessary information to address movements or consignments which present a risk.*

(Textual proposal by Korea, The Separate Customs Territory of Taiwan, Penghu, Kinmen and Matsu, and Switzerland, TN/TF/W/140).

2. Clarification of the main features of the suggested proposals

2.1 What is risk management?

As a part of customs reform programmes, customs are being increasingly urged to apply risk management techniques in the examination of documents and in the physical checking of imported goods upon arrival. The technique could also be applied to the examination of documents and to the physical checking of goods to be exported.

In order to understand how the technique is applied, it is necessary to know what risk management is.

2.2 The use of the risk management technique in the private and Public sectors

Risk management is a management technique that is widely used both in the public and private sectors. In the public sector, ministries and government departments routinely examine the risks involved in not being able to achieve the aims and objectives of the economic and social policies they propose to adopt. The technique is applied when they invest money in new projects aimed at providing services to the public. This enables the concerned government departments to determine priorities, and to direct the limited resources available to them for the development of projects in which there are minimal risks involved in achieving successful results. The technique is also used by government departments responsible for the collection of taxes, particularly by customs.

2.3 The application of the risk management technique by customs in the clearance of imported and exported goods

Customs authorities perform two main tasks in relation to imported and exported goods. First, they are under obligation to ensure that all duties, charges and fees payable on such goods are collected, and to see that importers and exporters comply fully with the customs rules and procedures, including those relating to security. Second, they are expected to ensure that trade is facilitated by ensuring that both imported and exported goods are cleared through customs without delay.

Traditionally, most customs administrations allow the clearance of imported and exported goods only after the relevant documents are fully scrutinised, and all goods are physically checked. These practices ensure that they conform to the information provided by the importer/exporter regarding technical specifications, quality, quantity, and value.

The application of the risk assessment technique enables customs to identify transactions in which past experience has shown that there is a high degree of compliance with customs rules regarding the declaration of value, tariff classification, and the origin of goods. Thus, the technique can be helpful in identifying importers/exporters that have no record of rule violation.

By identifying clearly the nature of transactions and the reputations of importers/exporters, customs can classify them into different risk assessment categories depending on whether they have been rule compliant or not. The common practice among customs authorities is to categorise every imported product after they have assessed the risk of non-compliance involved in its import/export into high risk, low risk, and medium risk, respectively.

Such categorisation can also be made with reference to the country of origin of the imported goods. For instance, it may be decided that all imports originating in certain countries should be placed in the high risk category because a large percentage of their imports are undervalued. Similarly, consignments from certain exporters of that country known to be indulging in such a practice could be placed in the high risk category while others (from the same country) with a better reputation could be placed in the low risk category. Thus, customs authorities can apply this technique of classification to all importers or agencies associated with imports and exports.

Another, more sophisticated system often used is to categorise imports/exports as well as importers/exporters by rating them on a scale of 0–100. Zero implies that the transaction involves no risk to any of the objectives of the customs administration, and 100 means that the transaction is bound to contravene some of its regulatory provisions. The ratings falling in between convey the degree of risk regarding customs objectives involved in the transactions. Thus, customs use the information generated by the history of past transactions as well as other relevant information regarding the non-compliance of customs rules and regulations for classifying the risks involved.

By using such a system of categorisation, customs determine the level of regulatory controls that should be exercised at different levels of risk. To facilitate such controls, the criteria for the measurement of compliance at different risk levels are prescribed. For instance, for transactions with a low level of risk, customs may decide to release goods without the rigorous checking of documentary evidence or physical inspection.

For imports falling in the medium risk category, they may prescribe inspections only on a selective basis. For this purpose, the selection of transactions to be checked is made on the basis of criteria determined periodically by the higher management. These criteria are kept confidential in order to avoid the possibility of customs officials entering into collusive deals with traders for avoiding the payment of duties. This is particularly true in countries where customs related corruption is rampant, and the practice of the undervaluation of imported goods is widely prevalent. For the remaining high risk categories, rigorous documentation controls may be exercised, and a higher percentage of goods may undergo physical checking.

Thus, the adoption of risk management systems results in the speedy clearance of those imported and exported goods that fall under the low risk category. It also enables customs to devote more resources to the examination of goods falling under the high risk category, and helps in dealing more effectively with customs malpractices such as the undervaluation of goods and other customs frauds.

However, risk management systems have to be adjusted and tailored to suit the situation prevailing in every country. Thus, each country is required to adopt a 'risk management profile' as well as define 'criteria for measuring compliance at different levels of risk' after undertaking risk assessment procedures. These profiles and criteria could vary from country to country. In countries where corruption in customs is widespread, and there is a tendency on the part traders to resort to the undervaluation of goods and other customs frauds, a larger number of transactions are likely to be put in the high risk category. Thus, the adoption of risk management profiles involves considerable preparatory work.

Such work is generally undertaken in four stages. These are:

● The identification of risks;

● The analysis of risks;

● The assessment of risks; and

● The preparation of risk management profiles.

Box 24 provides an overview of the elements that have to be taken into account in preparing a risk management profile, and in adopting the appropriate strategy for measures of compliance at each level of risk.

Box 24: The preparation of risk profiles and the criteria for the management of risk at different levels

Identification of risks

The first step in preparing a profile or a plan for risk management is to identify the risks of non-compliance of customs rules and procedures. The risks facing customs administration include:

◆ Loss in the collection of customs duties due to, *inter alia*, the undervaluation of imported goods or their classification under tariff headings subject to lower duties;

◆ The avoidance of rules relating to licensing requirements or prohibition of imports under, *inter alia*, safeguard actions;

◆ False declarations of the country of origin of goods in order to benefit from preferential access under GSP, or other preferential arrangement, or to avoid payment of anti-dumping or countervailing duties; and

◆ The avoidance of other customs regulations, including security regulations.

Risks of non-compliance in relation to each of the elements mentioned above have to be identified for:

- ◆ Goods originating in different countries, and

- ◆ Importers, exporters, and other stake holders.

Such identification has to be made after taking into account the 'strengths and weaknesses of the present control systems' and 'the chances or risks of the rules being circumvented.'

Analysis of risks
Once the risks are identified, an assessment is made of their likelihood and consequences by assessing the 'likelihood of the event to happen' and the 'potential consequences and their magnitude' if they were to happen, taking into account statistical and other information available with customs and elsewhere. In most cases, customs seek the cooperation of the associations of industries, and of importers and exporters in preparing such risk assessment.

Assessment of risks and the determination of priorities
On the basis of such assessment, risks are classified into different categories. The systems adopted for categorisation vary considerably. The most common system is to categorise them as low, medium, and high. Traffic light terminology (green, orange, and red) is often used to describe these three categories. More sophisticated and complex systems provide for more detailed categorisation, such as on a scale of 0 to 100.

The preparation of risk profiles for the management of risks
On the basis of such identification and risk assessment, risk profiles can be prepared and strategies for the management of risks can be adopted. For each risk category, the strategies should provide the criteria which customs appraisers and inspectors are expected to apply for measuring compliance with customs rules and procedures.

These strategies may provide for accepting low risks by clearing goods without the rigorous scrutiny of documentation and physical inspection. However, random checks can be made of certain transactions. The criterion for such random checks can be determined by the senior management team and be changed from time to time. The criteria used for random checks are kept as a highly guarded secret, in order to avoid importers and exporters from entering into collusive deals with customs appraisers for the evasion of duties.

For medium and high risk categories, a more rigorous system for the scrutiny of documents and physical checking can be prescribed. These have to take into account the availability of human and technical resources, the prevalence of customs malpractices on the part of traders, and of corruption in customs in general.

3. Proposals on authorised importers

Risk management procedures also enable customs to adopt special or fast track methods for the clearance of the goods of traders who have built a reputation for full compliance with customs rules and regulations. Such traders are deemed 'authorised persons' by customs. The criteria which a trader must meet before being declared an 'authorised person' include a record for each of the following:

- ● Accurate and correct declarations;

- ● Adequate security provided to meet obligations;

- ● Timely duty and payment of taxes;

- ● Correct declaration of tariff classification and country of origin; and

- ● No history of significant recurring errors or violations.

In addition to these requirements regarding the compliance with customs rules and procedures, customs also insist that a trader wishing to be treated as an 'authorised person' must also maintain an adequate system for managing commercial records.

For such authorised persons, customs:

- Permit the release of goods on the basis of minimum information necessary for the identification of goods, and permit the subsequent completion of the final goods Declaration, and

- In certain cases, permit the clearance of goods at the premises of the importer.

In addition, customs may permit authorised persons to:

- Make lodgement of the goods Declaration covering imports and export transactions over a certain period of time (e.g. six months), and

- Authorise them to self assess their duty and tax liability, and to ensure compliance with other customs requirements.

4. Proposals on post-clearance audit

In order to facilitate the early release through customs of goods both imported exported, the risk management system envisages that customs should, where possible, rely on a post-audit to check the information provided in documents rather than pre-check such information prior to the release of goods. The selection of persons or companies to be subjected to such audits is made on the basis of risk profiles. The special privileges extended to 'authorised persons' described above are generally subject to their agreeing to have their accounts audited by customs after the release of goods. The objective of such audits is to check the information provided in customs declaration form (regarding the value of imported or exported goods, their origin and tariff classification, and the duty relief obtained under drawback/remission programmes) from the accounts and the records of the company. The post-audit is considered to be an effective tool for customs control, as customs auditors are able to get a clear and comprehensive picture of the relevant transactions from the books and records of traders. Depending on the type of business the importer is engaged in, and the customs revenue involved, such audits may be conducted by customs periodically (every six months or once per year), or even on an occasional basis.

5. Relevant Kyoto Convention standards

The Kyoto Convention has prescribed standards regarding all the subjects discussed above. All the countries that have ratified the Convention are expected to comply with them. The Convention has also laid down guidelines to be followed by all countries while applying these standards.

Box 25 lists the standards relating to the application of 'risk assessment and management techniques' as also to the 'post-clearance audit.'

The standards relating to imports by 'authorised persons' are described in Box 26.

Box 25: Customs Control

Chapter 6, WCO Kyoto Convention (General Annex)

6.1. Standard
All goods, including means of transport, which enter or leave the Customs territory, regardless of whether they are liable to duties and taxes, shall be subject to Customs control.

6.2. Standard
Customs control shall be limited to that necessary to ensure compliance with the Customs law.

6.3. Standard
In the application of Customs control, the Customs shall use risk management.

6.4. Standard
The Customs shall use risk analysis to determine which persons and which goods, including means of transport, should be examined and the extent of the examination.

6.5. Standard
The Customs shall adopt a compliance measurement strategy to support risk management.
General Annex/Chapter 6 25.

6.6. Standard
Customs control systems shall include audit-based controls.

6.7. Standard
The Customs shall seek to co-operate with other Customs administrations and seek to conclude mutual administrative assistance agreements to enhance Customs control.

6.8. Standard
The Customs shall seek to co-operate with the trade and seek to conclude Memoranda of Understanding to enhance Customs control.

6.9. Transitional Standard
The Customs shall use information technology and electronic commerce to the greatest possible extent to enhance Customs control.

6.10. Standard
The Customs shall evaluate traders' commercial systems where those systems have an impact on Customs operations to ensure compliance with Customs requirements.

Box 26: Special Procedures for Authorised Persons

Chapter 3, WCO Kyoto Convention (General Annex)

3.32. Transitional Standard
For authorised persons who meet criteria specified by the Customs, including having an appropriate record of compliance with Customs requirements and a satisfactory system for managing their commercial records, the Customs shall provide for:

◆ release of the goods on the provision of the minimum information necessary to identify the goods and permit the subsequent completion of the final Goods declaration;

- clearance of the goods at the declarant's premises or another place authorised by the Customs;

and, in addition, to the extent possible, other special procedures such as :

- allowing a single Goods declaration for all imports or exports in a given period where goods are imported or exported frequently by the same person;

- use of the authorised persons' commercial records to self-assess their duty and tax liability and, where appropriate, to ensure compliance with other Customs requirements;

- allowing the lodgement of the Goods declaration by means of an entry in the records of the authorised person to be supported subsequently by a supplementary Goods declaration.

6. Overview of the findings and conclusions of case studies on the experience of developing countries in introducing and implementing trade facilitation measures

Many issues need to be examined before deciding upon the approach that could be adopted in the WTO negotiations for the development of rules regarding the measures dealt with in this Chapter. However, before doing so, some of the findings and conclusions of the case studies undertaken by international organisations such as the World Bank and OECD about the experience of developing countries in introducing and applying trade facilitation measures have to be taken into account.

6.1 Findings relating to the adoption of risk management techniques and systems for the designation of authorised traders

- The results of the programmes providing for the use of risk management techniques vary widely from country to country. Countries in which information technology is well developed, and its use widely prevalent among traders, the information needed for categorising transactions as well as importers/exporters into different risk categories is readily accessible. Thus, they are able to permit the clearance of goods falling in the lower risk categories after a limited scrutiny of documents and without physical checking. Countries in which considerable progress has been made in the use of risk management techniques in the clearance of goods imported include Morocco, Peru, and the Philippines, all of which have been the subject of case studies. In Morocco, for instance, the customs administration has set a goal of releasing 90% of filed declarations without immediate physical inspection.[69]

- The legislation of Peru has modified the provisions relating to the physical inspection of cargo (the previous requirement was 100%) with a view to encouraging customs to reduce the percentage of goods checked physically. However, it provides that at least 15% of shipments must be physically checked.[70]

- In other countries, where the practice of the undervaluation of goods by traders and other customs frauds are widely prevalent, there is a reluctance to rely entirely on the results of risk assessment systems in the clearing of goods. Countries in which risk management systems have been adopted but where customs malpractices are widely prevalent, the customs authorities often ignore the results of

---

69 Marcel Steenlandt and Luc De Wulf, Case Study on Morocco, p. 40
70 Adrien Goorman, Case study on Peru, p. 77.

such systems. They tend to classify a greater percentage of goods in the high risk categories (orange or red) because they fear that if they did otherwise, the revenues due would not be fully collected. This practice is more prevalent in those countries in which, at the beginning of the year, the Ministry of Finance prescribes targets for the collection of revenue as well as exercises vigilance on the progress being made during its collection.

- Experience shows that the adoption of risk assessment measures is the most expensive amongst all the measures taken by countries to facilitate trade because of the expenditure needed for infrastructure and training. Thus, the development of an effective and well functioning system takes a number of years, and depends on the ability and willingness of donor countries to continue meeting the expenditure necessary for building up the information technology infrastructure.[71]

- A number of countries are reluctant to adopt the system of 'authorised importers' as they fear that some companies may have to be included (because of their political connections) despite their records showing that they have not been fully rule compliant. The adoption of the system also presents practical problems: in many developing countries, imports are made by a large number of firms whose past records are needed for establishing compliance with customs rules but which are not readily available.

6.2   Findings on the post-audit of imported goods

Case studies about the experience of some countries show that although they have adopted the programme of the post-audit, its generalised use has been limited because of resource constraints. A number of countries do not have a sufficient number of trained personnel to undertake such audits. The training of officials also poses practical problems. The period of training is long; sending officials for training involves their absence from the workplace for an extended period of time. The other alternative is to recruit new staff with the necessary background and training. The budgetary resources required for this purpose are generally not available. It is often suggested that a way around this problem could be to rely on the deputation of auditors from the offices of other tax authorities and departments. However, this may not be a long term solution as the other departments are also generally short of staff.[72]

In countries where corruption amongst customs officials is widely prevalent, there are apprehensions that an increased reliance on post-audit – which has to be undertaken at the premises of the importer – may provide opportunities to customs auditors to enter into collusive deals with the firms whose accounts are being audited and, thus, lead to increased corruption.

6.3   Points for consideration

Any consideration of the possible approach to be adopted in the discussions on the proposals for the development of rules in the WTO covering the application of risk management systems, the designation of authorised importers, and the adoption of the post-audit should be undertaken in the light of the following lessons learnt from the findings and conclusions of the case studies described in the previous section, and the experience of the application of the risk management technique as a management tool in the countries included in the case studies.

- First, the provision of technical assistance covering all aspects of customs clearance procedures, even if given over an extended period of time, does not guarantee that the customs administration will be

---

71   OECD, Trade Policy Working Paper No. 8, pp. 12-13.
72   *Ibid*, pp. 13-14.

able to implement effectively the reform programme based on the applications of a) risk management techniques, or b) special procedures of imports by authorised persons. Thus, it would be necessary to ensure that the provision of technical assistance is not linked to the acceptance of binding obligations under WTO rules in these and other similar areas by assistance receiving countries.

- Second, as noted previously, risk management techniques are being applied both by the business community and by governments in a number of diverse areas. It is recognised that the extent and level of the risk involved in the non-fulfilment of the objectives of the policy, and the level of the non-compliance of rules that can be deemed acceptable should be left to the decision of the management.

- Third, for the effective application of the system, managements need considerable discretionary authority. It is generally accepted in all analytical literature about the theory and practice of management that it is not desirable to restrain or limit such discretionary authority by rules or regulations. As a paper on 'The Risk Management of Everything' emphasises, risk management should be characterised more by '...learning and experiment, rather than rule-based processes.'[73] Consequently, if rules are adopted, their only aim should be to encourage countries to use such techniques. Decisions regarding how the techniques should be applied should be left to the management.

- Fourth, many countries, particularly those that are least developed or at a lesser stage of development, may find it difficult to continue to meet the additional recurring expenditure needed for the effective implementation of the reform programme from their own budgetary resources after the technical assistance programme comes to an end. This could be the case even when the reform programme has resulted in an increase in the revenues being collected. In most countries, the revenue collected from customs and other duties are credited to the general revenue account. As such, the availability of the additional funds needed for the maintenance or strengthening of the reform programme depends on the priorities the government proposes to attach to the reform of customs clearance procedures as compared to other projects more likely to have a direct impact on economic and social development and on poverty alleviation.

The above lessons suggest that it may be difficult for a number of countries to accept binding obligations to introduce and implement the reform of customs clearance procedures by applying risk management techniques and adopting procedures for imports by authorised persons. There is, however, increasing awareness on the part of customs authorities in most countries regarding the need to adopt these innovative methods. Thus, the aim of the negotiations in this area may have to be directed towards seeing how the new rules can provide incentives, and encourage countries to adopt these innovative methods for the speedy and effective clearance of goods. Against this background, it may be necessary to examine carefully whether, as suggested earlier, it would be desirable for the Agreement to encourage countries to apply the standards that have been developed by the WCO instead of writing new rules covering these measures.

---

73   Michael Power, The Risk Management of Everything – Rethinking the Politics of Uncertainty, (Demos, London: 2004), p. 61.

Chapter 15: Facilitating the release of goods through customs: pre-arrival clearance, one time shop, and single window clearance

General

The previous chapter described three techniques that are being advocated for adoption by customs authorities in all countries to expedite the clearance of goods. These include the application of risk management techniques to significantly reduce the number of imported/exported goods needing to be physically checked, the designation of 'authorised importers,' and the reliance on a system of post-audit.

This chapter aims at describing the proposals that call upon countries to adopt other, more specific, complementary methods and techniques in the day-to-day administration of customs procedures in order to facilitate trade.

These include:

* The pre-arrival clearance of goods;
* The establishment of a 'one time shop' and 'single window' clearance of goods;
* The release of goods on the basis of 'security of payments;'
* Special procedures for the clearance of goods, including express shipments; and
* Advance rulings.

1. The pre-arrival clearance of goods

1.1   Explanation of the term

The general practice of most customs administrations is to accept documentation after the goods have arrived. Increasingly, however, customs are encouraging importers to submit their documents before the arrival of the goods at the port. The development of information technology (IT) facilitates the submission of documentation to customs before the arrival of goods at the customs ports of the importing country.

The submission of documents before arrival speeds up the clearance process, as customs have time to complete their scrutiny before the arrival of goods. This leads to the saving of time spent on documentation scrutiny while the goods wait in the customs port.

In the case of imports by 'authorised persons' who have been given the special privileges of obtaining the clearance of their goods without physical checking, customs may agree to release the goods immediately upon arrival on the basis of the pre-arrival scrutiny of documents. In all such cases, the authenticity of the information provided in the documentation is checked by undertaking 'post-audits.'

The pre-arrival examination of documents may be used for all types of cargoes, or may be limited to certain types of cargoes where speedy clearance is of crucial importance. The latter could include fresh foods, other perishable articles, and products with limited shelf life or seasonal selling periods.

1.2   Provisions of the Kyoto Convention

The Kyoto Convention calls on countries to provide 'the lodging and registering or checking of the goods Declaration and other supporting documents prior to the arrival of the goods (standard 3.25) under their national laws.

1.3   Proposals made by delegations

The proposals to make the adoption of procedures for pre-arrival clearance mandatory are listed below.

Box 27: Pre-arrival clearance

◆ Members shall maintain or introduce pre-arrival processing, which is defined as administrative procedures of customs and other relevant border agencies to accept and examine import documentation and other required information upon the submission by traders prior to the arrival of goods, in order to further expedite the clearance of goods where appropriate. In cases where it is decided that no further examination is required, goods should be cleared immediately upon arrival (Japan, Korea, Mongolia, and Switzerland, TN/TF/W/117).

◆ *"Clearance in advance of arrival enabl[ing] importers to file their entries prior to the arrival of merchandise at the port of entry. Importers may claim their goods immediately after importation, so long as they are not selected for document review or physical examination"* (Chinese Taipei, TN/TF/W/10).

◆ *"Introduction of procedures for accepting and examining documents prior to the arrival of goods..."* (Japan, Mongolia, Peru and Chinese Taipei, TN/TF/W/17).

◆ Introduce and utilise pre-arrival processing (Korea, TN/TF/W/18).

◆ *"Establishment of disciplines on (....) pre-clearance (...) of goods"* (Peru, TN/TF/W/30).

◆ *"A commitment by each member to introduce simplified customs release and clearance procedures including the possibility of pre-arrival processing of documentation..."* (European Communities, TN/TF/W/46).

1.4   Points for consideration

Most developed countries and a few developing countries have now well functioning systems for the pre-arrival clearance of goods. The system facilitates trade by reducing pressure on the regular staff responsible for examining documents after the arrival of goods.

However, the implementation of the system, in most cases, requires additional staff. Many developing countries, with their resource-starved budgets, find it difficult to allocate the funds needed for the adoption of the system of pre-arrival clearance.

2. The establishment of a 'one time shop' and 'single window' clearance facilities

2.1 The 'one time shop'

Even though customs is the primary agency responsible for the clearance of goods, it can release them only after the importers have been able to get approvals from other agencies responsible for ensuring that they conform to technical regulations and requirements regarding their quality, safety, and conformity with health standards. The clearance of goods is often held up because of delays in obtaining approvals from these agencies.

2.2.1 Proposals tabled by delegations

It is proposed that one of the ways to resolve this problem is to ensure greater coordination among the various agencies, *inter alia*, through the establishment of 'one time shops.' The various agencies should be required to undertake, to the extent possible, a one time only 'documentary and physical verification' at this shop, and at hours that meet the needs of the trader (European Communities /N/TF/W/46).

2.2.2 Provisions of the Kyoto Convention

The Kyoto Convention recognises that the convergence of controls into a single control to meet all government requirements is an important trade facilitation measure. Towards this end, it calls on countries to ensure that their inspections are 'coordinated and are carried out at the same time' (standard 3.5).

2.2.3 Points for consideration

The establishment of such 'one time shops' at all customs ports would, no doubt, greatly reduce the difficulties faced by traders in obtaining approvals from various government bodies such as the Ministries of Health and Industry, and other national standard setting bodies. However, a number of developing countries may have to weigh the benefits of such 'one time shops' accruing to traders and to a general reduction in clearance time against the additional recurring costs incurred in establishing them.

2.3 The 'single window' clearance system

Most developed countries and some developing countries (in which the use of information technology (IT) among traders is well established) are complementing the efforts of other agencies for greater coordination by adopting the system known as the 'single window' clearance system. Under this system, traders submit a single declaration containing all the data and information required by customs and other agencies involved in the clearance of imported and exported goods.

Different models of the single window system have been developed and applied. In some countries, a single authority has been established to coordinate and enforce all border related controls (e.g. Sweden and The Netherlands). Other countries may not have such centralised agencies; however, they often require traders to submit their declarations electronically in a single form to various agencies for processing and approval. Approval permits are then transmitted electronically to the traders (e.g. Singapore).

2.3.1 Proposals

The specific proposals on the adoption of the single window system that have been tabled are listed in Box 28.

Box 28: Single window

◆ *"Introduction of procedures for allowing one-time submission of import or export documentation to one authority (...) (including coordinating the timing and place of physical inspections among the relevant authorities to the extent possible"* (Japan, Mongolia, Chinese Taipei and Peru, TN/TF/W/17).

◆ *"Acceptance of single documentary submission of import or export documentation requirements in cases of repeated transactions of same products; exemption of documentary submissions for each importation or exportation should be permitted"* (Japan, Mongolia, Chinese Taipei and Peru, TN/TF/W/17).

◆ *"Recommendation to establish a single-window mechanism at borders or ports with efficient computer back-up"* (Peru, TN/TF/W/30).

◆ *"... efforts toward the one-stop service clearance/release facilities through inter-agency coordination, plus remote filing and local clearance facilitates, are crucial." (...) "... should consider whether rules could be developed to ensure that the activities and requirements of all agencies present at borders are coordinated in a manner designed to facilitate trade." (...) "An agreement on trade facilitation may cover provisions on a Single Window approach whereby Members gradually undertake necessary measures"* (Turkey, TN/TF/W/45).

◆ *"Progressive implementation of the principle of a single, one-time presentation to one agency, normally the customs, of all documentation and data requirements for export or import, subject to any exceptions to be identified"* (European Communities, TN/TF/W/46).

◆ See also reference to input by Canada in TN/TF/W/20 as reflected in section J:1.

◆ *"Progressive" implementation of the principle of a single, one-time presentation of documentation and data to one agency "subject to any exceptions to be identified." "This should be a best endeavour provision and the commitment would be to making progressive efforts, rather than to any fixed deadline." "Flexibility will be needed – especially for some developing countries... "* (European Communities, TN/TF/W/46).

◆ *Members shall establish or designate a single entry point, hereinafter referred to as the "single window," where documentation and data requirements for exportation and importation are submitted one time only. The single window shall undertake onward distribution of the aforementioned documentation and data requirements to all the relevant authorities or agencies.*

◆ *In cases where documentation and data requirements have already been by the single window, the same documentation and data requirements shall not be requested by other authorities or agencies.*

◆ *Members shall notify other Members through the WTO Secretariat of the contact information of the single window.*

◆ *Members are encouraged to use, to the extent possible, information technology to support the single window.*

◆ *Members shall, where practicable, refer to relevant international standards and practices such as the WCO Revised Kyoto Convention and UN/CEFACT Recommendation No.33.*

◆ *With regard to the scope of participating authorities or agencies and documentation and data requirements, Members are allowed to implement the single window in a progressive manner taking into account each Member's administrative capacity.*

(Textual proposal by Korea,TN/TF/W/138)

2.3.2 Points for consideration

The adoption of a 'single window system' by a particular country depends greatly on whether information technology is widely used among traders. For many countries in which IT facilities are in a nascent stage of development, the adoption of the single window system envisaging the electronic submission of a single document is likely to be a long term goal at present.

3. The release of goods against security provided by the importer for the payment of duties

In cases where the clearance of goods is likely to be delayed, the customs laws of most countries allow traders to obtain the release of goods by providing collateral security, or another appropriate instrument guaranteeing the payment of duties and other taxes. Such situations could, *inter alia*, arise:

- Where there are differences between customs and the importers regarding the declared value of the imported goods, or on their tariff classification; and
- Where goods are imported for exports after processing in the country.

3.1 Proposals tabled by delegations

The proposals tabled by delegations envisage that any future international rules that may be developed should recognise the right of traders to secure the release of goods by providing collateral security in the above and other similar situations.

Box 29: Collateral Security

- *"Maintain a system by which goods may be released from the custody of customs before final payment of duties or resolution of customs matters (such as classification or customs valuation), utilizing as necessary a guarantee as a surety, bond, or deposit"* (United States, TN/TF/W/21).

- *"Possibility of establishing an enhanced customs clearance system with provisions on the security (bonds, financial guarantees, etc.) or other forms of collateral required to ensure that the obligations of importers, warehouse operators or international goods carriers towards the customs authorities are properly discharged"* (Peru, TN/TF/W/30).

3.2 Relevant provisions in other legal instruments

In this context, Article 13 of the Agreement on Customs Valuation is of relevance. It provides that national laws should grant rights to traders to withdraw their goods from customs by providing a 'sufficient guarantee' in the form of a surety, a deposit, or some other appropriate instrument. This should be adequate to cover the ultimate payment of the customs duties to which the imported goods are liable, and should even be adequate for those cases in which 'it becomes necessary to delay the final determination' of the customs value of the goods.

The Kyoto Convention also contains standards that aim at granting a right to traders to secure the release of their goods before the formalities regarding their clearance have been completed. These standards are listed in Box 30.

Box 30: The Release of Goods

Chapter 3, WCO Kyoto Convention (General Annex)

3.41. Standard
If the Customs are satisfied that the declarant will subsequently accomplish all the formalities in respect of clearance they shall release the goods, provided that the declarant produces a commercial or official document giving the main particulars of the consignment concerned and acceptable to the Customs, and that security, where required, has been furnished to ensure collection of any applicable duties and taxes.

3.42. Standard
When the Customs decide that they require laboratory analysis of samples, detailed technical documents or expert advice, they shall release the goods before the results of such examination are known, provided that any security required has been furnished and provided they are satisfied that the goods are not subject to prohibitions or restrictions.

3.43. Standard
When an offence has been detected, the Customs shall not wait for the completion of administrative or legal action before they release the goods, provided that the goods are not liable to confiscation or forfeiture or to be needed as evidence at some later stage and that the declarant pays the duties and taxes and furnishes security to ensure collection of any additional duties and taxes and of any penalties which may be imposed.
General Annex/Chapter 3 16.

3.3   Points for consideration

As countries are already under an obligation to ensure that their customs shall release goods even in cases where there are differences between customs and the importer on the 'value' of the imported goods on the basis of a security for the payment of duties provided by the importer, the adoption of the proposals would only mean a broadening of this obligation to cover other differences between customs and traders on matters such as tariff classifications or the origin of goods.

4. Advance Rulings

4.1   The term 'advance rulings'

If it is possible to know before hand the exact amount of duty that has to be paid to customs, it considerably facilitates a company's business decision regarding whether or not certain goods should be imported. For this purpose, the laws of some countries provide that customs should, if requested by a trader, make available information in the form of a ruling on such matters as the tariff classification of the goods to be imported, and how their origin and value will be determined. To be able to do this, customs generally require traders to furnish the following information:

- The name and address of the applicant;

- The full details of the goods, such as their commercial description, nature, composition, quality, price, origin and use, packaging, and where applicable, the manufacturing process;

- The particulars of any previous importation of goods of the same kind by the applicant, together with the tariff heading applied; and

- The customs office through which goods are to be cleared.

In addition, the applicants are generally required to provide samples of the goods to be imported and, where this is not possible, they may be called upon to provide photographs, plans, drawings, or a complete description of the goods.

Such rulings may be provided by customs only for the information of the importers in some administrations; however, the rulings provided are binding on both the customs administration and the applicant for a number of years.

On the basis of such rulings, importers and exporters can secure the speedy clearance of goods. However, customs officers may, if they consider it necessary, make risk-based checks in order to see whether the goods in question are identical to those that are subject to the ruling.

The ruling is generally valid for a period of one to five years. It may be annulled by customs if it becomes incompatible with new measures adopted by it, or by judicial decisions.[74]

4.2   Proposals tabled by delegations

The proposals tabled by delegations envisage that new rules should require customs to provide 'binding advance rulings' at the request of traders. Such requests could be made by importers and exporters, as well as foreign producers. Specific proposals tabled are listed in Box 31.

Box 31: Advance rulings

Establishment and development of an advance rulings system (Japan, Mongolia, Chinese Taipei, Pakistan and Peru, TN/TF/W/8).

Development of disciplines on the provision of advance rulings on tariff classification (including any applicable rate of duty or tax applicable upon importation (Canada and Australia, TN/TF/W/9).

Advance rulings on tariff classification (Chinese Taipei, TN/TF/W/10).

"Make available, upon request of a trader in advance of trade, binding rules in certain specific areas (e.g., tariff classification, customs valuation, duty deferral)" (United States, TN/TF/W/12).

Advance rulings on "... matters such as tariff classification, applicable duties and valuations" upon written request within a certain time period that "would be binding on customs authorities for a period of time, provided that the facts and circumstance on which the rulings are based remain unchanged" (Singapore, TN/TF/W/38).

Advance rulings covering "the main elements of import requirements, such as tariff classification and applicable duties and taxes" and "tariff preferences". The provisions on advance rulings in the Agreement on Rules of Origin "might serve as a model to be applied more generally" (Turkey, TN/TF/W/45).

---

74   Kyoto Convention, General Annex, Chapter 9, Para 3.10 ‚'Time-limits for validity of rulings'.

4.3 Points needing further examination

Work on the preparation of such rulings requires coordination among the different sections of the customs department. The general practice in countries that have adopted the practice of advance rulings is to establish a separate unit staffed by experts in such areas as tariff classification, valuation, and determination of origin. In deciding whether or not to take up the system of advance rulings, countries that do not have it may have to consider carefully the administrative and financial costs involved in its adoption.

PART FIVE

Transit Trade and Landlocked Countries

Chapter 16: Transit trade and landlocked countries

General

There are many countries in the world today which have no sea coasts and are surrounded on all sides by other countries. These countries are known as landlocked countries. Except in cases where they are imported/exported by air, in such countries goods have to be transported by rail or by road through the territory of the country in order to reach a sea port. In some cases, the goods may even have to be transported through more than one country in order to reach the importing landlocked country.

The countries through which the imported/exported goods have to pass are known as 'transit countries.' The procedures for the clearance of goods in landlocked countries call for close cooperation between the customs administrations of both coastal as well as transit countries. The latter always want to ensure that the goods in transit to the landlocked country are not leaked into their domestic markets without the payment of import duties and domestic consumption taxes, or by circumventing rules relating to the prohibition of the imports of certain products. At the same time, landlocked countries are keen on ensuring that 'customs transit procedures' under which goods are transported from the customs port of the transit countries to their own customs ports, are kept simple and do not increase costs or cause excessive delays.

Poor and inefficient customs transit procedures constitute a major obstacle to the trade of landlocked countries. Research conducted by the World Bank and other organisations shows that, for a typical landlocked country, transport costs are higher by 50% than in a typical coastal country, even while the volume of trade is lower.[75]

These findings are of great concern to landlocked countries, 31 of which are developing countries; of these, 16 are classified as highly indebted poor countries (HIPC); 20 out of 50 least developed countries are also landlocked.

However, it is important to note that customs transit procedures is only one among the many factors that leads to higher transport costs for landlocked countries. Other factors include:

- Cross border vehicle regulations;
- Visas for truck drivers;
- Insurance;
- Police controls;
- The poor quality of the transport services available and poor road conditions; and
- The inefficient organisation of the private trucking sector.

1. Overview of the international rules governing transit trade

Custom transit procedures are generally regulated by national legislations providing for transit codes, or by bilateral or plurilateral agreements between customs and the parties affected by the transit operations. The core provisions of such transit procedures include the following:

---

75   Jean Francois Arvis, 'Transit and the Special Case of Landlocked Countries', p. 244, in Luc De Wulf and José B. Sokol, Customs Modernization Handbook, (World Bank, Washington D.C. 2005).

- Sealing of the shipment at the point where the transit operation is initiated;
- Providing financial security to customs in the country of transit which will guarantee the payment of duties if the goods do not leave the country of transit; and
- Using an efficient information system about when the transit goods have effectively left the country of despatch so that the security is released.

1.1   GATT rules

Article V of GATT contains rules governing transit trade. Para 1 of the Article defines the term 'transit traffic' to include goods and vessels as well as other means of transport. It clarifies that goods shall be deemed to be in transit when they are in passage across the territory, with or without transhipment, warehousing, breaking bulk, or change in the mode of transport. Transit traffic is completed when the goods cross the frontier of the transit country and reach the destination country.

Para 2 of the Article provides the right to countries of freedom of transit. It further clarifies that 'there shall be freedom of transit through the territory of each country, via the routes most convenient for international transit, for traffic in transit to and from the territory of other countries.' In order to ensure that countries are able to derive full benefits from the 'right of transit,' the rules also provide that 'no distinction shall be made which is based on flags of vessels, the place of origin, departure, entry, exit or destination, or any circumstances relating to the ownership of goods, of vessels and other means of transport.'

It further affirms that 'except in cases of failure to comply with the applicable customs law and regulations, such traffic coming and going to the territory of other contracting parties shall not be subject to unnecessary delays or restrictions and shall be exempt from customs duties and all forms of transit duties or other charges imposed on transit, except charges on transportation or those commensurate with administrative expenses entailed by transit or with the costs of services rendered.'

Transit countries are also under obligations to ensure that transit charges and regulations are:
- Reasonable, having regard to the conditions of traffic, and
- Do not result in the collection of fees or the application of regulations or formalities to traffic in transit to and from any country, treatment that is less favourable than that it accords to traffic in transit to and from any other country.

1.2   The Revised Kyoto Convention

The Kyoto Convention clarifies these provisions by focusing on the applicable customs formalities. Its revised version lays down standards which countries should apply in their regulations providing for:
- Formalities at the office of departure;
- The application of customs seals;
- Formalities en route; and
- The termination of customs transit.

It also lays down the standards which should be followed when the goods are 'transhipped' under customs control, from the importing means of transport under customs control to the exporting means of transport within the area of one customs office' (see Kyoto Convention: Specific Annex E and Guidelines: Customs Transit).

1.3 Other International Conventions

A number of other Conventions have been adopted for facilitating transit traffic and the trade of landlocked countries. These include:

- The Convention on the International Transport of Goods under Cover of TIR Carnets, known as the 'TIR Convention' (Geneva,14 November 1975);

- The Convention on Temporary Admission, 'Istanbul Convention' (Istanbul, 26 June 1990);[76] and

- The Customs Convention on the A.T.A. Carnet for the Temporary Admission of Goods, 'A.T.A. Convention' (Brussels, 6 December 1961).[77]

As the first mentioned Convention is the most widely used in the inland transport of goods by a number of countries, its main features are worth noting.

The five pillars on which the Convention rests are listed in Box 32.

Box 32: The Five Pillars of the TIR Convention

The TIR Convention is not only one of the most successful international transport conventions but also the only existing universal customs transit system. In this sense, it serves as a benchmark for any future effective regional transit framework. Its main pillars are the following:

Secure vehicles. Goods are to be transported in containers or compartments of road vehicles constructed in such a way that there is no access to the interior when secured by a customs seal, so that no goods can be removed or added during the transit procedure, and so that any tampering will be clearly visible.

International guarantee valid throughout the journey. In a situation in which the transport operator cannot pay the customs duties and taxes due, this system ensures that the customs duties and taxes at risk are covered by the national guaranteeing system of the operator.

National associations of transport operators. National associations control access to the TIR procedures by transport operators, issue the appropriate documents, and manage the national guarantee system.

TIR carnet. This is the standard international customs document accepted and recognised by all members of the TIR Convention.

International and mutual recognition of customs control measures. The countries of transit and destination accept the control measures taken in the country of departure.

The system created by the Convention requires close cooperation among all stake holders involved in transit traffic, viz. customs, transport operators and their associations, insurance companies, and other legal

---

76 The Istanbul Convention groups various facilities for the temporary admission of goods into a single instrument. Consequently, it does not deal with matters of customs transit.

77 A.T.A. Carnets can be accepted for the transit of goods under temporary admission, which have to be conveyed to or from their destination under Customs Control, either in the customs territory of temporary admission or through a customs territory or customs between those of exportation and importation (Kyoto Convention, specific Annex E Chapter 1 Guidelines on Customs Transit).

bodies. One of its main features is that 'national associations of transport operators' are responsible for the application of the procedures by transport operators. They issue the appropriate documents and provide the guarantee for the payment of customs duties and other taxes in cases where, because of the leakage of goods/or other reasons, the transport operators are required to pay them to the customs authorities of the transit countries.

From the point of view of the customs administrations, the main advantages of the system are:

- Duties and taxes for risk during international transit movements are guaranteed up to US$ 50,000 (with higher maximum for alcohol and tobacco), and

- Only registered transport operators are permitted to use TIR carnets, thus emphasising the reliability of the system.

The TIR Convention has been a great success mainly in Europe. The number of TIR carnets (standard international customs documents accepted and recognised by all members of the Convention) has increased from 3,000 in 1952 to 2.7 million in 2001.[78]

Though the TIR system has been set up in Central Asia, the Caucasus and the Maghreb, and in some parts of the Middle East, its use by transport operators in these countries has so far been modest. In June 1982, sixteen countries belonging to the Economic Community of West African States (ECOWAS) have established a system (commonly known as TRIE – Transit Routier Inter-Etats) which is similar to that of the International Convention. However, it is being ignored by most transport operators in the membership countries: about 70% of transit procedures in the ECOWAS region stem from bilateral accords and national regulations and procedures.

The main reasons for the unsuccessful use of the Convention among most developing countries is the general absence of efficient and well functioning national associations of transport operators. Even in countries where effective and credible national associations exist, they encounter serious difficulties in successfully operating systems for guaranteeing payments of duties to customs of transit countries, should there be a leakage of goods. This is due to the under development of the local financial infrastructure, and the unwillingness of international insurance companies to provide cover, given their perception of the political and commercial risks existing in these countries.

1.4   Regional Agreements

A number of regional agreements regarding transit trade have been adopted in recent years. These include:

- The mentioned Transit Routier Inter-Etats (TRIE) of ECOWAS, the only example beyond TIR of an agreement dedicated only to transit;

- The Association of Southeast Asian Nations (ASEAN) Framework Agreement on the Facilitation of Goods in Transit;

- The Greater Mekong Sub-region (GMS) Agreement for Facilitation of Cross-Border Transport of Goods and People;

---

78   Jean Francois Arvis, 'Transit and the Special Case of Landlocked Countries', pp. 255.

- The Economic Cooperation Organization's (ECO) Transit Transport Framework Agreement - formed by the Islamic Republic of Afghanistan, Republic of Azerbaijan, Islamic Republic of Iran, Republic of Kazakhstan, Kyrgyz Republic, Islamic Republic of Pakistan, Republic of Tajikistan, Republic of Turkey, Turkmenistan, and the Republic of Uzbekistan; and

- The Common Market for Eastern and Southern Africa (COMESA) Agreement on a Single Administrative Document.

Box 33: Proposal on the Promotion of Regional Transit Agreements or Arrangements

Members shall promote bilateral and regional transit agreements or arrangements which are consistent with all other commitments on Trade Facilitation and with a view to reducing trade barriers. Members agree to cooperate and coordinate in designing and applying bilateral and regional transit agreements or arrangements. Members shall take full account of international standards and instruments when designing and applying those agreements or arrangements. It is recommended that such agreements or arrangements go beyond customs matters relevant in the context of transit, such as road and transport issues. Members shall not enforce unilateral rules affecting traffic in transit which are not in accordance with the bilateral or regional transit agreements or arrangements in which they participate. Members participating in regional transit agreements or arrangements shall give a positive consideration to reasoned requests to participate by other Members who meet the requisite participation criteria.

(Mongolia, Paraguay, Rwanda, and Switzerland, TN/TF/W/119)

However, except for the TRIE (an agreement negotiated among ECOWAS countries), these regional agreements tend to lay down broad goals and policy directions. Actual customs transit facilitation may be dependent on other existing agreements or procedures. A 2001 UNCTAD report points out 'there has not been any shortage of measures and initiatives to improve the facilitation of transit traffic. COMESA, ECA and SADC all have various measures that are in place to address transit facilitation. Unfortunately, the major problem has been poor implementation.'[79]

2. Transit Corridors

A recent development in the area of transit facilitation at the regional level is the emergence of 'transit corridors' which aim at ensuring efficient and secure transit along specific routes, to the benefit of landlocked and transit countries. The corridors focus on policies and initiatives for facilitating 'transit by specific routes and border crossings.' Such policies are formulated and implemented with the involvement of all stakeholders – private and public. Box 34 contains examples of transport corridors adopted by some countries in Africa and elsewhere for customs transit. However, the experience of transit corridors, as in the case of regional agreements on trade facilitation, has been mixed.[80]

---

79   InfraAfrica Ltd. 2001, p. 45, quoted by Jean François Arvis, see p. 260.
80   Jean François Arvis, p. 261.

Box 34: Transit Corridors

Bay Development Corridor. The Walvis Bay Development Corridor (now Trans Kalahari) became operational in late 1999. The driving force of the project was the Walvis Bay Corridor Group (WBCG), a public/private partnership. In November 2003, the Trans Kalahari Corridor Memorandum of Understanding was signed. It introduced a new single customs administrative document which, until then, had been in use on a pilot basis. This new simplified approach provides a streamlined and effective tool for managing customs transit transactions throughout Namibia, Botswana and South Africa, and will replace a cumbersome set of procedures involving up to 10 national documents in each country transited.

Northern Corridor: This corridor provides a lifeline through Kenya to the landlocked economies of Uganda, Rwanda, Burundi, and the landlocked areas within the Democratic Republic of Congo. The corridor is governed by the Northern Corridor Transit Transport Coordination Authority, which aims to help harmonise and simplify the procedures involved in transporting goods within the region. Significant achievements accomplished so far include the following:

◆ The simplification of port clearance procedures;

◆ Documentary simplification, achieved, through the creation of the Road Transit Customs Declaration (RTCD), which is meant to be the single administrative document attached to a shipment through the corridor. However, in practice, the RTCD is often copied at the border onto another RTCD issued by the next country, an illustration of how difficult it may be to change old habits;

◆ The use of the COMESA Customs Declaration Document by Northern Corridor countries; and

◆ Reduction by half of the transit time between Mombassa, Kenya, and Bujumbura, Burundi, from over 30 days to about 15 days. Some unnecessary border formalities along the corridor have been removed.

TRACECA. TRACECA is an EU-initiated programme, launched in 1993, to develop a transport corridor on a west-east axis from Europe, across the Black Sea, through the Caucasus and the Caspian Sea to Central Asia (a modern Silk Road). It aims at harmonizing the legislative base in the transport and transit sectors of its member states, and places great emphasis on infrastructure development and improvement. During its 10-year existence, TRACECA has implemented 53 projects and channeled over US$120 million in infrastructure investment and technical assistance.

3. Proposals regarding the modification of Article V and the issues needing examination

A number of proposals have been tabled for the clarification of the provisions of GATT Article V relating to transit trade. This section analyses the issues that may have to be taken into account in a further examination of the proposals.

3.1 Strengthened non-discrimination

It is, *inter alia*, suggested that countries should be required to apply the principle of non-discrimination to:

● Modes of transport used in transit;

● Carriers of goods in transit;

● The routes chosen; and

● The types of consignments in relation to transit procedures.

The general points made in Chapter 11 about the difficulties that may be encountered while applying the
MFN principle strictly to customs control procedures will also be relevant in the case of transit trade. The

extent of documentary control and physical inspections could vary depending on the existing risks regarding the non-compliance of customs rules. For instance, if customs of the transit country finds that because of collusive links among traders there is a greater risk of goods transported by road being leaked during transit into domestic markets, they may like to insist that imports originating in countries where such risks exist must be:

● Transported by rail and not by road or [vice-versa]; and

● Use a more direct route than that permitted for transit from other countries

In considering the proposal, it would also be necessary to consider that Article V already contains provisions calling on countries to apply the principle of non-discrimination. In particular, it imposes an obligation on countries:

● Not to make any distinction which is based on the flag of the vessel, the place of origin, departure, entry, exit, or destination or any circumstances relating to the ownership of goods, vessels or other means of transport, and

● Not to accord, in the collection of fees or the application of regulations or formalities to traffic in transit to and from any country, treatment that is less favourable than that it accords to traffic in transit to and from any other country.

3.2   National Treatment

It is further suggested that 'with respect to all laws, regulations and procedures affecting the internal passage of traffic in transit across the territory of a member, and all fees and charges imposed in connection with transit, (including transportation charges, transit fees and charges) and without prejudice to the legitimate customs control and supervision of goods in transit, each member shall accord to traffic in transit to or from the territory of any member, treatment no less favourable than that accorded to domestic goods and imports and their movement.'

The proposal itself recognises that it may not be possible to apply the 'national treatment' principle to goods which are allowed to be transported through transit countries under customs control and supervision. It may also become necessary to levy higher transportation charges to cover the costs of customs control. In this situation, if the 'national treatment' rule is to be included in the rules applicable to transit trade, the exceptions that would have to be made for goods transported under customs control would have to be clearly identified.

3.3   Fees and charges

The proposals suggest that the rules should be clarified to provide that:

● All fees and charges should be published;

● Fees that are not published should not be collected;

● There should be periodic reviews of fees and charges; and

● The provisions of Article VIII (which require that fees and charges should not exceed the cost of services rendered by customs) should apply to transit trade.

In general, the same obligations which apply to the publication of fees and charges payable on non-transit trade should apply to the publication of fees and charges on transit trade. In determining the level of fees payable on transit trade, it should be possible for the customs administrations to take into account the expenditure incurred on introducing simplified procedures, other reform programmes, and the adoption of information technology. However, such fees should be kept under constant review and their level reduced as the direct and other non-direct costs get recovered from the fees collected.

3.4   Simplification of transit procedures

The proposals suggest that the new rules should, *inter alia*, impose obligations for:

- Periodic reviews;
- The adoption of common customs and documentation procedures;
- Limitations on inspections and controls, and
- Improved coordination among the authorities of transit and landlocked countries.

Box 35 lists some of these specific proposals.

Box 35: Proposal on the Simplification of Transit Procedures

Common customs documentation and procedures:
For goods entering a Member under customs transit procedure, Members should accept commercially available information, included as part of transit declarations.
Contracting parties to regional transit agreements or arrangements should agree on common, simplified documents that are aligned with international standards. In both cases, Members involved in transit shall allow the same set of documents to accompany the consignment from the country of departure to destination.

Limited physical inspections of goods:
Members shall limit physical inspections of goods in transit to the case where circumstances may require them. Consignments secured by customs seals shall not, as a general rule, be subjected to customs examination. No quality control and no veterinary, medicosanitary or phytosanitary inspection shall be imposed on goods in transit, except in cases where risks have been identified. This shall not prevent customs from carrying out spot checks on the goods, based on risk management. Only when customs consider such a measure indispensable in relation with the characteristics of the goods as referred in Article [2] shall they (i) require goods to follow a prescribed itinerary; or (ii) require goods to be conveyed under customs escort surveillance. Normally, customs shall not impose such treatment to sealed consignments conforming to the national regulatory requirements.[81]

(Mongolia, Paraguay, Rwanda, and Switzerland , TN/TF/W/119)

Efforts to simplify documentation and inspection requirements as well as other procedures applicable in transit trade have been made over the last few decades by almost all countries. This has been done by entering into agreements on a bilateral and regional basis. International conventions also provide models of procedures that should be applied in transit trade in order to keep documentation requirements and inspection to the minimum. For instance, the above-mentioned TIR Convention requires member countries to use its 'standard international customs document in transit trade (TIR carnet)' and prescribes procedures that could be applied in cooperation with national associations of operators for facilitating transit trade. It also encourages transit and landlocked countries to reduce inspections by entering into arrangements for

---

81   Members shall consider using Annex E, Standard 3 of the Revised Kyoto Convention as the basis for the national requirements on seals and fastening.

the mutual recognition of one another's customs control measures. The revised Kyoto Convention also provides guidelines on the formalities to be followed at the commencement, en route, and at the termination of transit trade.

In this context, it may be necessary to examine very carefully whether there is any need to develop new rules in this area in the negotiations. The problems in transit trade arise not because international norms do not exist, but because of the practical difficulties that are encountered while applying them.

3.5 Sealing requirements

Containers or compartments of road vehicles in which goods in transit trade are to be transported are 'sealed by customs' in order to ensure that they are not removed or added to during transit. Sealing requirements often cause delays in transit trade. It is suggested that rules relating to sealing should be reviewed and appropriate guidelines be adopted.

As regards sealing requirements, the Kyoto Convention lays down detailed standards governing methods to be used in applying customs seals (standards 10 and recommended practice 11) in its special Annex E. It also includes 'minimum requirements' that customs seals and fastenings must comply with (standards 16, 17 and 18 and Appendix).

3.6 Bonded transport regime guarantee

Article V of GATT provides that transit countries should not collect duties or other taxes on goods in transit which customs normally collect on imported goods. Such duties should be collected at the termination of transit by the landlocked country of destination. However, the customs administrations of transit countries require transport operators to provide guarantees to cover the payment of customs duties and other taxes (such as value added tax) in cases where the goods are removed from the containers during transit and introduced clandestinely into the domestic market. It is proposed that new rules aiming at the more effective discipline on the level, nature and management of guarantees which are required from transit operators, including rules to ensure that they are not used as an instrument to raise revenue should be adopted (see Box 36).

Box 36: Proposal on an International, Regional or National Customs Guarantee System

International, regional or national customs guarantee system[82]

In order to avoid provisional taxation while securing revenue in the case of inland diversion of goods, Members shall operate bonded transport regimes that allow the transit of goods through the territory without payment of customs duties, taxes or other charges subject to the provision of an appropriate guarantee. Members shall ensure that guarantees required from transit operators are (i) reasonable having regard to the conditions of transit and the characteristics and the value of the consignment, and limited to the amount of customs debt or other charges which may be incurred in respect of the goods; (ii) designed and applied on a regional or international basis to as great an extent as possible; and (iii) released promptly and in full after the completion of the transit operation. Guarantees shall be renewable for subsequent consignments once a previous one is proved to have reached its destination.
(Mongolia, Paraguay, Rwanda, and Switzerland, TN/TF/W/119)

---

82 This text is an almost identical copy of the text contained in TN/TF/W/113.

These proposals would have to be examined against the background of the main features of the practices followed by customs for obtaining transit guarantees described in Box 37.

Box 37: Main features of the transit guarantees used in transit trade

The guarantees acceptable by customs are defined by the regulations of the transit country. Within the open options of financial securities, the choice is the exclusive responsibility of the principal. A guarantee can be provided by a bank (in the form of a bond) or as a form of insurance by a guarantor that can be reinsured internationally by well known and reliable insurance companies. Non-guarantee forms of security, such as deposits, may still be in place in some transit countries, although they are obviously not recommended. A principal may also be its own guarantor. This is a common practice for rail transport, and grants customs access to more direct recourse mechanisms.

There are two categories of transit guarantee:

◆ An individual guarantee covers only a single transit operation effected by the principal concerned. It covers the full amount of duties, taxes, and other charges for which the goods are liable.

◆ A comprehensive guarantee covers several transit operations up to a given reference amount, which is set equal to the total amount of duties and other charges that may be incurred with respect to goods under the transit operations of the principal during a period of at least one week.

In general, the calculation of the guarantee is based on the highest rates of duties and other charges applicable to the goods, and depends on the classification of the goods by customs. The amount covered by the comprehensive guarantee is 100% of the reference amount. If the principal complies with certain criteria of reliability, the amount of guarantee to be specified to the guarantors may be reduced by customs to 30% of the reference amount.

In case of the movement of high-risk goods, customs can be allowed to calculate the guarantee at a percentage that is related to the risk of non-clearance. International transit regimes such as the TIR allow for further savings.

Source: Jean Francois Arvis, 'Transit and the Special Case of Landlocked Countries', in Luc De Wulf and José B. Sokol (eds.) *Customs Modernization Handbook* (World Bank, Washington D.C. 2005).

In normal circumstances, guarantees are issued by banks and insurance companies. Customs administrations usually publish lists of financial institutions that are authorised to act as guarantors. In the case of the International TIR Convention, such guarantees are issued by national associations of transport operators.

It is clear from the information in Box 37 that customs wish to have considerable discretion in determining the level of guarantee. If the transport operator meets with the 'criteria of reliability,' the amount of guarantee is reduced by customs to as low as 30% of the estimated value of the goods in transit. On the other hand, in the case of high-risk goods, customs often demand a guarantee for an amount that is higher than the value of the goods in transit, and the amount may be linked to the risk of non-clearance.

The above practices followed by customs in deciding the level of guarantees raise doubts about whether it would be desirable to adopt a rigid discipline in the WTO on the nature, level, and management of guarantees. Customs need considerable discretion while determining the nature of guarantees and the level of the amount, taking into account the services provided by domestic and international banks and insurance companies and the risks that exist of goods being clandestinely introduced in the domestic market during transit trade.

A. Publications

George B. **Barman**, 'Comments on Natalie McNeil's Paper', in Thomas Cottier and Petros C. Mavroidis, (eds.) Patrick Blatter (associate ed.), *The Role of the Judge in International Trade Regulation - Experience and Lessons for the WTO,* (The University of Michigan Press, 2003).

J. Michael **Finger** and John S. **Wilson**, 'Trade Facilitation, Implementation, the Doha Development Agenda', (World Bank), 12 April 2006 (draft).

Natalie **McNeils**, 'The Role of Judges in the EU and WTO: Lessons from the BSE and Hormone Case' in Thomas Cottier and Petros C. Mavroidis, (eds.) Patrick Blatter (associate ed.), *The Role the Judge in International Trade Regulation - Experience and Lessons for the WTO,* (The University of Michigan Press, 2003).

Michael **Power**, *The Risk Management of Everything – Rethinking the Politics of Uncertainty*, Demos, (London, 2004).

Vinod **Rege** and Shyam **Gujadhur**, *Influencing and Meeting International Standards*, Vol. One and Two, The Commonwealth Secretariat and the International Trade Centre (ITC), 2004.

Vinod **Rege**, 'Theory and Practice of the Harmonisation of Rules on a Regional and International Basis – Its Relevance for the Work in WTO on Trade Facilitation', *Journal of World Trade,* Vol. 36, No 4. , August 2002.

Vinod **Rege**, 'Customs Valuation and Customs Reform', in Bernard M. Hoekman, Aditya Mattoo and Philip English (eds.), *Development, Trade, and the WTO: A Handbook,* (World Bank, Washington D.C., 2002).

Vinod **Rege,** 'Developing Country Participation in Negotiations Leading to the Adoption of the WTO Agreements on Customs Valuation and Preshipment Inspection: A Public Choice Analysis', 22(1), World Competition, 1999.

Joseph E. **Stiglitz** and Andrew **Charlton**, 'Aid for Trade' in *After Hong Kong: Some Key Trade Issues for Developing Countries* (Commonwealth Secretariat, London, 2007).

Luc de **Wulf** and José B. **Sokol** (eds.), *Customs Modernization Handbook*, (World Bank, Washington D.C., 2005).

Luc de **Wulf** and Gerald **McLinden** (eds.), *Customs Modernization Initiatives - Case Studies*, (World Bank, Washington D.C. 2004).

B. Reports: Organisations

AITIC, Agency for International Trade Information and Cooperation, Background Note, Aid for Trade, Moving Target, April 2005.

CUTS, 'Trilateral Development Cooperation: An Emerging Trend', Economics and Environment, No. 1, 2005.

OECD 'An Analysis of Non-Tariff Measures: Customs Fees and Charges', OECD Trade Policy Working Paper No. 14, 8 March 2005.

OECD: Trade Facilitation Reform in the Service of Development, OECD Trade Policy Working Paper No. 12, (22 February 2005).

OECD: Quantitative Assessment of the Benefits of Trade Facilitation (TD/TC/WP/(2003)31/Final).

OECD: Business Benefits of Trade Facilitation, Working Party on Trade Committee, (TD/TC/WP(2001)21/Final).

UNCTAD E-Commerce and Development Report 2001 (UNCTAD/SDTE/ECB/1), 20 Nov 2001.

UN Millennium Project, Task Force on Trade, 'Trade for Development' (Earthscan, London, Sterling Va., 2005).

WCO Fact Sheet on the 'The WCO Customs Data Model', (see the WCO website http://www.wcoomd.org/ie/En/Topics_Issues/FacilitationCustomsProcedures/facil_wco_data_model.htm)

World Bank and IMF (Development Committee), 'Doha Development Agenda and Aid for Trade', (DC2005-0016, 12 September 2005).

WTO Guide to GATT Law and Practice, Vol. 1, (WTO, 1995).

INDEX

S

T

U

W